CELEBRATING
50 YEARS
Texas A&M University Press
publishing since 1974

PICNIC

Willie Nelson's Fourth of July Tradition

TEXAS MUSIC SERIES
Sponsored by the Center for Texas Music History
Texas State University
Jason Mellard, *General Editor*

PICNIC

TEXAS A&M UNIVERSITY PRESS • College Station

Willie Nelson's Fourth of July Tradition

DAVE DALTON THOMAS
Foreword by Joe Nick Patoski

Copyright © 2024
by Dave Dalton Thomas
All rights reserved
First edition

This paper meets the requirements of
ANSI/NISO Z39.48-1992 (Permanence of Paper).
Binding materials have been chosen for durability.

Library of Congress Cataloging-in-Publication Data

Names: Thomas, Dave Dalton, 1971– author. | Patoski, Joe Nick, 1951– writer of foreword.
Title: Willie Nelson's Fourth of July Picnic / Dave Dalton Thomas ; foreword by Joe Nick Patoski.
Other titles: Texas music series.
Description: First edition. | College Station : Texas A&M University Press, [2024] | Series: Texas music series | "Texas music series, sponsored by the Center for Texas Music History, Texas State University."--ECIP title page. | Includes bibliographical references and index.
Identifiers: LCCN 2023052509 | ISBN 9781648431944 (cloth) | ISBN 9781648431951 (ebook)
Subjects: LCSH: Nelson, Willie, 1933—Performances. | Nelson, Willie, 1933—Friends and associates. | Willie Nelson's Fourth of July Picnic (Festival)—History. | Country music festivals—Texas—History. | Fourth of July celebrations—Texas. | Fourth of July—Songs and music—History and criticism. | Country musicians—Texas. | Country musicians—United States.
Classification: LCC ML420.N4 T56 2024 | DDC 782.421642092—dc23/eng/20231201
LC record available at https://lccn.loc.gov/2023052509

Frontispiece photo by Rick Henson
Cover photo by Jay Janner

For Mom & Dad

They took me backstage, and I went to Willie's bus, and they opened the door and, lo and behold, Willie came out, pigtails and all. And he shook my hand and said that he was sorry, he would like to visit with me, but he had to go jam with Leon Russell.

—*Robert Earl Keen, "No. 2 Live Dinner"*

Contents

Foreword, by Joe Nick Patoski	ix
Preface	xi
Acknowledgments	xiii
Introduction	1
Chapter One	**8**
1973: Dripping Springs	8
1974: College Station	33
1975: Liberty Hill	35
Chapter Two	**37**
1976: Gonzales	37
1977: Tulsa	63
1978: Kansas City, Dallas, and Austin	63
1979: Pedernales	64
Chapter Three	**66**
1980: Pedernales	66
1981 and 1982	86
1983: Syracuse, New Jersey, and Atlanta	87
Chapter Four	**88**
1984: South Park Meadows	88
1985: South Park Meadows	102
1986: Farm Aid II at Manor Downs	103
Chapter Five	**105**
1987: Carl's Corner	105
1988 and 1989	119
1990: Zilker Park, Austin	120
1991–1994	121
Chapter Six	**122**
1995: Luckenbach	122
1996: Luckenbach	147
1997–1999: Luckenbach	149
2000: Southpark Meadows	149
2001 and 2002	150

Chapter Seven — 152
    2003: Two River Canyon — 152

Chapter Eight — 172
    2004: Fort Worth Stockyards — 172
    2005: Fort Worth Stockyards — 192
    2006: Fort Worth Stockyards — 193
    2007: Washington State — 194
    2008: San Antonio (July 4) and Houston (July 5) — 194
    2009: South Bend, Indiana — 195

Chapter Nine — 196
    2010: The (New) Backyard — 196
    2011–2012: Fort Worth Stockyards — 211
    2013–2014: Fort Worth Stockyards — 212

Chapter Ten — 214
    2015: Austin360 Amphitheater, Circuit of the Americas — 214
    2016–2017: Austin360 Amphitheater, Circuit of the Americas — 228
    2018: Austin360 Amphitheater, Circuit of the Americas — 229
    2019: Austin360 Amphitheater, Circuit of the Americas — 230
    2020: The Virtual Picnic — 231
    2022: Q2 Stadium, Austin — 232
    2023: Q2 Stadium, Austin — 233

Conclusion — 235
Appendix A: Artists Who Played the Fourth of July Picnics — 239
Appendix B: Events Often Confused with Fourth of July Picnics — 251
Appendix C: Suggested Reading — 253
Sources — 255
Index — 269

A gallery of photos follows page 174

Foreword

Around most of the world, a picnic means a basket filled with food and drinks on a blanket spread over a bed of thick grass, under a shady tree in an idyllic natural setting on a warm sunny day, with lots of birds singing, but no bugs or varmints, and very few people around.

In Texas and in certain quarters of the music and concert trades, "picnic" translates to multiple thousands of people of all ages and body types gathered in an open space, many stripped down close to naked, most sweating profusely, (hopefully) hydrating madly while feeling good from doing a little of who knows what, starting with beer and letting the imagination run wild from there, topped by lots of music.

Which leads to the inevitable sixty-four-dollar question: What on earth compels someone to sit, squat, or stand in the middle of a sun-burned pasture, hooting and hollering in torrid, hundred-degree Texas heat?

Easy answer: Willie Nelson, Mr. Picnic himself.

The world of Willie Nelson is wide-ranging and complex and covers all sorts of territory, beginning with the many strains of music he performs, starting with traditional country and western and extending to Django Reinhardt jazz and Grateful Dead jams, all while reaching far-and-wide cultural corners that include the independent family farmer, the movie business, and cannabis.

For all the excitement and ritual of a Willie Nelson show (and "show" is precisely how Willie describes his live performances), nothing really, not even Farm Aid, comes close to being the definitive touchstone that the Willie Nelson Fourth of July Picnic is.

The annual event, (almost) always staged outdoors, has been part of the singer-songwriter's professional and personal life ever since his post-Nashville move to Austin in the early 1970s, where he reinvented himself as the Godfather of Texas Music. A Willie Nelson Fourth of July Picnic is an excuse to see Willie, of course, and an all-day party for most of the audience. For the musicians, it's something of a family reunion. For one day, in the middle of everyone crisscrossing the continent in the name of entertainment, the tour buses circle like a wagon train, and crews and players pause to visit, catch up, and renew relationships before going to work making music.

You might not be an outdoors person. Or you don't appreciate being around marijuana smoke or sweating in tight quarters with others in various states of inebriation/ecstasy on a hot day. Live music out in the open just might not be your thing. Stay inside with the AC on full blast and spread a blanket and basket of goodies with cool drinks on the living room floor. Put some Willie on the sound system and dive into *Picnic*. It's sort of like being there, minus the inevitable hassles.

These stories say a lot about one of the most interesting people on earth and how family, community, and reunion weirdly figure into his personal and professional life, especially on Independence Day. *Picnic* is the biography of an annual rite. It's the story of Willie Nelson, too. There's stuff in here that even an old Williephile like me didn't know.

The Fourth of July Picnic left a lot of memories behind, even some that are best forgotten. But that was what it was really like, living inside a Willie Nelson song every Fourth of July.

—**Joe Nick Patoski**

Preface

The phone rang in the Luckenbach bar. Bartender Jimmy Lee Jones picked it up, then handed it to me. I had been there most of the afternoon, drinking beer on my day off. Jalapeno Sam Lewis was on the other end. He told me he had an opportunity for me, that I needed to come up the road and meet a few people. This wasn't infrequent. Ever since my initial story on Luckenbach for the *San Angelo Standard-Times* had been picked up by the Associated Press and had run in a few other Texas newspapers, Sam had pretended—and told others—that I was a bigger deal than I was.

I drove to a bed-and-breakfast a mile up the road, walked in, and found myself in front of Tim O'Connor, Larry Trader, and Jack Yoder. I didn't know that they worked for Willie Nelson, but I recognized this was a much more serious situation than I had expected. The men had been meeting with Luckenbach leadership, and it had just been decided that the 1995 Willie Nelson Fourth of July Picnic was going to happen in the historic spot in a few months.

"Do you want to get the story out?" Larry Trader asked me.

I was all of twenty-three years old, I had seen Willie play only once, I had never been to a music festival, and I knew very little about the Fourth of July Picnic.

"Hell yes," I said.

I didn't plan to become the chronicler of the Picnic's history.

The Picnic picked me.

Acknowledgments

This book would not have happened without a lot of help. I need to start by thanking my "command crew" of advisers: Peter Blackstock, Rob Clark, and Chad Swiatecki all offered invaluable help and support.

I interviewed 117 different people for this book, and some of them absolutely changed the course of the chapter I was writing about. Tim O'Connor, however, is the bedrock of the entire book. This would be a lesser work without the hours I spent with him.

I'm also particularly indebted to Eddie Wilson, Woody Roberts, Joe Nick Patoski, Mike Benestante, Laurie Kelley Taylor, VelAnne Clifton, Connie Nelson, Pam and Billy Minick, John and Cris Graham, and Dahr Jamail.

Some people were patient enough to talk to me multiple times throughout this journey. I am grateful to Ray Wylie Hubbard, Ray Benson, Paula Nelson, Amy Nelson, John T. Davis, Scott Newton, Roger Collins, Freddy Fletcher, Steve Brooks, Bob Wishoff, Budrock Prewitt, and Jack Yoder.

I want to thank the photographers who let me include their wonderful images in this book, including Watt Casey Jr., Bob Daemmrich, Ron McKeown, Rick Henson, Scott Newton, John Carrico, Gary Miller, Scott Moore, and Jay Janner. I also want to thank the artists who allowed me to include their posters: Danny Garrett, Steve Brooks, Greg Ice, Billy Perkins, Chris Gates, and Jim Franklin.

Thom Lemmons, my editor at Texas A&M University Press, believed in this project from the start, and his calm encouragement allowed me to believe I could do this.

Melinda Wickman was one of the first people I interviewed, and she encouraged me to enjoy the journey of creating this book. It was among the best advice I received.

Most important, I'm grateful for the support of my friends and family. My wife, Shannon, and kids, Matthew, David, and Amy, have shared my successes and struggles over the past four years, and I couldn't have done it without their support.

PICNIC
Willie Nelson's Fourth of July Tradition

INTRODUCTION

Willie Nelson was standing backstage at the Dripping Springs Reunion in 1972. Grover Lewis, writing for *Rolling Stone* magazine, asked Willie if he would return the next year if the Reunion became an annual event. Willie thought about it for a minute, Lewis wrote, then said, "You mean if the same people was runnin' it, or if somebody else was?"

Was that moment the genesis of the Willie Nelson Fourth of July Picnic? It seems reasonable, though there's more than one set of roots: Willie has credited a Leon Russell show in Albuquerque with inspiring him to do the Picnic. Lana Nelson had excitedly told her father about attending the Atlanta International Pop Festival in 1969. Of course Woodstock, also in 1969, changed everything. But at that moment on March 19, 1972, Willie could see it.

The Dripping Springs Reunion is often misremembered as a Willie-organized event, though he was just part of the lineup. It was a remarkable gathering of country music and bluegrass artists, but there was little promotion and few people came. Terry Allen, who was recruited to play between sets along with other young songwriters Lee Clayton and Billy Joe Shaver, said the idea that the festival would bring rednecks and hippies to the same event caused some concern.

"There was some tension over that," Allen said. "On every hillside around the place there was a Texas Ranger with a shotgun on horseback. I don't think there was one bit of trouble . . . but there wasn't a huge crowd either. Part of that might have been because of that anticipation there might be some kind of violence."

A sequel to the Dripping Springs Reunion was quickly announced, but once the money was counted, those plans faded away. Allen said he kept the check he received from promoters in his kitchen for years. It had been returned to him, marked "insufficient funds."

Still, Willie thought it was a hell of an idea. And so it happened that in late spring of 1973, a forty-year-old country musician, inspired by a failed festival the year before, decided he was going to hold his own music festival. He would hold it in the same remote and rocky field where the previous festival had withered. And he would do it in July—not the hottest part of the Central Texas summer, but damn sure close enough.

It didn't make a lot of sense. When Johnny Bush found out about his friend's plan, he said it was foolish. "Willie, there ain't no way in hell a bunch of cowboys are going to come out in the hundred-degree heat to watch us pick our guitars," Bush told him. "He proved me wrong."

Today the Willie Nelson Fourth of July Picnic is a part of the Texas cultural fabric. The massive events in the 1970s are part of our mythology, and decades later college kids and pale office workers who had no business standing in the sun for eight hours still went to Luckenbach, Fort Worth, or a racetrack east of Austin to be a part of it.

After my initial run of writing about the Luckenbach Picnics, I remained a fan and continued attending each year. I was fascinated by the history of the Picnic and sought out every account that I could find. For a newspaper copy editor, it was frustrating. Different histories of the event would conflict with each other, mixing up years and missing Picnics entirely. By 2007, I had had enough and decided to compile my own history, using only immediate media coverage from the shows.

This book is an extension of that research. In addition to all the written and video accounts I could gather, I did nearly 150 interviews. The driving desire behind the book was to get it right, to establish a definitive history of the event, and to separate fact from fiction. This wasn't easy. Not only is the Picnic an event where reality turns to legend almost as soon as it happens, but people love their Picnic mythology—particularly during the chaotic 1970s events. Memories are fuzzy because of the chaos, the beer, the drugs, and the years.

In a conversation with Steve Kirk, who produced shows for Willie during the 1970s, he shared a memory of the 1976 Gonzales Picnic. "We were in our little campsite by our motorhome, and all of a sudden someone says, 'Isn't that Waylon Jennings?' And I looked over, and running through our campsite was Geno [McCoslin] running with a bag of cocaine and Waylon Jennings chasing him with a pistol."

"Wait," I said. "Is that right? Are you sure?"

Kirk backed down a bit. "I can't remember who had the cocaine and who had the pistol. I can't remember." So that anecdote didn't make that chapter, but rest assured it has plenty of drugs and guns anyway.

The fact that the Picnic was often held at the same location for two-to five-year stretches also blurred the memories a bit. When you call a musician who might play 150 shows a year and ask him to recall what happened

◀ *Where Woodstock meets Texas: A young fan gingerly picks her way among the crushed cactus in front of the stage at the Picnic in Liberty Hill.* © *Ron McKeown*

Billy Joe Shaver relaxes backstage during the 2000 Picnic at Southpark Meadows in Austin. Not getting to interview Shaver for the book was a significant loss. Photo by John Carrico

in Fort Worth in 2004, it's hard to blame him when he starts talking about things that happened in Fort Worth in 2005.

Fuzzy memories notwithstanding, I have made every effort to try to present an accurate picture of what happened and when, without leaning on myth and exaggeration. My secondary goal was to present a *full* picture of the Picnic. Most Willie biographies get up to and past his IRS troubles in the early 1990s and then slide into "and he lived happily ever after." It would be tempting to do the same with the Picnics—to focus on the first era of the Picnic at the expense of the later ones.

I didn't want to do that. My ten chapters cover the evolution of the Picnic and how it changed with age, expectations, and cultural shifts.

I wasn't able to interview Willie Nelson for this book, though I had done so a half-dozen times at various Picnics. Given his age and the Covid pandemic, it's understandable. There were other disappointments. In some cases, I was just too late to interview an aging artist—Jerry Jeff Walker, Johnny Bush, and Billy Joe Shaver all died as I was writing the book.

However, the blessings are even more numerous. Time and again, I stumbled—or was guided—into good fortune. When my friend Peter Blackstock introduced me to record producer and music industry legend Bill Bentley, I had no idea who he was or that he had attended the 1973 Picnic. But Bentley added quite a bit of frankness to my first chapter.

"The last thing I remember was waking up the next day and having boils all over my face," he told me. "I'm pretty sure it was first-degree burns. I'd been out there in the sun for like ten hours with no protection. But you take the psilocybin or the acid, you don't really worry about what the elements are going to do to you. You're just too high to care."

It was just as unlikely that I would get to interview Dahr Jamail, but we somehow connected. Dahr would prove to be the most unguarded of all my interviewees.

"It was all thieves," he said of producing the 1976 Picnic. "Everybody around us was a fucking thief and a liar. Geno was promising a Paul McCartney and John Lennon reunion and every fucking thing else he could think of—anything he could think of, he'd say it."

Now Dahr is a lawyer, and a considerably wealthy one at that. It's not my policy to do so, but I called him back after a while and asked him if that's what he meant to say. "Yeah," he said. "I'd say 'a criminal, a thief, and a liar,' if you want to know the bottom line. Now, the music business is so cut-and-dried. Like you're going to Whole Foods. But back then it was some pretty hard-core people."

"Hard-core" seemed to apply to Tim O'Connor. When I met him in Luckenbach in 1995, he was gruff and had little patience for my inexperience. But when I started writing this book twenty-five years later, I knew I had to interview him, and I pursued him relentlessly.

"When you talk about the Willie Family, you're talking about some pretty ornery people," he told me at our first meeting at his home. "The old saying used to be 'you cannot buy a ticket to this parade.' It wasn't ego; it wasn't any of that. It's just that none of us put up with any bullshit."

When I told Tim I wanted to ask some pointed questions about the trouble at the 2010 Picnic, his first response was, "I think I need to go get the shotgun." He was kidding, but there was a time that wouldn't have been an idle threat.

Tim knew his battle against cancer wasn't going well. At this point in his life, he was happy to tell his story, even the bad parts, and have someone hear him. We started talking in the fall of 2020. In July 2021 he called me one last time from his hospice bed, telling me he was sorry he wasn't going to see the book.

Willie and Family perform alongside Kimmie Rhodes during the mini-Picnic in 1993 at the Backyard. No matter how small the Picnic was at various points, it still carried the weight of its history with it. Photo by John Carrico

Me too, Tim.

The Picnic was many things over the years: It was big, it was small, it was legendary, it was infamous, it was great, it was bad, it was hot, it was . . . well, it was hot. Janis Tillerson, a Willie superfan, told me she went to every Picnic except two. She was able to sum them up succinctly: "Some were hell. And some were wonderful."

That's enough introduction. Let's kick things off with Delbert McClinton telling us how the Picnic began: "In the beginning, it was not a commodity. It was a gathering. And it was magic. The air tasted different. Everything about being a part of that explosion that Willie brought about was just magic. And still is. I mean, it always will be."

Meet the Picnic VIPs

Willie Nelson

Willie began the Picnic in 1973 when he was 40 years old. He was still hosting them mostly-annually in 2023 at the age of 90.

Throughout the half-century run of the Fourth of July Picnics, these guys — and the Picnic was a boys' club — were part of the tradition. Other stars would come and go, but the regulars kept coming back. Total numbers are through 2023, including the 2020 virtual Picnic.

Ray Wylie Hubbard

Ray Wylie played at 28 Picnics, more than anyone — except for Willie, of course. Ray started in 1974 and played in the 2020 virtual Picnic.

Asleep at the Wheel

The band led by Ray Benson played 26 Picnics ranging from 1974 in College Station through the Picnic in 2023 in Austin.

Billy Joe Shaver

Billy Joe played at 23 Picnics, starting with the inaugural 1973 Picnic. Billy Joe played his last Picnic in 2019.

David Allan Coe

David Allan played at 23 Picnics, most infamously at Gonzales in 1976. His first was in 1974 and he played his last Picnic in 2019.

Johnny Bush

Johnny performed at 23 Picnics and was the classic country heart of the event. The longtime Willie friend played his last Picnic in 2019.

The Geezinslaws

The band led by Sammy Allred were longtime friends of Willie and played at 21 Picnics. Their last Picnic was in 2010 at the Backyard.

Leon Russell

A huge star at the time of the first Picnic, he helped it succeed. Leon performed at 17 Picnics, the last a year before his death in 2016.

Kris Kristofferson

Kris performed at 16 Picnics, staying connected with the event across the decades. His last Picnic was in Austin in 2016.

Ray Price

Ray got a late start, but was steady in the later years, playing 15 Picnics. His last Picnic was 2011 in Fort Worth at the age of 85.

Waylon Jennings

Willie's friend and collaborator was there at the start. Waylon played 12 Picnics, mostly in the early years. His last was 1996 in Luckenbach.

Jamey Johnson

Jamey played his first Picnic in 2010 and was a vital addition to the aging group of regulars. He played 10 Picnics, ending in 2020.

Merle Haggard

Merle only played at 8 Picnics, though he canceled appearances at three more. His last Picnic was in 2015, where Willie joined him onstage.

OTHER FREQUENT PICNIC PERFORMERS INCLUDE: Steve Fromholz, Paula Nelson, Folk Uke, Jessi Colter, Lukas Nelson, Micah Nelson

Photos: Scott Moore (Willie, Kristofferson, Coe, Johnson, Shaver, Bush), Rick Henson (Russell, Jennings, Allred), Gary Miller (Haggard, Benson, Hubbard), Luckenbach, Texas (Price)

CHAPTER ONE

1973: Dripping Springs

SITE: *The Hurlbut Ranch on McGregor Lane west of Dripping Springs, about seven miles from US 290*
ATTENDANCE: *Estimated at 40,000*
HEADLINERS: *Willie Nelson, Leon Russell, Kris Kristofferson, Waylon Jennings, Rita Coolidge, Tom T. Hall, Charlie Rich, John Prine, Sammi Smith, Billy Joe Shaver, Lee Clayton*

Picnic VIP Update

Willie Nelson: Willie had just released the *Shotgun Willie* album on Atlantic Records and was settling into his new Austin home. He had recently struck up a friendship with Leon Russell.

Leon Russell: Leon had just released his three-LP *Leon Live* album on Shelter Records. He lived in his hometown of Tulsa, Oklahoma, and was one of the biggest rock stars in the world.

Waylon Jennings: Waylon had just released the Billy Joe Shaver–written *Honky Tonk Heroes* on RCA Victor. He was changing the rules in Nashville and on the verge of superstardom.

Billy Joe Shaver: Billy Joe had just released his first album, *Old Five and Dimers like Me*, on Monument Records and was riding high on the attention from Waylon's *Honky Tonk Heroes*.

To hear Eddie Wilson tell it, the Picnic was in need of a hippie intervention. Willie Nelson's friends had their talents. Friends like Joe Jamail and Darrell Royal had money and influence. Friends like Larry Trader and Geno McCoslin collected money and exercised their influence as well—just not in quite the same way. There were many more who were loyal, enterprising, and occasionally unhindered by the law.

But, Eddie argued, Willie's friends weren't selling enough tickets to make the 1973 Fourth of July Picnic a success. "Willie already had delusions of grandeur about the thing, but there was no word about it out anywhere at all," Eddie said. "All the tickets were in boxes still under everybody's bed."

Dahr Jamail would tell you that is bullshit. By the time Eddie and his Armadillo World Headquarters colleagues were involved, "we already had tickets in place, selling them and doing interviews on radio in Houston and San Antonio and Dallas. So I don't really know what they did."

The son of powerful Houston lawyer Joe Jamail, Dahr was not yet nineteen years old during the inaugural Picnic, but he had been close with Willie's Family for years. Dahr already counted himself as one of the promoters who handled Willie's business in Texas, along with Larry, Geno, Tom Gresham, and Tim O'Connor.

Willie's Texas promoters and inner circle then thrived on the chaos of the night life during a more lawless time. Some of them hustled and swindled when they could. Some brandished guns if they thought they were the ones being swindled. Or disrespected.

The hippies at the Armadillo had little tolerance for that. An ugly split was coming. Ugly enough that forty-seven years later, Dahr would still bristle at the idea that the Armadillo's survivors would take any credit at all for the success of the Dripping Springs Picnic.

At first, Willie and the Armadillo seemed destined for a long partnership. His first show at that iconic Austin venue on August 12, 1972, sparked the cultural merger of "the long-hairs and the rednecks" over country music—a moment so long and widely celebrated that it might seem to be more legend than truth if *American-Statesman* columnist Townsend Miller hadn't predicted it in a story the day of the show: "If Willie's conservative, traditional fans will follow him tonight to the Armadillo to join with his young 'now' fans, it's going to be quite a night!"

Colleague Joe Gracey confirmed it in print a week later: It was "a sizable and sociable crowd made up of the most amazing assortment of country music fans I have ever seen."

On that monumental foundation, Eddie and Willie were building a business relationship and a friendship. "Willie and I used to take rides," said Eddie (who would later cement his name in Austin, Texas, history by taking Kenneth Threadgill's defunct tavern and running it as Threadgill's restaurant for forty years). "We would just pile in the car and go riding and get high and talk about whatever came up."

And things did come up. Eddie recalls stopping with Willie to visit some "smuggler buddies" who were so enamored with meeting the emerging country star that they spelled out "WILLIE" in giant block letters on their glass coffee table . . . in cocaine.

It was during one of those drives through the Hill Country that Eddie told Willie he was "worried sick" about what he felt was the lack of buzz surrounding the inaugural Picnic and offered to help. Willie accepted, and Eddie soon convened a meeting at his West Austin home.

Woody Roberts and Eddie Wilson remained lifelong friends after teaming up to help the inaugural Picnic become a success. This 2000s-era photo shows the pair at Wilson's downtown Threadgill's restaurant and concert venue. Photo courtesy of Sandra Wilson

THE SMELL OF POT hung in the air, and cold beers were passed around. Eddie's living room was crowded enough that some men sat on the floor. The Willie side included Larry Trader and Billy Ray "B. C." Cooper, both of whom did whatever Willie needed doing, with B. C. often serving as Willie's personal driver. The Armadillo side included Eddie, artist Jim Franklin, all-around manager Bobby Hedderman, and lawyer Mike Tolleson. Tolleson would spend the meeting on the phone with Francois de Menil—an investor who had already put fifteen thousand dollars toward a Picnic film—and Hedderman would later be at the center of the dispute that would end the partnership between the Armadillo and Willie.

Eddie had also brought in someone else. Woody Roberts had left a distinguished radio career in San Antonio the year before to become a media consultant. He knew both the music business and the radio business—what would excite the DJs, what advertising worked, what would get people talking.

Eddie steered the conversation around the room, taking stock of what had been done and what needed to be done in the two weeks left before the Picnic.

The concert site had already been selected: It would be at the Hurlbut Ranch, which had hosted the Dripping Springs Reunion the year before—Dahr Jamail said he got a loan on his car to get the twenty-five hundred dollars for Burt Hurlbut and claimed he bribed the Dripping Springs mayor and sheriff with five hundred dollars each.

The Armadillo staff would handle production of the show, building a stage and arranging local services from ambulances to Porta Potties.

Many of the performers were lined up: Waylon Jennings, Kris Kristofferson, Rita Coolidge, Sammi Smith, John Prine, and Tom T. Hall were on the bill, though what was originally advertised as a 4:30 showtime would grow into a daylong event as more and more artists joined.

The poster had already been done. Jim Franklin had drawn up a blue-and-yellow poster with an armadillo emerging from under an American flag. Franklin would do five more Picnic posters over the years, and Danny Garrett's frequently used "Uncle Willie" design would become iconic—but the first poster would prove hard to top.

And with the help of Joe Jamail, Willie had set up a company—Nelson Prospecting Corporation—and printed up tickets by the thousands. Dahr Jamail was in charge of selling tickets in Houston, Tom Gresham in Waco, Larry Trader in San Antonio, and Geno McCoslin in Dallas. Radio advertising and drive-time promotions on country stations had moved some of those tickets.

But Woody felt that the Picnic was following in the footsteps of the Dripping Springs Reunion. "They had put together a country show that was somewhat similar to but I think weaker than the show that ran the year before," Woody said. "A lot of the same musicians, but none of the big stars. There was just no way they were gonna have a crowd with that lineup and promoting it on country music [radio]—it wasn't the kind of thing that was gonna have a big turnout."

What they needed, Woody realized, was not a country music festival but a modern music festival with rock stars that could draw a crowd to a rugged and rural site. Eddie agreed: "The country folks were used to going out and wearing slacks and slow dancing. It took a youth element to be willing to sit in the heat on a bunch of rocks."

Woody hardly had time to worry about the fix he had gotten into when someone mentioned—almost as an afterthought—that Leon Russell was going to be there. "I said, 'Leon Russell, for Christ's sake! Well, now we got a show!' I could build an event around Leon Russell, without any trouble, because he was at that time, a mega-mega-star."

Willie and Leon had recently become friends—Jim Franklin had arranged the introduction—and Willie had asked Leon to join the Picnic. Leon's manager wasn't excited by the idea of the big star playing a strange festival outside Austin with a bunch of relatively little-known country musicians. The compromise was that Leon would attend and help emcee but couldn't be promoted as a performer.

That didn't matter. Woody knew all he would have to do is let DJs know that Leon Russell would *be there*. And they would do the rest.

The meeting wrapped up with the consensus to pull most of the advertising from country radio stations around the state and focus on rock 'n' roll stations in Central and South Texas. Not all of Willie's friends would take it well, but when Willie agreed, the debate was over.

As folks filed out, leaving Woody and Eddie to make promotional plans, Woody was still thinking: Doug Sahm was on the bill. He had just recorded *Doug Sahm and Friends* on Atlantic. Bob Dylan had played on that album . . .

And one of the most enduring mysteries of the Picnic was born right there: Woody Roberts made up the rumor that Bob Dylan would appear at the Picnic. "I'll own up to that now," Woody said. "I never really said, 'Tell people that Bob Dylan is going to show up.' But I did say when talking with the radio people, 'As far as we know, there is no truth to the rumor that Bob Dylan will show up to play with Doug.' And of course, that's all you needed to say."

In mid-June, the inaugural Picnic wavered between two futures. It could become an iconic event for the next half century, a national phenomenon for the next decade, and the jet fuel for Willie's rise to Lone Star royalty. Or it could become a kind of Dripping Springs Reunion Part 2—a musical masterpiece barely remembered.

So who was right, Eddie Wilson or Dahr Jamail? Tim O'Connor is not an impartial judge, but the longtime Willie friend and promoter doesn't hold any enmity toward Eddie or the Armadillo. He said they were an important cultural force in 1973, and it's fair to say they helped drive some of the ticket sales. But he said claiming sole credit for the Picnic's success is stepping over the line.

However, in the spring of 2022, Mike Tolleson could still bring out a stack of paperwork half a foot high, including yellow legal papers scrawled with performer budgets, promotion plans, and receipts for supplies ranging from Winnebagos for dressing rooms to flashlights and salt tablets. The paper trail is there to prove that the Armadillo did a hell of a lot to make the Picnic happen.

Willie's team took the idea and ran with it, creating legend out of chaos. They did sell tickets across the state. The Armadillo did a lot of the work on the site and made the last push on ticket sales in Central Texas, bringing in a diverse counterculture crowd that made the Picnic unique. Both sides agree on the genius of Jim Franklin's artwork and the vital presence of Leon Russell.

However, Woody Roberts's contribution has been mostly overlooked. If Eddie Wilson is claiming any credit, he's giving it to Woody: "From my perspective, the success that it became was due entirely to the involvement of Woody Roberts. That was the wrench that broke the lug nut loose. And it was a beautiful thing to watch."

DRIPPING SPRINGS in 1973 had a population of about five hundred living along US 290 between Austin and Johnson City. Sandy Gravenor, who graduated from Dripping Springs High School that year, was one of a graduating class of just twenty-seven. "We were just a bunch of old country folk," she said.

The town had survived the Dripping Springs Reunion the year before, tolerating the hippies and enjoying the added business. The Reunion promoters hired a lot of locals, even paying the high school seniors to clean up the grounds nightly during the three-day event to raise funds for their senior trip.

"They were my friends so I had to help them," Gravenor said. "We'd go out there with trash bags and pick up beer cans and Coke cans and drugs and whatever else we could find. It was pretty wild for a seventeen-year-old country girl."

The Reunion site was at the Hurlbut Ranch on McGregor Lane, west of Dripping Springs and just over seven miles of twisty Hill Country caliche road from US 290. Brothers Burt and James Hurlbut had recently inherited the ranch and had a "million-dollar debt from Uncle Sam on the property," James said. "We were trying to figure out a way to save the ranch" when they agreed to host the Dripping Springs Reunion.

Reunion promoters set their stage in a natural depression between two small hills, providing an amphitheater effect. Electrical power was established. A well was put in, feeding a couple miles of galvanized piping. Contractors worked around the clock in the last few days to pull it off. Fifteen months later, the infrastructure remained, more or less. Picnic workers swarmed over the grounds. The stage was reconstructed, a medical shack was built, portable bathrooms were put in place, and an entrance gate was set up—an optimistic combination of insufficient fencing, a Winnebago, and a small box office.

At $5.50 in advance, tickets were selling in Austin at the Armadillo and its typical outlets (such as Oat Willie's, Texas Hatters, and Inner Sanctum), which was important because Mike Tolleson said ticket money was essentially all they had to pay the contractors on-site. "It was being promoted in Dallas and San Antonio and Houston and Austin. But whatever Geno McCoslin collected in Dallas, we never saw. Whatever got collected in San Antonio, Houston, we never saw. We were assuming that that money was going back to Willie and the company account for paying talent and things like that."

Tolleson, an Austin lawyer who handled the "business nuts and bolts" of the Picnic for the Armadillo—along with friend and CPA Randy McCall—was troubled but focused on managing what he could with the money the Armadillo had.

Woody Roberts had secured an office at the Armadillo and was hurriedly carrying out a last-second-panic marketing plan. Randy's wife, Diane McCall, volunteered to help, and together they placed newspaper ads, called Texas TV stations, and appealed to all the major music magazines. The focus, however, was radio. Woody had written a seventy-second ad that just impressed the hell out of Eddie Wilson. "It was just absolutely titillating," Eddie said. Amid song snippets from the featured performers, "it had fireworks going off, big explosions after everyone's name as they were listed off."

Woody went to Willie's house to record a canned interview—shrewdly set up so that DJs could ask a half-dozen provided questions and then play a tape of Willie's answer, letting listeners think it was a live conversation with their local station. There were a few real on-air interviews, particularly with Bill Mack, whose all-night country music show on WBAP out of Fort Worth was heard across the country.

And everyone, from small-town radio stations to national magazines, would receive the same one-page press sheet saying that Leon Russell would be there and noting that "there's no verified truth to the rumor that Bob Dylan might show up." At rock stations across Central Texas, DJs were giving away Leon's latest album along with tickets to the Picnic, and Woody's Dylan rumor took on a life of its own.

"Whenever a radio station would play a Bob Dylan song, going up to that Picnic, they'd say, you know, there's a rumor Dylan might show up— we don't know; we can't confirm it," Woody said. "It gave us extra promotional mentions, and it also gave us glitter, which the event needed—rock 'n' roll glitter—real bad."

The phenomenally successful *Woodstock* documentary may have been what Houston's Francois de Menil had in mind when he agreed to give Willie fifteen thousand dollars for the right to film the Picnic and secure the necessary artist releases—one of the weirder subplots of the Picnic.

In his book *The Improbable Rise of Redneck Rock*, Austin writer Jan Reid said magazine publisher Michael Price was steering the film, but years later Mike Tolleson could only recall dealing with Francois. Ultimately, it wouldn't matter because the film never stood a chance at happening. The artists' releases weren't signed: "They were pretty expansive," Tolleson said. "The contracts were asking for a lot and paying nothing."

And Tolleson said the contract that Francois presented to Willie wasn't much better. "Basically, he wanted to come in and shoot the film and to control everything and walk away with it, and Willie had no control over it whatsoever." When Tolleson told Willie that the contract wasn't in his best interest, Francois got hot about it for a few days, then dropped the whole thing cold.

"At some point, that conversation—what I don't remember is how or why—it just simply stopped," Tolleson said. Francois had to sue Willie to get his fifteen thousand dollars back—or threatened to sue at least, depending on the source. The issue was ultimately resolved, and hard feelings eventually faded.

Despite later reminiscing by some that the stage at the first Picnic was uncovered or was actually a flat-bed truck or whatever exaggerated

Leon Russell and Willie Nelson perform on the morning of the 1973 Picnic as the crowd begins to arrive. They had been up all night and decided to welcome the morning arrivals with a little gospel music. © Ron McKeown

hardship they could dream up, the Armadillo crew had done pretty well. "The stage was a big, beautiful, well-built structure," Eddie Wilson said. "It had walls and a roof. Nothing flimsy about it all. And we got a call a couple days before the show that the roof had blown off." Sabotage was suspected. "We looked for tracks," Eddie said. "We were just flabbergasted. But we didn't have time to get too deep into forensics because the show was coming up."

Eddie had recently hired a company to seal some basement rooms at the Armadillo with polyurethane spray foam, and he had a sudden moment of inspiration. He called Lloyd Fortenberry at Austin's Uranus Urethanes, and a new roof was made, more or less instantly, with spray foam and chicken wire. With a little effort it was raised into place.

"I like to think that all of us have at least three or four really great moments in life," Eddie said, "and I had one of mine in the middle of that particular stress." The inspiration didn't come without a price. "It was such a magical piece of insulation that the shade underneath it was remarkably cooler," Eddie said. By the afternoon of the show, the stage would be a crowded, chaotic, stressful mess.

Woody's ad campaign was paying off. Nobody knew just how many, but it was clear that the fans were coming.

"THIS IS A VOICE from the time when the outlaws rode."

Lee Clayton is telling a story about the night before the inaugural Picnic. He was at Willie's house, not far from the Hurlbut Ranch. "In the living room were Willie Nelson, Waylon Jennings, Coach [Darrell] Royal, Kris Kristofferson, Billy Joe Shaver, and myself," the musician said. "It was in the evening and we're playing songs and stuff like that. And around midnight, Jerry Jeff Walker came through the door."

Jerry Jeff, Clayton said, was wearing a T-shirt and a short bathing suit, complemented by a cowboy hat and boots, and he was carrying a quart-sized plastic mug of beer. "He says, 'I want to play a song I'm gonna record.'" Jerry Jeff put down his beer, picked up a guitar, and played the Guy Clark song "Desperados Waiting for a Train"—which he did record the next month in Luckenbach for his landmark *Viva Terlingua!* album.

"That's the first time that me or anybody else in that room had ever heard that song," Lee said. "Every hair in that room stood straight up. And I've seen and heard many performances of that song . . . but that was maybe the best that I ever heard because he *was* a desperado waiting for a train at that moment. We all were."

It was now the Fourth of July. The Picnic was under way. At the Hurlbut Ranch, the press had gathered for a pre-party that ended up being short on the promised barbecue, beer, and artist access. Jan Reid described it as a bust. Woody Roberts said it started rough but got better as the night cooled and the beer eventually flowed.

Willie and Leon Russell eventually showed up at the site, staying up all night picking and singing before deciding on a whim to open the Picnic at dawn. In his book *It's a Long Story*, Willie wrote: "When the light broke on that Wednesday morning of the Fourth of July we were feeling jittery. To calm down, Leon and I went onstage, turned on the sound, and started playing gospel hymns as the sun rose over the great expanse of the empty land set out before us."

Photographer Ron McKeown was there at sunrise to document the moment, photographing Willie and Leon from behind as they sat on chairs to play for the fans who were already there—and those trickling in from the hills. Camping on-site wasn't allowed, so those who came the day before pulled off to the side of the road outside the ranch and came in with the sun. They would have a long, hot day ahead of them, but they weren't alone.

"We were one of the first bands and due to the [traffic], we arrived with just enough time to set up and play," said Tony Airoldi, who was part of the Austin band Greezy Wheels. "As I was dragging my gear onstage, I remember seeing Leon Russell sitting on a Fender Twin amp, holding a guitar, and looking like he might fall over at any moment."

Leon would rally. The traffic would just get worse.

One of the lasting mental images of the 1973 Picnic is the young picnicker, trudging down a dusty caliche road, doggedly lugging a cooler of beer, for miles on end. It didn't have to happen. There was plenty of parking on-site—hundreds of acres of it.

American-Statesman columnist Townsend Miller put forth an authoritative theory in the newspaper a few days after the event: Fans driving to the site in the morning came across the cars parked alongside the road outside the ranch from the night before. Naturally, they just pulled in behind them, figuring this was it. At first, they weren't too far away. But as the line of cars kept stretching back, the walk got farther and farther. There were no clear directions, no road signs—fans parking later in the day had no clue how far away they were. Townsend claimed some fans walked as far as seven miles.

Some performers got caught in the traffic jam, too. Townsend said Billy Joe Shaver had to hoof it in from four miles away or risk missing his afternoon set. Dripping Springs native Sandy Gravenor had no such problem. "I knew the backroads. They had advertised this one way in . . . but we knew other ways to get around and get back in there; it wasn't hard for local people to figure it out."

Adding to the problem on the advertised route, Mike Tolleson explained, was that when cars pulled off to either side of the barely-two-lane caliche road, it became a one-lane road, clogged with pedestrians. Even people determined to try to drive to the site were caught in a massive traffic jam.

Tolleson said he felt bound by duty to "gravitate toward wherever [he] thought the problems were" on the day of the Picnic. That doesn't mean he felt good about it. "Well, the reason why I can't tell you definitively [who performed] from personal experience is because it seems as though I spent all my time out on the fucking road trying to deal with traffic. When I discovered what was going on there, it ended up taking up a whole lot of my time in my day because nobody was out there dealing with that."

Eddie Wilson recalled that the Picnic "had so much forward momentum that even that kind of [parking] silliness couldn't stop it. People went tromping through the weeds to get there and over the fences, through the brush."

Bill Bentley, who would become a famed music industry executive and producer, was a self-described "hippie kid from Houston" who ventured out in the back of a pickup with his bandmates in the Bizarros. They abandoned their truck in the "mayhem" that was parking without really thinking about how to find it later. "At that point, who cared?" he said. "We were just kind of crazed and going for it."

The Picnic was more than a big show, photographer Alan Pogue said. "I think everybody knew this was a historic moment."

They came walking in by the hundreds. Then thousands. Later, the Texas Department of Public Safety estimated that forty thousand attended. Other published estimates range from twenty thousand to seventy thousand.

"They stormed the gate, somewhere between *The Red Badge of Courage* and Gettysburg." Eddie Wilson is talking figuratively. Perhaps it did resemble a battlefield, but there wasn't much of a gate to storm. Did the picnickers knock down fencing and come streaming in? Eddie and others said yes. Mike Tolleson said there really wasn't fencing of any kind at the entrance, just a little box office set up in front of a Winnebago.

"There was just no security there other than it was being handled like a typical venue box office; you're supposed to walk up, pay your money, and get your ticket and walk on in," Tolleson said. "Well, there were hundreds

The crowd at the inaugural 1973 Picnic reached forty thousand. This was more than either the Armadillo crew or Willie's people were prepared to handle. Photo by Duncan Engler, Austin American-Statesman

of people coming, and there was no proper fencing . . . or security staff there to control the way those people came in."

Carlotta Pankratz manned the box office. Tolleson stood in the road trying to take money. Some paid, but most did not. In the chaos many never even noticed there was anyone to take their money. "The people were just coming in such waves that they weren't even gonna stop at that box office," Tolleson said. "They were just coming in. . . . It was not well organized or well structured or secured." What money they managed to get went in the Winnebago, where Willie associate Larry Trader was collecting and counting.

In her book *Heartworn Memories*, Willie's daughter Susie Nelson described what fans encountered once they made it to the Picnic site:

> [Fans sat] on an overgrazed hillside while a hot wind coated them with caliche dust as fine as talcum powder and the hot Texas sun baked every bit of exposed flesh. . . . There were hippie girls running around with nothing on but a pair of cutoffs and a pair of sandals. I also saw a couple of hippie guys running around without either cutoffs or sandals. . . . People drank up all the beer they'd brought with them before they got to where they could park their cars. There was no beer available on the grounds. In fact, the water was running out. There weren't enough restrooms to handle the demand and first aid facilities were stretched to the breaking point. . . . But even so, the hillside was covered with people who stayed and stayed and stayed.

Like most written recollections of the Picnics, some of her account is conflated with memories from other Picnics or exaggerated in the telling. But nobody disputes her assessment of the site. "I do remember just a skiff of caliche dust on everything," Eddie said. "It was exactly the opposite of a dark and eerie night. It was a bright and dusty day."

Sandy Gravenor said there had been little rain in the area and described the site as "dusty and dirty." "There weren't any improvements made to the area where you sit," she said. "It was just sort of, you know, the side of the hill, and people took their blankets and lawn chairs and whatever else they could carry in."

For Bentley, what they could carry in was a supply of psilocybin, which they took when they arrived. "We got to kind of where the huge crowd was building and the psilocybin hit and we all just scattered away from each other. I never saw anybody that I had gone out there with that whole day."

Historical data from the National Oceanic and Atmospheric Association (NOAA) says the temperature hit ninety-two in nearby New

Braunfels on July 4, 1973, and Austin reported a high of ninety-three, but firsthand accounts from Dripping Springs describe the heat in terms ranging from over one hundred to just shy of hell. "It was miserable," Dallas artist Steve Brooks said. "God, it was so hot. Just really, really hot."

Gravenor snuck backstage—not to meet the performers but to hide underneath the stage, "because that was one place there was shade."

"I didn't go outside again on the Fourth of July for twenty years," Eddie said. "Lord God, it was hot."

Thomas Chapman, a Texas Tech student who had driven down from Lubbock, had a plan for the heat: "[We] had this huge Styrofoam ice chest; it was just gigantic. So we filled it up with beer and ice and put it in the back of a pickup." But the beer was gone by 2 p.m. and the sun was relentless. "We tried to pull anything we had with us over us to keep the sun from hitting us directly," Thomas said.

Bill Bentley, tripping on psilocybin, was freaked out by a Charlie Rich song that mentioned snakes and decided to go find a tree to sit under. "I knew I was burning up, and I needed to find some shade. I think I found one like about half a mile away and stayed there for about an hour, hour and a half."

Louis Karp, who would go on to found Austin's iconic Waterloo Records, attended with his future wife and her friends. They had a different plan for beating the heat. "There was a creek where we all went skinny-dipping." It was great, until the sheriff's deputies rode up on horseback. "They scooted us back: 'Put your clothes on and get out of here.'"

Dripping Springs resident Thomas Sheldon told a similar story from the other side. He had been friends with an old cowboy who had worked security on horseback at the Picnic. The cowboy—a lifelong bachelor who went by "Pud"—loved to tell stories of all the young, naked girls he saw at the event. "These girls would hop on the back of his horse; they wanted to get rides on the horse," Sheldon said. "He'd go, 'It was crazy. I didn't know what to do; they would come over and ask for a ride, and they were half-naked. I never seen anything like it.'"

The Hays County cowboy went home that day with a new appreciation for hippies. "He said they were sweet, nice, and wonderful people," Sheldon said.

With all the sun and heat, it's no surprise that the cots at the medical shack were quickly full. "I was friends with the People's Community Clinic," photographer Alan Pogue said. "They had kind of like a MASH unit. Somebody had been selling bad mushrooms, so there were a lot of people throwing up, needing care."

A cowboy watches the growing crowd. Local volunteers kept an eye on the proceedings and occasionally rounded up naked hippies. © Ron McKeown

Ultimately, several patients were transferred to Brackenridge Hospital in Austin because of the mushroom poisoning, heat exhaustion, and one accidental shooting. Eddie Wilson pointed out the shooting was nothing outlaw—it turned out that a young fan had a little pistol in the back seat of his jeans and sat down hard enough for it to go off and blow "a tiny little piece of his ass off."

Just how outlaw was the original Picnic? Willie biographer Joe Nick Patoski said it was pretty crazy but stopped short of being notorious. "So many people showed up, unlike the year before," he said. "And, yeah, the fences got knocked down and all that shit . . . but it was more of a hippie deal."

Brad Hurlbut remembered his father calling the sheriff to run off a group of bikers who decided that they should serve as the show's security: "He met them at the front of the ranch with the sheriff to hold them off because he didn't want that in there."

Photographers Pogue and Melinda Wickman (who took the photos for *The Improbable Rise of Redneck Rock*) described a mellow, marijuana-fueled crowd where people took care of each other and law enforcement kept a low profile.

It's possible that some of the memories of Dripping Springs may be a subconscious overcorrection, fueled by a desire to assign a Utopian aura to the first Picnic. Willie, no doubt, was thinking of his legacy when he described it in *It's a Long Story*:

> We might have been more than a little unorganized, but we pulled it off. The music was great. The crowd was happy. Buzzed on beer or high on weed or tripping on acid, the different cultures got along great. No name-calling, no pushing and shoving, no cracked skulls. I have to say that, given the potential for disaster, I felt relieved. In my name, a peaceful Fourth of July picnic had unfolded under sunny skies.

Picnicker Louis Karp agreed. "It was very mellow. It felt disorganized and disjointed, but we didn't care. . . . I don't remember anything negative about it. Everybody fell in love with Willie Nelson."

"LEON RUSSELL comes out and says, 'Well, they said Bob Dylan could write songs.' And everybody went 'wow!'" Thomas Chapman is describing how Leon acknowledged the Dylan rumor before introducing John Prine. Chapman recalls the moment because it was when he became a lifelong fan of Prine: "That's the first time I heard of him or heard him. And he blew everybody away."

Bob Dylan didn't come, of course. Doug Sahm didn't show up either. But there were plenty of surprises. The advertised lineup on the Jim Franklin poster was just a start. Artists kept asking to join the Picnic, and Willie wasn't good at saying no. A scheduled 4:30 showtime kept moving up until the concert lasted all day.

Freda and the Firedogs—arguably the hottest Austin band at the time—were among those who were expected to play, but instead they were victims of the chaos. "We told 'em we were there and were waiting around, and it just kept getting later and later," Bobby Earl Smith said. "People kept getting added to the bill. Finally, the sun's about to set. And the band, especially me, I'm starting to get frustrated."

He says bandmate John Reed went to talk to Willie about playing and came away with no answer. Marcia Ball confirmed that they never ended up playing but remembers the circumstances a little differently. "I remember being up on the hill with my friends; we were up there watching from

CHAPTER ONE \ 25

The rocky grounds of the Hurlbut Ranch were not a deterrent for some in the crowd. Photo by Stanley Farrar, Austin American-Statesman

the ridge at the back of the crowd. And we heard them announce 'Freda and the Firedogs, please come to the stage, Freda and the Firedogs.' And I thought, 'I can't get there!'"

Lee Clayton remembered the Picnic as good times and great music, saying he never saw anything negative—then recalls "but, you know, Billy Joe [Shaver] took a handful of acid and was crazy the whole time."

The story of Billy Joe at the first Picnic is one where the legend can hardly be pried away from the real story. In at least one interview, he claimed he had been bitten by a venomous spider and started hallucinating that he was Jesus and began healing picknickers and baptizing them in mud puddles. It's a great story if you don't start wondering how many mud puddles happened to be around this thirsty Texas ranch in July.

Often Shaver's 1973 Picnic story is confused with (or combined with) his epic introduction to Waylon Jennings at the Dripping Springs Reunion, though the '72 meeting is well documented. All we can be sure about when it comes to '73 is that Billy Joe was there, but definitely not *all* there.

Bill Bentley recalled that Shaver was the first artist he saw after he arrived. "He kind of had a scowl on his face and played about two or three songs by himself. And then he just said, 'Me and my mama got out and here we had to walk a mile in to even get to the stage. To hell with this.' And he got up and walked off.

"I felt like, boy, this is gonna be a very different day."

Lissa Hattersley, who wasn't all that far removed from graduating high school in Upstate New York, has the distinction of attending both Woodstock and the inaugural Picnic. She performed with the Austin band Greezy Wheels. "I don't remember a lot, but I do remember that it was really dusty. Salt tablets were being handed out to artists so they wouldn't suffer heatstroke!"

Bandmate Tony Airoldi said he has certain memories of the Picnic that stick with him, but the rest is "kind of a blur." "Even though we had played many sold-out shows at the Armadillo World Headquarters, I'd never been in front of that many people. I loved it."

Tony said he recalls standing on top of the hill as the sun went down and someone was shooting bottle rockets into the crowd. "People were screaming," he said. "It was pissing me off. Then [Kris] Kristofferson came up to the microphone and said, 'Hey, cut the shit. That's just fucking stupid' in that voice of his. And it stopped. Who's going to argue with Kris?"

If you were looking for trouble and guns and hard feelings at the '73 Picnic, your best bet was backstage. "It was total chaos backstage," Woody Roberts said. "The backstage was out of control. Because every

Willie Nelson and Leon Russell watch Charlie Rich perform during the 1973 Picnic. Photo by Watt Casey, WattCasey.com

band—and there were a lot of bands—had their road crew and they had their girlfriends. Plus you had the regular backstage Willie gang that had to be near Willie. It had nothing to do with work; they were just Willie's entourage."

Then came the stage crew and sound crew, working like hell in the heat to load and unload equipment. Woody said most everyone was feeling no pain. "Whether it was beer or whether it was coke or whether it was pot or whatever, people were having a party. It was the Fourth of July, and they were getting as loose as you get on the Fourth of July at a big outdoor festival like that."

Things quickly got heated onstage, where VIPs and wannabes were huddled in the shade of the urethane roof. Bobby Hedderman was doing his best as stage manager, but the rules clearly did not apply to Willie's entourage, and sometimes they flashed a gun to remind him.

Eddie feuded with Dallas promoter and Willie friend Geno McCoslin. Hedderman fumed over his inability to keep the stage clear. At one point, Jan Reid wrote, Waylon Jennings said he wouldn't play because he didn't have enough room.

Adding to the drama was a good number of actual working press and even more imaginary press with real passes. A too-late effort to instill some control over the chaos just managed to make things worse.

Willie, telling the *Los Angeles Free Press* that he would feel bad about asking people to leave the stage, said, "I don't know if it's such a good idea to throw a party in your own hometown."

Fortunately, a truce was declared that evening when Willie drummer Paul English got married to Dianne Huddleston onstage in front of the crowd. Billy Cooper's father, the Reverend George W. Cooper, conducted the ceremony. Sammi Smith served as matron of honor, while Waylon was the best man. Dianne wore blue denim; Paul wore a black cape.

The closest the Picnic would come to disaster was later that evening when the power went off. Woody Roberts said it happened at night while Rita Coolidge was singing. The consensus is that a transformer blew somewhere in Hays County, the system overloaded by the sound and lighting set up by Showco Sound out of Dallas—although Eddie Wilson favors the conspiracy theory that the transformer was shot by "a redneck with a big deer rifle."

Either way, the Picnic was suddenly dark and quiet. Woody feared a rattlesnake-prompted stampede. Eddie feared the show was over before the biggest stars had even performed: "That would have been a tremendous disaster."

Waylon Jennings performs during the 1973 Picnic. Waylon had been unhappy about the crowded conditions onstage and had threatened not to perform. Photo by Watt Casey, WattCasey.com

Fortunately, the Showco crew were seasoned professionals. After much experimentation, the system was wired into a few generators, the lights and sound returned, and the Picnic headed for the finish line.

Tom T. Hall threw his guitar into the crowd. A young Stevie Ray Vaughan played with Marc Benno and the Nightcrawlers. Leon Russell fired up the remaining crowd, and Willie eased them down with "The Party's Over," closing the Picnic sometime after 2 a.m.

There are no media descriptions of how anyone who stayed until the end actually found their cars spread across miles of darkened Hill Country. But Louis Karp remembered how it felt. "We just all managed to stumble our way back down that long caliche road under the beautiful starry night and got in our car and went home."

As Willie played his set, Bill Bentley, feeling like he was close to heatstroke, started walking toward where he thought he might find his ride. "I just started wandering around, thinking how in the world was I ever going to find the truck. But I remember just somehow miraculously walking into this monster parking lot and directly to [the truck]. When you're that high on psychedelics, you just feel like some things are preordained."

NEARLY FORTY YEARS after the Picnic, Burt's brother James Hurlbut said there was no pride in having hosted the first Picnic. "The Dripping Springs Reunion was really a wonderful thing to happen," he told the *American-Statesman*. "The Willie Nelson Picnic was a disaster. The way they handled it, the messes . . . people were swimming in our creeks and walking up to our house and doing weird stuff. . . . I'm sorry we had it."

Years later, his nephew Brad Hurlbut was much more excited at having a family connection to the event but admitted the mess left behind was terrible. "The next few days, I helped clean up a lot of the trash down there. I think my dad had to spend quite a bit of money to clean it up."

Coolers were strewn everywhere, abandoned in the night. Wallets were found. Most surprising were the dogs left behind. "I remember particularly, we had a three-legged dog that wandered up to our house from the Picnic," Brad said. "The owner was looking for it. It was crazy."

The money was bound to be an issue. The accusations and recriminations started quickly after the music stopped and lasted for years. Willie's people said the Armadillo staff were the only ones who made money. The Armadillo pointed at the unaccounted-for ticket money collected by Larry Trader at the gate.

But the end result was just hard feelings, not financial ruin. Mike Tolleson said the money the Armadillo collected covered their expenses—barely. "By the time we cleaned everything up, it seemed to be that everybody we knew that we had worked with got paid."

He runs through a couple of expenditures to illustrate his point: "Looks like the Oak Hill Fire Department got paid $100. We had to write a check to KRMH radio for $119.25. . . . There was a golf cart damaged—we paid $75. There was a site telephone that we paid $100 for. We wrote a check to Dependable Dodge, probably for a Winnebago rental, $250."

The musicians got paid—most of them. A couple thousand dollars went to the big stars, but some of the smaller names played simply for the exposure (whether they planned to or not). Jan Reid wrote that Willie was able to pay back a twenty-five-thousand-dollar loan and recoup his personal investment, but that was it.

"I have this recollection of Randy McCall and I going out to Willie's house at some point afterward," Tolleson said. "We gave Willie an accounting of everything that we had come into our hands, and we gave him a breakdown of where that money went and basically told him that we paid all the bills, but there wasn't anything left over. We collected some money; we paid the bills and barely escaped not in debt."

The hard feelings never rose to the level of legal action, but there in Tolleson's files from the Picnic is a kind of warning. "Here's a note from somebody saying, 'Burt Hurlbut is mad because he says that he was supposed to sit in on the money count at Dripping Springs,'" Tolleson said. "Since he didn't, he is threatening to tell the IRS that we walked out with a bag full of money."

In the end, it wasn't money that caused the split between Willie and the Armadillo; it was guns. Bobby Hedderman was bitter enough about the threats coming from Willie's gun-toting friends while he was trying to manage the stage at the Picnic. But he wasn't about to let this kind of outlaw vibe infect the Armadillo World Headquarters. "A lot of the guys around Willie were pretty rough characters," Tolleson said. "Willie's crowd were not love and peace people. They were coming from kind of another place philosophically."

Some subsequent collaborations between Willie and the Armadillo led to a couple more tense showdowns between Willie's entourage and the hippies. By the end of the year, when Willie showed up to arrange another show, Hedderman told Willie that he'd have to control his friends and keep the guns out. Willie didn't take that well. A few days later,

Hedderman called Willie's manager. One "fuck you" later, that was it for the Willie-Armadillo partnership.

Dahr Jamail remembers it differently. "I told [Eddie], Willie drove me down there and [said], 'Go in there and tell Eddie Wilson they'll never see me again.' And I'm like, you gotta be shitting me; what the fuck's going on here? There was a lot of backstabbing, and not necessary because nobody was in charge of any fucking thing."

Eddie got the message. "I believe Willie said that if his friends weren't good enough for the Armadillo, then he wasn't either, which is, you know, kind of a schoolboy way of thinking about it," Eddie said. "It was the guns, not the friends. But that was pretty much the end."

Asked if he and Willie ever got back together and resolved their differences, Eddie's answer was uncharacteristically brief: "I don't think that we did."

The '73 Picnic didn't make Willie any substantial money, but the publicity that he received was far more valuable. For the next three years, the Picnic would be one of the dominant Texas cultural events of the summer. Even more rewarding for Willie was the national attention. Woody Roberts

Willie Nelson, Kenneth Threadgill, and Leon Russell perform during the 1973 Picnic. Threadgill, an old-school country stalwart, said he had no problems performing with rock icon Russell. Photo by Watt Casey, WattCasey.com

said it "really put Willie in the spotlight that he hadn't been in before. That huge crowd turned out . . . over the Fourth of July weekend when the news media is hungry for something, right? Here's this weird event down there in Texas with country singers and Leon Russell and hippies and cowboys. . . . It caught everybody's eye."

Photographer Melinda Wickman described it as "Texas and country music's Woodstock," but it was more than a peaceful gathering of Willie's friends and fans. You can see it in what Kenneth Threadgill told *Denton Record-Chronicle* reporter Greg Thompson: "I think the time for music segregation is over with now. I had never met Leon [Russell], but the only problem he and I had was picking up my right key."

Bill Bentley takes pride in being a survivor of the first Picnic. "Just being at the start of the cosmic cowboy-redneck rock movement, that was really sort of the watershed beginning of that whole cultural change."

Willie didn't just bring the hippies and rednecks together in Texas, Woody argued. His Picnic cemented a long-simmering merger of rock and country music. "The Dripping Springs Reunion was the end of the old Nashville era," Woody said. "If you take a look at the people that played the Reunion, they had all the big Nashville stars. And it didn't work. Willie's Picnic was the start of the brand-new era."

Woody acknowledged the mixture of rock and country predates the Picnic, pointing at albums such as the Byrds' *Sweetheart of the Rodeo* or Bob Dylan's *Nashville Skyline*. "But in reality, that Picnic is where it started to really emerge," he said. "After that, country music was never the same."

Joe Nick Patoski didn't go quite so far but did agree that the Picnic marked a liberation from Nashville. "This was an Austin deal. What epitomized that was the unholy alliance of the Armadillo becoming co-promoters along with Willie's thieves. . . . The Armadillo was on board, and that brought in a whole different audience. And everything seemed pretty cool. That all fell apart before '74, and it was back to Willie and his thieves."

The outlaw era was coming.

"I WAS A BORED KID in August. The grass had grown up. I found a can of Sterno and a lighter and some [tree] stumps." Eight-year-old Brad Hurlbut was wandering around the seven-thousand-acre Hurlbut Ranch a month after the Picnic, when he found something to do. He lit a fire and watched it burn before thinking better of it.

"I just remembered I went home and laid down on the couch thinking that I had put the fire out. My dad came in the door and said, 'Eighty acres

The Picnic site off McGregor Road outside Dripping Springs was still relatively unchanged forty years later. Photo by Dave Dalton Thomas

up in smoke!' I knew exactly what eighty acres it was." He had burned down what was left of the Picnic site, including the "concession stands and some of the medic booths . . . and damn near most of the stage."

Brad said that for decades afterward, you could walk up and down the creek on the property and find pieces of the urethane- and chicken-wire stage roof.

1974: College Station

SITE: *Texas World Speedway, south of College Station*
ATTENDANCE: *Estimated at 20,000 per day, July 4–6*
HEADLINERS: *Willie Nelson, Waylon Jennings, Leon Russell, Larry Gatlin, Lefty Frizzell, Rick Nelson, Doug Sahm, Michael Murphey, Jimmy Buffett, Bobby Bare, B. W. Stevenson, Doug Kershaw, Nitty Gritty Dirt Band, Jerry Jeff Walker, Freda and the Firedogs*

Willie Nelson wasted no time scaling up his new event, taking the Picnic to the concrete confines and shadeless infield of the Texas World Speedway, expanding it to three days and packing it with a lineup that would be unrivaled until 2003.

Tickets to the Picnic, held Thursday, July 4, through Saturday, July 6, were eight dollars per day or twenty dollars for all three days. Tickets were supposed to be capped at fifty thousand per day, but that wasn't a problem. The heat and the influx of young "freaks" kept most of the area's older country music fans away.

The community had put up a weak fight prior to the Picnic, but afterward many would be outraged by the nudity and open drug use. Between the searing heat, prostrated fans, cowboy hats, and Lone Star Beer, it was part Woodstock from Texas and part Woodstock from hell. As seen in the Yabo Yablonsky concert film *Willie Nelson's 4th of July Celebration*, which was released in 1979, the performers were every bit as stoned as the crowd, just not baked into submission by the sun.

Still, for many, it was a great fun. "I do remember how fun and free it felt," said Judy Hubbard, who watched future husband Ray Wylie from the crowd. "Everyone was happy and shared food, booze, and weed. The music was unique and incredible."

It was the last gig for Austin band Freda and the Firedogs, and Bobby Earl Smith recalls the chaos. "We played our *ass* off," he said. "Marcia [Ball] was doing 'I Wanna Be a Cowboy's Sweetheart,' and it was sounding great, and these two guys came skydiving in. Marcia takes her hat off, starts waving it. People thought she was waving at the skydivers, but what she was actually saying was, 'Don't piss on our parade; this is our show; get out of here.'"

Marcia Ball had a more Zen outlook on it years later. "I'm standing up there yodeling my little heart out, and the whole crowd has turned around and they're looking up in the sky. Which maybe wasn't for the worst, considering I was just learning how to yodel."

The lineup was in a constant state of confusion. In addition to the normal Picnic chaos, the NBC program *Midnight Special* kept trying to get good footage of Waylon, bumping other performers from the bill. Yet somehow *Kung Fu* star David Carradine kept his spot. "I don't know what he was doing, but it was some hippie dippie bullshit," Smith said.

The Picnic may be best remembered by Generation X Texans as the Picnic where Robert Earl Keen, then a young Willie fan, lost his car to a fire in the parking lot. "Someone said, 'Oh my God, look at the smoke,' and I remember running up the grandstands," Smith said. "Looking over into this field, the black smoke was just billowing. One car would catch on fire, and then another would catch on fire. It was pretty amazing."

Keen recorded a hilarious five-minute story of his time at the '74 Picnic on his album *No. 2 Live Dinner*, telling the live crowd about getting relaxed "in the Willie way" and waking up to hear his car had burned down and to see his date leaving him for a pair of ridiculously fit and tanned men.

Asked how much poetic license went into the story, Keen said it wasn't much. "The girl, the golden gods that ran out there with her and took her away . . . all of that stuff happened. The license plate deal, that was exactly how I remembered it—the car burned to the ground and that was pretty much it."

He hitchhiked home to Houston alone, but not before a brief meeting with Willie. Twenty-one years later, the two would meet at another Picnic. This time, it would be Keen's career that was on fire, not his car.

1975: Liberty Hill

SITE: *A pasture west of Liberty Hill along FM 1869 by the South Fork of the San Gabriel River*
ATTENDANCE: *Estimated at 70,000*
HEADLINERS: *Willie Nelson, Kris Kristofferson, Rita Coolidge, the Pointer Sisters, Doug Sahm, David Allan Coe, Johnny Bush, Charlie Daniels Band, Delbert McClinton*

Before the Picnic, the Texas Senate declared July 4 "Willie Nelson Day," though people in Liberty Hill weren't so sure. Even though Willie had scaled back from the three-day event held in College Station in 1974, the normal assortment of conservative and religious townsfolk didn't like the idea of hosting the Picnic and were not reassured by the promises of promoter Geno McCoslin.

Willie hosted the event in a five-hundred-acre pasture owned by an Austin friend. Camping was allowed the night before. Tickets were $5.50 in advance, $7.50 at the gate. An estimated seventy thousand showed up, creating a traffic jam extending from the site to US 183. As they did in Dripping Springs, people began to park along the road outside the site, and many ended up walking miles and miles.

But what they found was quite different from the rocky hills of '73. A legion of concessionaires stood ready, selling food, drink, clothing, and more. The Floating Head Shop was said to have done brisk business. The crowds sizzled in the sun and swam in the San Gabriel River. As people feared in Liberty Hill, many were some combination of naked, drunk, and stoned. One Williamson County deputy sheriff said, "If we had arrested all the naked and drunk people I saw, we'd have filled our jail and yours and all the jails from here to Dallas."

The show went on for seventeen hours, ending just before dawn on July 5. Reviewers praised the sets by the Pointer Sisters and David Allan Coe. Coe's set was delayed by an early-evening rain shower, which turned the pasture to mud and threatened to collapse the canvas covering the stage. Willie sideman Paul English solved the problem by pulling out a pistol and shooting a couple holes in the canvas, safely draining the water and instantly creating a legendary Picnic moment.

"Liberty Hill in '75, that was the classic Picnic in my mind," said Willie biographer Joe Nick Patoski. "In '75, [the Picnic] really became a national act, and the presence of the Pointer Sisters kinda affirms that. That's when it all came together. There was a shitload of people, there's a shitload of national press, and Willie had an album [*Red Headed Stranger*] that was about to change his life."

Not everyone in Liberty Hill was impressed. A newspaper publisher said the town had been "raped." Trash was heaped at the site and littered the roadways and the river. One couple said they took their children to see the mess left behind and got more than they bargained for when a naked man emerged from beneath a bridge.

McCoslin shrugged off the criticism over trash and inadequate water, toilet facilities, and sanitation, saying he had "no idea" so many people would show up. Willie was charged with violating the Texas Mass Gatherings Act and was eventually fined one thousand dollars.

CHAPTER TWO

1976: Gonzales

SITE: *The Sterling Kelley Ranch on FM 532, about eight miles east of Gonzales*
ATTENDANCE: *Estimated at 80,000*
HEADLINERS: *Willie Nelson, Waylon Jennings, Leon and Mary Russell, Kris Kristofferson, Rita Coolidge, David Allan Coe, Jerry Jeff Walker, Doug Sahm, George Jones*

Picnic VIP Update

Willie Nelson: Riding on the wave of popularity of his massive hit album *Red Headed Stranger*, Willie was suddenly nationally famous and the subject of enormous media attention.

Kris Kristofferson: An established country music star, having won multiple Grammys, Kris was a rising presence in Hollywood. Of his three films in 1976, he would win a Golden Globe for his role in *A Star Is Born*.

David Allan Coe: Having recently released the album *Longhaired Redneck*, David Allan was living the outlaw persona to the hilt. He was a great singer and songwriter but remained on the fringes of the industry.

Ray Wylie Hubbard: Known for "Up against the Wall Redneck Mother," Ray released his first album in 1976, *Ray Wylie Hubbard and the Cowboy Twinkies*. The producer had changed the sound, and Ray Wylie hated it so much that the first time he heard it, he cried.

It was about time for the citizens of Gonzales County to go to work on Monday morning when the rain came down. But at the Picnic site, Willie Nelson and his fans had been partying all night—Willie had just sat in with Leon and Mary Russell. The 1976 Picnic had officially been going strong for twenty-four hours, though for some the party had started Saturday, or even Friday.

Or, in the case of promoter Geno McCoslin, the party wasn't measured in hours or days but in alcohol- and drug-fueled manias that could go on for weeks before he melted down. An enormous number of people had joined Willie and Geno in the impossibly tiny community of Little New York, Texas, about eight miles east of Gonzales, descending en masse despite a pretty remarkable community effort to reject the Fourth of July Picnic.

The weekend was its own alcohol- and drug-fueled mania, an orgy of nudity and drunkenness and drug consumption that the people of Gonzales County had scarcely been able to imagine—at least not until many of them stopped by the Kelley Ranch to witness it happen.

Now the skies had opened up. The canvas roof over the stage had collapsed. The sound system was fried, and Leon's piano was soaked. The freshly bulldozed ground in front of the stage turned to mud, and the mud mixed with effluent from the few overflowing Porta Potties. The picnickers packed up and fled toward Interstate 10, stopping only to clean out area restaurants and food stores like a swarm of locusts.

Given the religious fervor of those who opposed the Picnic, there's no doubt some saw a higher power at work—a cleansing flood to wash away the wicked. Mike Benestante, who worked for promoter Dahr Jamail and did much of the advance work in Gonzales, doesn't disagree. "It's divine intervention that ended the concert," he said forty-four years later. "That's what it was."

The kidnapping, though . . . that probably wasn't part of the spiritual script. "Walking back to the trailer, I felt a gun in my back," Mike said. "I turned around and it was Geno. 'You're coming with me kid.'"

Texas writer Joe Nick Patoski didn't stay until it all came crashing down. He left early after seeing enough. "Gonzales was conflict," he said. "It was like all the bad elements that existed in this thing kind of came to the surface. Things turned sour. Gonzales was the end of the first iteration [of the Picnic]. And it ended poorly."

Dahr Jamail would remind us here that at least eighty thousand people showed up, making Gonzales the largest Picnic, and a great many of them had a great time. Despite Willie and Waylon Jennings's sets being rained out, much of the music was great and the experience was like no other. That Dahr, Mike, Geno, and others managed to create this experience in an empty field in *rural* Texas—far removed from Austin, at least culturally—was improbable and impressive.

But Patoski is right. Conflict was at the heart of the Gonzales Picnic, right from the start. The Willie Family had always been driven by the energy that accompanied chaos, yet at the height of the outlaw country era, that chaos spilled over into violence and depravity. There were rapes

Early morning on the last day of the Willie Nelson Fourth of July Picnic outside Gonzales, just before the rain ended the show. The photographer noted: "It is 8:30 and Leon Russell has just been called back for an encore. Many have not awakened yet. Trash is everywhere." Photo by Ed Malcik, Austin American-Statesman

and stabbings and overdoses. A man died. Guns were openly carried, and hard drugs were openly sold and used.

The first four Willie Nelson Fourth of July Picnics were all epic and are all legendary. But only the Gonzales Picnic is infamous.

Laurie Kelley Taylor is the daughter of Sterling Kelley, the rancher who hosted the 1976 Picnic. She and her husband, Steve Taylor, found that they could hardly leave that legacy behind. "Whenever we would travel, Steve would say [we're from] Gonzales, Texas," she said. And people would immediately associate it with the Picnic. "Well, yeah, that happened on my daddy's place. . . . Everybody had an opinion about it."

GONZALES IN 1976 was home to about six thousand people, many of whom worked in the poultry industry. About seventy miles south of Austin and an equal distance east of San Antonio, Gonzales was decidedly nonurban Texas. Its citizens were proud of their town's role as the spark that

Houston Munson and Willie Nelson at Munson's home in Gonzales before the Picnic. Photo courtesy of the Munson family

inflamed the Texas Revolution, but in the mid-1970s, most were plenty happy to keep things the way they were.

Houston Munson wasn't one of them. The forty-year-old Gonzales County district attorney was a big Willie Nelson fan and had reached out to Willie in late 1975, hoping to host a concert on his ranch near Shiner for his birthday. It didn't happen then, but when Willie started looking for a place to hold the '76 Picnic, he called Houston back.

Houston's daughter, Beth Munson Bumpass, recalled that one day that spring she stopped by her dad's office after school and Willie was there. "I was just starstruck," she said. "My dad said, 'We're getting ready to look at places to have the Picnic; you wanna go with us?'"

She sat in the pickup between her dad and Willie, and on the way out of town, they stopped at a convenience store so Willie could get a cooler, some ice, and some Lone Star Beer. When they stopped at a ranch, "my dad got out to open the gate and Willie said, 'You want a beer?'" Beth said. "I was fifteen years old, and I'd never had a beer before, but I said 'sure.'"

On April 29, Townsend Miller announced in the *Austin American-Statesman* that Gonzales would be the site of a three-day Picnic on July 2–4: "This is beautiful country, and I'm told that the camping site is blessed with a small warm-water river and numerous small lakes." All of that would prove to be a bit of an exaggeration.

With District Attorney Houston brokering the deal, Willie had reached an agreement with Sterling Kelley to host the Picnic on approximately 850 acres of mesquite brush and pasture along FM 532. The deal gave Kelley twenty thousand dollars and guaranteed "payment of expenses necessary to clean up and restore the premises." Willie would foot the bill for getting the site ready.

In a sign of problems to come, the agreement quickly came under fire. As it turns out, some of the land in question actually belonged to Sterling Kelley's mother. "My grandmother was real big in the Baptist church, and she wasn't very keen on them having that kind of party on her land," said Mark Kelley, cousin to Sterling's daughter, Laurie. "My uncle had leased the place from her, and he turned around and leased it to Willie, and she was really upset about it."

Mike Benestante. Photo courtesy of Mike Benestante

Ultimately Leona Kelley's son persuaded her not to fight the deal. "She was dead-set against it, but she went ahead and let her son do it because there was gonna be a lawsuit over it," Mark Kelley said. "She still wasn't happy about it."

Dahr Jamail met Mike Benestante in 1975 while the two were attending the University of St. Thomas, a private Catholic college in Houston. "Dahr came to a party we had at our house in Montrose, and we became instant friends," Mike said. After that, "he came to our house every night and generally played his guitar."

Mike was at school on a golf scholarship but shared Dahr's love of music and soon started helping his new friend promote shows, beginning with the 1975 Fourth of July Picnic in Liberty Hill and continuing with a string of highly successful shows in Houston. Dahr, connected to Willie through his father since childhood, was the boss, but Mike was a go-getter. "Anything that needed doing, [he'd say,] 'I got it covered,' and he'd go handle it," Dahr said.

In the spring of 1976, Dahr was still going to college in Houston, two hours away from the Picnic site. Mike, however, had lost his golf scholarship, dropped out of school, and was completely taken by the "excitement and glamour" of the music business. "I was all in," Mike said.

So he moved to Gonzales, set up Picnic headquarters in a rented house, and opened a credit account with the town's foremost lumberyard. Both the house and the lumberyard were owned by County Judge Henry Vollentine, making a key connection that Mike says was a stroke of luck—he had rented the house from Vollentine's wife, he said, without having any idea who she was. "I met Mr. Vollentine and we just hit it off real good," Mike said. "I think they saw that I was honest, and I loved what I was doing and we had good intentions." Others weren't so sure about that last part.

The unironically named CLOD—Citizens for Law, Order, and Decency—had formed after the Picnic was announced. Under the leadership of chairman Upton Ruddock and Reverend Jimmy Darnell, they were more than 120 strong and had circulated petitions against the Picnic. "To allow this invasion is to invite the anti-American, anti-Christian hippie subculture right into our homes," read a handbill distributed by Darnell's non-denominational church. They were offended. They were indignant. And they had a real shot at stopping the Picnic.

At the time, the Texas Mass Gatherings Act required any mass gathering with five thousand or more people that ran longer than twelve hours to receive a permit from the county judge to ensure sanitation and health standards were met. Houston Munson filed an application listing Willie as the promoter. The application said one thousand portable toilets had been reserved but was breezy on other topics, saying medical facilities would be "more than adequate" and security would be "sufficient." Three typed pages of easy promises and a five-dollar application fee . . . there was an expectation on Willie's side that the permit was simply a formality.

The Gonzales County Commissioners Court, presided over by Judge Vollentine, agreed to hold a hearing on the application on May 19 at 10 a.m. Dahr and his lawyer friend Richard Mithoff come to town for what would be a six-hour showdown. "Houston has sworn it's all wired and everything is hooked up," Dahr said. "And we go down there, and they have this hearing, and there's five hundred people against it called the Citizens for Law, Order, and Decency. And the fucking bunch of judges vote it down. So this was all supposed to be like wired, and Richard's looking at me like what the fuck is this?"

All four county commissioners rejected the application. Perhaps they were swayed by the CLODs, who denounced expected immorality, drunkenness, and drugs. Or maybe they were swayed by Williamson County Commissioner Wesley Foust, who made the trip to warn about what had happened in Liberty Hill the year before. Or perhaps it was, as one commissioner would insist later, a legal decision based on traffic, sanitation, and health concerns.

Either way, Willie got the message. Despite an immediate promise by Mithoff to appeal, by the next day Willie had issued a statement: "I can't go against the law on this thing."

The Picnic was off.

Dahr Jamail had told Mike Benestante to come home, but Mike wasn't ready to give up. The Picnic headquarters was just around the corner from Houston Munson's home in Gonzales. Houston would come over to Mike's rented house, and they would drink Lone Star and scheme. They would have to change the commissioners' minds.

For a few days it seemed pointless. There was open talk about where else the Picnic could go, though Willie had said that too much money had already been invested in Gonzales to move it. Willie was firm: it wasn't happening.

But soon petitions were circulating around town in favor of having the Picnic. "When the CLODs became a threat, I started a rival entity, 'Friends of Willie,'" Mike said. "I solicited Eddie Scheske to be the founder. When they released negative information, we countered. Most of the young people were on our side."

CLOD stood firm, putting their moral objections on the back burner to emphasize the law: "Similar musical festivals have caused health problems, law enforcement problems and traffic jams. It is for the overall good of the community that we oppose this event."

Houston's daughter, Beth Munson Bumpass, said the community was "definitely divided. But my dad loved Willie, and he wanted it to happen. All the controversy was quite scary back then, especially for our family, because there was so much opposition toward it."

Mike told the *Austin American-Statesman* that Willie should go ahead and do the Picnic without the permit, noting that the worst that could happen was a one-thousand-dollar fine.

Within a few days, they had backed off that stance. Dahr was quoted by the *Statesman* saying that they would not go ahead without a permit. "We must obey the law," Dahr said. Houston Munson got to work. On May 28, he filed an amended application for a permit, this time going into careful detail about the site and the health, safety, and security preparations. Among the promises:

> The maximum number of persons allowed to attend will be 150,000 and this will be controlled by sale of tickets. . . . No one will be allowed to attend without one of such tickets.
>
> Preparations for sanitation and security and parking [will be] made for 200,000 people.
>
> The promoter also has made preparations to fully and completely abide by all regulations contained in the requirements issued by the Texas Department of Health Resources.
>
> There will be 50 qualified security officers in the entertainment site and an additional 75 undercover security personnel in the crowd . . . to negate any drug problems and to aid in enforcement of the laws.
>
> Separate toilet facilities for men and women shall be provided at a rate of no more than 50 persons per toilet seat. Over 1,500 porta-cans have been rented. . . . All toilet facilities shall be serviced at least twice a day.

It looked good on paper. But it's worth noting that Houston told the *Statesman* that he had filed the amended application without contacting Willie.

It seems big promises were part of the plan. A local preacher who had opposed the Picnic dropped his opposition after being told he could preach to the crowd on Sunday, July 4, and that Willie and Johnny Cash would sing in his choir. It didn't happen.

Houston told the county that Phases and Stages Productions out of Austin was going to film the event and give the local hospital district up to one million dollars. This didn't happen either.

The reported lineup now included Roy Clark, Michael Murphey, and the Marshall Tucker Band, as well as Bob Dylan and Joan Baez arriving in Gonzales as part of a special train tour. None of them played the Picnic.

Houston said the TV rights to the Picnic had been sold to NBC for $650,000. The company handling Willie's contracts said that wasn't true.

In the midst of this Willie was set to perform on June 4 at Houston Munson's ranch near Shiner as a benefit for the medical clinic in Moulton, a small town north of Shiner. The fund-raiser was originally set to include the Gonzales Hospital, but after the local dispute over the Picnic they refused to accept any funds from Willie.

Strictly a Friday-night affair, the ranch benefit didn't require any permit and drew at most four thousand people, buying tickets at five or six dollars each. The day before, Judge Vollentine told the *Statesman* that he assumed Willie would announce, again, that the Picnic was off. At a

CHAPTER TWO \ 45

Page 24 ICONOCLAST, Dallas, Texas, July 12, 1976

WILLIE'S FOURTH FOURTH OF JULY PICNIC

E PLURIBUS WILLIE

**JULY 4
IN GONZALES
TEXAS**

TICKETS AVAILABLE AT:
DALLAS—PRESTON TICKET AGENCY
FT WORTH—AMUSEMENT TICKET SERVICE
AUSTIN—INNERSANCTUM
HOUSTON—FOLEY'S
SAN ANTONIO—SAN ANTONIO TICKET SERVICE

THE NATIONS' LARGEST ANNUAL MUSIC EVENT

This advertisement for the Picnic ran several times in the Iconoclast, an alternative newspaper in Dallas. Curiously, the ad ran a week after the show was over. Dave Dalton Thomas collection preshow cocktail party for VIPs, Willie, as expected, told reporters that there would be no Picnic in Gonzales, though he teased the idea of a one-day show near Lake Livingston or Lake Travis.

But just before taking the stage, Willie met with a group of Gonzales County officials that included Judge Vollentine. During his performance, Willie announced to the crowd that the Gonzales Picnic was back on. Beth Munson Bumpass remembers that her father went up onstage and told Willie that the show was on and Willie gave Houston Munson a kiss right there in front of everyone. "As my dad said, 'a kiss on the mouth-hole,'" she laughed.

It's not exactly clear what sparked the deal. Mike Benestante said they had already gained the approval of one county commissioner and the benefit show helped sway a second commissioner—the one whose district was closest to Moulton. Judge Vollentine told the *Statesman* that Willie had promised that the show would be a one-day, twelve-hour event, easing county concerns.

Looking back, Willie's nephew Freddy Fletcher was a lot more direct: "They had to bribe a bunch of people down there. They had to pay a lot of cash to be able to do that show." He didn't offer specific details, but Joe Nick Patoski confirms that kind of approach wasn't unprecedented or even unusual at the time.

Mike offered a more wholesome explanation. "Willie met with the politicians directly. And Willie has a presence when you meet him. People just kinda go along with things. He has a reassuring presence."

With less than a month to go, the preparations—and the anxiety and the insanity—kicked into high gear. The rented house in Gonzales was Picnic Central. Mike had two phone lines and two young assistants named Cat and Angel, who were earning "twenty dollars a week and all the pot they could smoke," Dahr said.

"They would type my press releases and get people on the phone for us," Mike said. "I mailed hundreds of press releases to various newspapers and spoke to an equal number of radio stations pumping up the free publicity."

Joining Mike and the two assistants at the house was Peter Sheridan, a massive man linked to the Hells Angels. He sometimes served as bodyguard and driver for Willie, and he sometimes was just an intimidating presence in the Willie Family. He didn't really have a job in Gonzales but liked being where the action was. So he moved in and slept on the floor.

Within a week of the Moulton benefit, Judge Vollentine was saying that he intended to grant the permit for a one-day Picnic "if everything in the petition is in order." And already, Willie's promoters were saying the Picnic was "officially" a one-day show . . . but there may be some "parties" on July 3 and July 5 that ticket holders would be able to attend.

DOUGLAS EUGENE McCOSLIN often had his hands on either cocaine, vodka, a gun, or someone's money. The Dallas-based promoter and club owner, known to many as "Geno," was an old friend of Willie's, having often booked Willie in the early days when few others would. Geno was loyal to Willie, with the understanding that taking a little extra money here and there was just part of the game.

In the mid-2000s, *Fort Worth Weekly* writer Jeff Prince interviewed Roy Stamps, a one-time partner of Geno. Stamps described Geno as "a troubled genius—creative, funny, handsome, and charismatic, but also conniving, paranoid, criminally minded, seldom without a pistol, and cranked to the nth degree."

There was a reason for the madness. "Today we would know Gino as bipolar," Stamps told Prince. "Back then we just thought he was crazy."

Susie McCoslin, one of Geno's daughters, did confirm that her father

Geno McCoslin, center, with Willie Nelson and Larry Trader making plans in a hotel room on the road in the mid-1970s. Photo courtesy of Susie McCoslin

was manic-depressive. Geno essentially self-medicated with drugs and alcohol for years before ultimately getting sober and taking lithium regularly. "He was good" when he was home, Susie said. "It was when he was gone on the road when things went bad with drugs and alcohol."

These days, when Willie's friends discuss Geno, he seems to be more legend than person. If someone has one Geno story, you can bet there is another. A favorite is that he had a hot show at the Sportatorium in Dallas and put "Men" and "Women" signs over the exit doors. People would go through the doors, thinking they were headed for the restroom, only to find themselves locked outside. If they wanted back in, they would have to buy another ticket.

But Geno stories exist because he was a loose cannon, and this was particularly true in Gonzales, where the pressure was ramping up in the weeks before the Picnic.

Joe Nick Patoski remembers that he and fellow writer Nelson Allen went to interview Geno in mid-June for an advance story and Geno pulled a gun on them. "There were always guns in the background," Patoski said. "But Geno was so coked up and out of his mind with the pressure of the prep and having to deal with the media—he pulled a gun on us while we're interviewing him. It's like 'Geno, what are you doing this to us for? There's no negotiations, there's nothing here. What's going on?'"

The Picnic headquarters in Gonzales got a little dicey as well. "Geno was okay early in the morning for about thirty minutes to an hour," Mike Benestante said. "But then his vodka and cocaine self-medication" would kick in.

Geno and Peter Sheridan "hated each other," Dahr Jamail said, and one day Geno just ran over Peter's motorcycle. "This Hells Angel comes home, finds his motorcycle torn up, and he has me pinned up on the wall," Dahr said. "So I gotta either rat on Geno, who would fucking kill me right there, or this Hells Angel is about to tear me from limb to limb. Geno comes walking up and puts a gun to his head."

Freddy Fletcher finishes the story: "Geno takes Peter up in a helicopter, puts a gun to his head, and says 'jump.'" When Peter begged for mercy, Geno let him off.

There's no explanation of where the helicopter came from or how Geno got the big guy into the helicopter, but Freddy turns serious when asked if that part is more legend than truth. "No, no, that really happened," he said.

On Monday, June 14, Judge Henry Vollentine granted the elusive permit at a two-hour commissioners meeting. Hog raisers and egg producers protested, the *Statesman* reported, and the Citizens for Law, Order, and Decency made a last-ditch effort, asking the judge to recuse himself because he was renting out his home to the Picnic promoters. Vollentine refused to step down.

Mike Benestante remembers this as "courtroom drama" pitting "conservatives versus liberals, rural versus urban lawyers," but if there was any suspense, the newspaper reports didn't reflect it. The Picnic was too big to stop now, and many in Gonzales County were thinking about making money off this hippie invasion rather than fighting it.

When Willie called off the Picnic in May, there was no small amount of confusion on the part of the artists scheduled to play. Now that it was definitely back on, the promoters scrambled to confirm as many artists as they could.

Waylon Jennings, Leon and Mary Russell, Kris Kristofferson and Rita Coolidge, George Jones, David Allan Coe, and Roger Miller were all confirmed. But Geno didn't limit himself. Instead of the "Bob Dylan rumor" sleight of hand that Woody Roberts used in 1973, Geno would just tell people that Dylan was coming. Heck, maybe Joan Baez and the Charlie Daniels Band, too.

"Welcome to Geno's world," Freddy said.

Mike said it was just show business. "You know, Geno and myself and everybody else, we exaggerated things as some of the people who were going to be there, just to try to build it up," he said. "We did not know how or when this thing would end. We were just trying to make it big."

Dahr said they just wanted to draw as many people as possible but admits that "today if you did that in a musical setting, you'd have one hundred lawsuits." Then he added, "There was a huge amount of insecurity [among the promoters], which probably added to the insanity and the overkill in getting people to come."

By June 29, Geno told the *Statesman* that, despite the twenty-four-hour permit, it was going to be a three-day Picnic, as originally planned, except running July 3–5. "I think Willie's decided to break the law," he said. "It's only a one-thousand-dollar fine."

At the Sterling Kelley Ranch, preparing the site was an around-the-clock race. "There was this huge amount of fear and energy.... It was almost like panic," Dahr said. "I did shows at that time at stadiums, but it's not the same thing as going out in the woods and trying to drag electricity, water, and a stage and sound and lights out there."

The ranch had utilities, but nothing that would support the expected one hundred thousand people—about fifteen times the population of the

Early arrivals claim a spot in the pasture as the 1976 Picnic gears up. Photo by Ed Malcik, Austin American-Statesman

entire surrounding area. Water and electricity were fortified. Roads were built. Fields were scraped clear to serve as parking lots, and traffic plans were desperately made.

One area where they were ahead of the game was setting up the stage. "Mike Lam was our production wizard," Mike Benestante said. "He had abundant resources and expertise. Dahr and Mike would come to Gonzales often to plan for the stage, sound, and lights. Mike was the one guy that could pull off the difficult task at Gonzales."

Fencing off the area was just a matter of illusion, for the most part. "We would fence in the area that you could see coming from the road," Dahr said. "We're trying to put up the appearance of a fence for five hundred to eight hundred yards, maybe that's a half a mile, just to force people to walk to the ticket gate."

Portable toilets were a different issue. State health regulations called for one toilet per fifty people—or about two thousand for the expected crowd of one hundred thousand. But a July 1 *Statesman* article said that the site still didn't have any. The story said one man was moving toilets from Fort Hood but stopped when he didn't get paid.

The promoters "said they'd make their own," the man said. A follow-up story the next day said workers were constructing "150-foot-long wooden toilets." Ultimately, there would be conflicting reports of what was actually provided in terms of toilets, but it would fall far, far short of what was needed.

When asked whether the promoters might have been concerned about not meeting the requirements of the Mass Gatherings Act, Joe Nick Patoski was quick to answer. "Fuck no! Are you kidding me? They're doing whatever it takes to do the show. It might not be up to code, but sanitation was the least of their fucking worries."

By July 2, there were already two thousand people at the site, camping out and waiting for the "unofficial" start time of noon on Saturday, July 3. More than fifty concessionaires, who had paid Houston Munson one thousand dollars each with the hopes of getting rich, were setting up and stocking their stands.

"The concert site, equipped with two stock tanks, has been cleared with bulldozers and could turn into a muddy quagmire if it rains," warned a final preview in the *Statesman*. The official forecast said the weekend would be cloudy but dry. But that wasn't the only forecast: "Local prognosticators say the area's tarantulas are on the move toward higher ground—a sure sign of rain."

"THIS IS A TRUE STORY. We're sleeping in our sleeping bags, and all of a sudden, there's this ruckus all around us—on top of us, literally."

Photographer Scott Newton is telling a story from the first night of the '76 Picnic. He and his wife and a friend of theirs were sleeping in their tent when a fight broke out.

"It was like out of a kung fu movie. These three guys were taking on, I don't know, twenty-five or thirty cowboys, and they kicked all their asses. We're standing there with these sleeping bags over us, and we watch this fight unfold like nothing I've ever seen. These karate guys kicked all these cowboys' asses. It was astonishing, it happened so fast; it was over in three or four minutes. And they dusted their hands off, just like in a cartoon, and walked off. I don't know what they were, bikers, security guys, whatever they were, man, there were teeth lost and everything. Gonzales was absolutely wild. I've never seen that much anarchy in Texas before or since."

On July 3, the Picnic got under way, and it didn't take long for it to become Willie's largest ever. More than seventy-five thousand were there

The Gonzales Picnic was the largest, with a crowd of eighty thousand. Photo by Tom Lankes, Austin American-Statesman

by nightfall, the *Statesman* reported, pouring into Gonzales from all directions. Traffic was stacked up on 532—locals were selling beer and ice to idling motorists—but there would be no parking and walking like in 1973. Tow trucks were busy hauling off cars parked on the side of the road.

The music began just before 4 p.m., and concessionaires sold T-shirts, suntan lotion, watermelon, barbecue . . . even fireworks.

Still, Geno McCoslin was pushing for more.

"When we showed up, we're supposed to go to a little motel by the side of the road," Ray Wylie Hubbard said. "We went into the office there and said, 'We're looking for Geno McCoslin, Willie's Picnic.' And he said, 'Well, he's down there in Room 11.' We walked into the room and Geno's on the phone, and he's got a record player there. He's playing Waylon Jennings, and he holds up his hand like 'don't talk.' And he says, 'Yeah this is Geno, we're out at the site right now. Waylon's onstage, and we think Dylan and [Paul] McCartney may sit in with him; there's still plenty of tickets left.' You know, and then he would hang up. He was calling little radio stations."

Trying to sell tickets was a little optimistic at that point. "The fence was down before the show ever started," Dahr Jamail said. "Mauled it to pieces the night before." Dahr said there was a ticket booth, but people wouldn't walk out of their way to go buy a ticket when they could just walk in through holes in the fence "as big as a Suburban."

The same as in Dripping Springs, they just didn't have enough people to sell tickets on foot to the waves of people coming in. "We had ten thousand tickets sold in advance," Dahr said. "And you have one hundred thousand people drive up, mostly getting there at the same time. That's like trying to get all the fish in the school of fish."

Filmmaker Perry Tong was at the stage by dawn's early light on July 4, ready for the music to begin in earnest. "We had two camera trucks and a sound truck and a motor home and there was nobody there," he said. "It's like six in the morning and then at 6:15, there was nothing but humanity coming over the hill; it looked like a Roman invasion. They came over the hill like ants."

Leon Russell and Jerry Jeff Walker opened the Bicentennial Fourth at 8 a.m., followed by Steve Fromholz, Floyd Tillman, and Ray Wylie Hubbard, who played "The Star-Spangled Banner."

Many of the bands played up to a dozen songs, as Willie and the promoters had already decided that the Picnic would last as long as they could go. "We were pretty much letting bands play and do what they wanted to do," Dahr said. "Willie was letting everybody have the stage. He was really generous."

B. W. Stevenson and Rusty Wier got big applause, reviews say, but few moved the crowd like country legend George Jones.

Tyler Mahan Coe, then researching George Jones for the second season of his "Cocaine & Rhinestones" podcast, shared the story he heard from Evelyn Shriver, a close friend of Jones and a Nashville legend. "Jones had terrible stage fright," Tyler said. "That's why he would always skip out on shows—giving him the 'No Show Jones' nickname—he'd get drunk and scared and run away. He was at the Picnic, and he got to looking at the crowd. And he saw these, you know, long-haired hippie, biker, rough-and-wild type folks and here he is in a Nudie suit. And he's like, 'I can't go out there. Those people don't want to hear anything that I'm gonna sing about.'"

He was planning on bailing, and then he ran into David Allan Coe. "My dad asked him what the problem was," Tyler said. And after George told him, David Allan responded, "George, I got longer hair than anyone else here. And I think you're the best country music singer of all time. I'll escort you to the stage, and I'll stand on the side of the stage. No one will give you any problem."

Rodeo Barton, a longtime member of David Allan's band, remembers the moment. "George had respect for David as a writer and performer," Rodeo said of George's decision to play. "I always suspected there was a bit of fear as David was a very imposing figure . . . but David adored the Possum and would have gone through hell to help him."

Either way, George did what many recall as an incredible show. He opened with "I'm Ragged, but I'm Right" and received a "thunderous ovation," as he described it a month later to the *Valley News* in Van Nuys, California. "I imagine the biggest look of relief that ever fell over anybody's face fell over mine when I finished that song," George told them.

Willie wouldn't show up at his own Picnic until later that night but wasted no time in sitting in with Dough Sahm about 3 a.m.—another set that was highly praised.

"The music was so good," Dahr said. "I never talked to anybody who wasn't happy. You know that legacy wouldn't live that long and people wouldn't be back if the music wasn't good. So you gotta start there. They're not dragging their shit out in the woods in the weather and that fucking heat unless the music was really fucking good."

For some, though, the music was just the sound track to the party. Drug use was open and rampant. A reporter for the *Victoria Advocate* later wrote that "the festival air was punctuated with hawkers' shouts of 'CO-caine!'"

The *Advocate* quoted Judge Vollentine, who said that security was "sorely inadequate." "Some of these kids were there for days and were very spaced out," Vollentine said. "Not just on marijuana, but on hard drugs. The potential for violence was there."

Freddy Fletcher's brother was there with the Travis County Sheriff's Department and was among those who were in charge of security. "That's a rough one," Freddy said. "When [the crowd] crashed the gates, I mean, the shit broke loose. There was no way to contain it after that."

In the heat—it was ninety-five on July 3 and a few degrees cooler on July 4, according to NOAA data for Gonzales—some people took to the stock ponds to cool off. This took a tragic turn when twenty-six-year-old Paul Lenden Boatright of Pasadena drowned, the Picnic's first and only death. Filmmaker Perry Tong caught footage of Boatright just before his death. "We'd been filming a bunch of hippies swimming in a stock tank," Perry said. "And one of them kept walking in the water, and the others were going out and dragging him back up on shore. We shot a little bit of footage of him and went on about our business. When we came back by, he was drowned."

David Allan Coe poses for a photo backstage at the Gonzales Picnic. He was seen with the gun in his back pocket throughout the day. © Ron McKeown

Perry meant to produce a concert movie called *Sweet Willie*. The project got off to a great start, then fell apart. "We shot around four thousand feet of sixteen-millimeter film," he said. "There were squabbles between investors and eventually we bowed out after we sold part of it to Dick Clark. I don't know what happened to the rest of the footage—somebody ran off with it."

The 1976 Picnic came at the height of the outlaw country era, and despite what the survivors may claim these days, for many of the picnickers it was definitely not about declaring independence from Nashville . . . it was about being an outlaw. Booze, drugs, bad attitudes, and guns were prevalent. David Allan Coe was among the many who openly carried a pistol.

"That was the first time and the last time that I saw an uninhibited display of guns," photographer Melinda Wickman said. "It was pretty blatant. And that one was the roughest Picnic that I remember seeing. I didn't feel quite safe."

Violence against women was very much an underreported part of the Gonzales Picnic. At one point Melinda wanted to go through the crowd to take some photos. One of the sheriffs backstage told her not to do that. "They told me to get on one of their horses and go through the crowd with a deputy, not to wander by myself," she said.

Fellow photographer Scott Newton had a bird's-eye view of the reason why. "At the beginning there were men and women up in front of the stage, but after a couple of hours, maybe halfway through the day, there weren't any women left," he said. "They were all getting groped; they all had to get out of that front area."

It got worse.

Because of the shortage of toilets, Newton said women would wander off to look for a private place to relieve themselves and were sexually assaulted. "The women were going off into the surrounding area, and they'd go to pee and there were guys raping them," he said. "I couldn't believe it." There's no way to confirm Newton's claim, but the *Statesman* said that "at least three rapes were reported to medical personnel."

The wildness continued through the night. Newton recalls soldiers "coming from Fort Hood with bags of fireworks," planning on having roman candle fights that got out of hand. An announcer later told the crowd to stop it—a five-year-old boy had been hit in the head and his eye was injured.

Medical volunteers with Austin's Middle Earth Crisis Center reported they found a seventeen-year-old girl lying unconscious in a ditch who stopped breathing after a drug overdose. She was taken by ambulance to an Austin hospital. (Ultimately, she recovered and became a volunteer for the group that rescued her.) The final medical tally is twenty overdoses, fifteen stabbings, five snakebites, fifteen vehicle accidents, ten fireworks injuries, and "almost twenty major cuts."

Some still had a hell of a time.

"There was a lot of nudity going on," Mark Kelley said. "They just didn't really care too much; they were having a good time. The last night I was there, there was some guy who took an ax and stuck it in his leg. So we got an ambulance coming. When the man came to tell the ambulance where the injured guy was, he didn't have nothing on either; he was just running in front of the headlights, everything swinging. That was a wild party man."

Mike Benestante didn't see any of that party. Exhausted, he made it to the site, went backstage, and looked out at what he figured was a job well done. "Everyone was smiling backstage, but I had no energy left," he said.

"I went to the closest trailer, which was just a few feet away. There was a huge wadded-up American flag in the room, maybe twenty by twenty feet. I wrapped myself in it, secure in the thought that things were going to be beautiful, then rolled over and closed my eyes."

About ninety minutes after Leon Russell awoke the Picnic with "Jumpin' Jack Flash" at 7:30 a.m. on Monday, the rain came down. In short order, the roof collapsed, the sound system shorted out, and the Picnic crowd began to flee.

Mike Benestante was awakened by the thunder and staggered into the rain toward the stage. Mike Lam handed him a large Bowie knife and told him to climb the scaffolding and slash drainage holes in the canopy. "I did my best Spiderman imitation," he said. "It was difficult duty. The poles were wet, and at one point I had to hang by one arm and stab with the other."

It was no use. Everything on the stage was soaked. The Picnic was over.

"Walking back to the trailer to retrieve my glasses, I felt a gun in my back," Mike said. "I turned around and it was Geno. 'You're coming with me kid.'" Mike and Geno got in the back seat of Geno's big Lincoln. Wally Selman and Poodie Locke, whom Willie had tasked with keeping an eye

Willie was late arriving for the 1976 Picnic in Gonzales but wasted no time joining Doug Sahm onstage. Photo by Ed Malcik, Austin American-Statesman

on Geno, got in the front seat and they drove off. Geno was in a frenzy, Mike said, and held a knife to Mike's throat and started blaming him for everything that went wrong.

Was it an authentic kidnapping? At the time, Mike said, he felt his life was in danger "from a madman." But looking back, he's not as sure. "I think it was all a show. Everything was a show for Geno. He was a performer." As the car headed toward Austin, Geno changed his mind about halfway there. The car slowed to a roll, and they kicked Mike out of the car. He hitchhiked back to Gonzales.

What was left of the Picnic was statistics. It was "a three-day event that left one man dead, several hundred persons injured, 147 facing criminal charges and 800 acres of trash," the *Statesman* reported. The *Nashville Tennessean* quoted music writer Don Cusic, who was among the crowd: "You could describe the Picnic briefly as 'a bunch of dust that turned to mud.'"

"IN THAT LITTLE POND over there, there was 75 to 80 people stark naked." Sterling Kelley gave a *Statesman* reporter a tour of his ranch a few weeks after the Picnic, pointing out where the action took place and navigating through "a whole sea of empty beer cans." He was upset that his favorite herding horse died when it was overfed by concessionaires and that people had nowhere to put their trash during the event.

It wasn't just beer cans, Laurie Kelley Taylor's husband, Steve Taylor, said. "When they left here, they left like thirty or forty cars, vans, dogs. There was just crap everywhere." Laurie said her dad ended up getting the contract to clean it all up. "The whole thing about this was he could make more money doing [the Picnic] in one weekend than he could in a year," she said. "And he was gonna do it. I mean, we didn't have a lot of money."

In the months following the Picnic, the Gonzales community remained split over whether it was worth the trouble. "The community ended up really liking it because everybody made so much money," Laurie said at first. "From the gas stations to the convenience stores to grocery stores . . . I mean, they sold out everything."

But she admitted a lot of those who didn't benefit economically "just thought it was the devil. . . . They were really against it from a religious standpoint of what went on out here." Even her own family was divided. "My mother nearly had a nervous breakdown over it. She was very involved in the church."

And then there were those in the community who paid Houston Munson one thousand dollars to operate a concession at the Picnic. Many

The aftermath of the 1976 Picnic in Gonzales. Landowner Sterling Kelley ended up suing Willie over cleanup costs. Photo by Tom Lankes, Austin American-Statesman

of them lost money. Despite the Picnic being on her dad's ranch, Laurie had to pay Houston, then spent two thousand dollars more to build and stock a booth selling popcorn and sandwiches. She found the booths were nowhere near the stage and the crowds.

"Monday when we went to the bank and had our change and money calculated, I broke down crying," she said. "That was like my life savings." Her cousin Mark Kelley lost two thousand dollars selling barbecued chicken but still thinks fondly of the Picnic. "I thought I was going to get rich and that didn't happen, but I sure had a good time."

Not everyone was so forgiving. A *Statesman* story took aim at Houston Munson, saying that while many of the concessionaires had lost money, the district attorney and a partner, Paul Norris, stood to gain as much as eighty thousand dollars. Munson said that wasn't the case and that he hoped to clear five thousand dollars after expenses. The story quoted angry concessionaires who said the pair had made plenty of promises but didn't deliver.

Debbie Culak, who worked for the Munson family for more than fifty years, said people knew it wasn't Munson's fault. "He had no idea it was gonna be the way it was," Debbie said, explaining Munson figured the Picnic would be more like the fund-raiser the month before at his ranch. "He had no idea it was going to be as big as it was gonna be and rowdy and all the problems."

For a while after the Picnic, the county weighed taking legal action against Willie. An inspection report from the Texas Department of Health Resources had listed fourteen deficiencies, mainly with the water supply and toilet facilities.

County Attorney Bob Burchard told the *Statesman* he intended to file misdemeanor charges even though the fines were negligible, and he questioned why County Judge Vollentine didn't revoke the permit. Judge Vollentine said that though he had seen the site preparations and knew that facilities were inadequate, he never considered revoking the permit: "Revocation would have cost someone several hundred thousand dollars." Then he tried to shift the blame to the county public health officer and said that though the health hazards were an inconvenience, he didn't hear about anyone suffering from them.

In the end, Willie didn't face any charges from Gonzales County. Officials seemed to decide they just wanted the whole thing to go away. But Willie wasn't yet in the clear.

The lawsuits came tumbling in, starting in July and lasting for years. Among them, Capital Ambulance Services sued Willie to collect $6,875; a burn victim sued Willie for $150,000, saying he couldn't get proper medical care; and even Sterling Kelley sued Willie for an extra $17,420, including $7,420 in cleanup costs.

By September Willie had had enough. He said he was done with Picnics; Gonzales was the last one. "It's just too big a hassle," he told the *San Antonio Express*. "I lost money."

"Oh yeah, he said that a lot," Freddy Fletcher said. "I've heard him say a million times, 'that's my last Picnic.'"

Years later, in his biography *It's a Long Story*, Willie defended working with "hustlers" such as Geno McCoslin. "Of course, I regretted any harm or any injuries suffered by anyone. And I also couldn't deny responsibility for putting people like Neil [Reshen] and Geno in charge." But he admitted he enjoyed the chaos and insisted "a whole lot of people still had a whole lot of fun."

When asked if he has regrets, Dahr Jamail takes the same approach. "Shit no, we had fun. I think everybody was there to have fun. I would focus on how good was the show? How big was the show?"

Still one fact looms over the Picnic. Everything the Citizens for Law, Order, and Decency and Gonzales County officials feared up front—nudity, drug use, drunkenness, violence, health and sanitation problems, traffic problems—all came true.

Were the CLODs right to oppose the Picnic? Was the county right to deny the permit at first? Freddy Fletcher is surprised by the question, and there's a long pause before he laughs: "Well, I mean, I wouldn't want it in my backyard." He says Gonzales just wasn't equipped to handle that kind of event. "I'm sure it scared them to death, rightfully so. You got all these people converging on your local town, and everybody knows they're drinking and doing drugs. I can't blame them for going 'We don't want this,' you know?"

Mike Benestante says the town's values were well placed, though he didn't see it that way at the time. "They were right in the end; it was decadence. [The CLODs] were right to protest it, and you know what? I would have been a better person probably if I had just walked out and maybe [Willie] would have done a little show somewhere else, or maybe there wouldn't have been a Picnic. That would have been a better outcome in the long run."

Willie Nelson at his 1976 Fourth of July Picnic. By the time the lawsuits came rolling in, Willie said he was done with hosting the annual tradition. Photo by Ed Malcik, Austin American-Statesman

HOUSTON MUNSON resigned as Gonzales County district attorney in 1984 while facing a possible lawsuit charging he misused his office for personal gain. He continued his private practice and remained active in

Gonzales. His obituary in 2017 mentioned the Picnic but glossed over any drama, saying that the fund-raiser with Willie on his ranch the month before the Picnic caused most citizens to drop their objections.

"I think once the Picnic was over with and people saw that it didn't ruin Gonzales, then I think it was just kind of water under the bridge at that point," Beth Munson Bumpass said. "Everybody went on with their lives." Except for Munson, of course. "Until my dad's death, he was still talking about Willie Nelson and the Picnic."

Mike Benestante not only forgave Geno McCoslin for kidnapping him, but he moved to Austin, then Dallas to work and live with the down-and-out promoter. Mike was "disenchanted" with his pay after working on the Gonzales Picnic but still wanted to produce shows, so he joined forces with Geno.

Why would Mike work with Geno when he had proved to be downright volatile? "I think it was really because I was young and I thought I could help the dude, simple as that." It ended badly. Mike doesn't want to share details, but he eventually decided he just really wasn't cut out for that part of the music business.

Mike left it behind and returned to college, ultimately becoming a PGA golf professional and a happy grandfather. "Everything good happened to me after I got away from that scene," he said. "I liked the family atmosphere, but you know deep down inside, the outlaw image—intimidating and guns and all that—it's just not me. And it got the best of me."

Geno McCoslin wasn't as fortunate. The one-time wild promoter retired and lived on Lake Mexia in his later years. "He was a loving and very proud grandpa to my nieces and nephews," his daughter Susie McCoslin said. "My daughter never knew my dad."

Sometime after the 1976 Picnic, Geno spent some time at Rusk State Hospital for mental health treatment. But he truly started getting better in the early '80s when he moved to Lake Mexia and attended church with his mother. He lived a pretty peaceful life, Susie said, but "was never perfect."

The mental illness was always there. At one point, Susie said a new doctor at the VA took her dad off lithium cold turkey, even though he had taken the drug for three decades. Geno quickly went downhill and committed suicide. After coming so far, Susie said, it was a bitter end to her father's life.

"He had been sober for many years."

1977: Tulsa

SITE: *Tulsa Fairgrounds Speedway*
ATTENDANCE: *Nearly 60,000*
HEADLINERS: *Willie Nelson, Waylon Jennings, Lynyrd Skynyrd, Jessi Colter, Jerry Jeff Walker, Asleep at the Wheel*

Willie Nelson stuck to his guns, sorta. He didn't host a Fourth of July Picnic in 1977 but instead handed over the reins to prominent rock concert promoter Barry Fey. The Oklahoma event was moved to Sunday, July 3—the only time Willie would have a solo, single-day Picnic on a day other than the Fourth.

The crowds came. "The week of the show, we couldn't print tickets fast enough," Larry Shaefer told the *Tulsa World* in 2007. They were prepared for thirty thousand and got twice as many.

The music was hot—Waylon had a smash hit with "Luckenbach, Texas," and the show was a few months before the plane crash that would devastate Lynyrd Skynyrd. But many of the fans were just not prepared for sun-soaked temperatures in the nineties. "It was difficult to discern whether many of the prostrated youngsters littering the infield were suffering from an excess of alcohol, drugs or sun," the *Oklahoman* reported.

It was a financial success—an ad in *Billboard Magazine* bragged of a gross of $590,000—but trouble followed the Picnic. Neighbors were so upset by the event that there was a grand jury hearing into the Tulsa County Fairgrounds Trust Authority. Outdoor rock concerts were banned at the site.

1978: Kansas City, Dallas, and Austin

SITE: *Arrowhead Stadium, the Cotton Bowl, and the Austin Opry House*
ATTENDANCE: *From 50,000 in Kansas City to 20,000 in Dallas to under 2,000 in Austin*
HEADLINERS *(Kansas City): Willie Nelson, Waylon Jennings, Jessi Colter, the Grateful Dead, Jerry Jeff Walker, Missouri*
Headliners (Dallas): *Willie Nelson, Waylon Jennings, Jessi Colter, Ray Wylie Hubbard, Charlie Daniels Band, Kris Kristofferson, Rita Coolidge, Emmylou Harris*
HEADLINERS *(Austin): Willie Nelson, Steve Fromholz*

The low-key *Washington Post* headline was probably the most telling thing written about the Picnic in 1978: "Willie Nelson on Artificial Turf." This year, Willie took a peek at the future of his Picnics, with a pair of tightly secured stadium shows and a "Picnic" in Austin that was really more of a lengthy concert. "It's too controlled," Willie told the *Post* in Dallas. "I liked it better when it was out in the pasture."

The show in Kansas City drew a well-behaved Midwest crowd on July 1. The second day of the inaugural Texxas Jam on July 2 in Dallas drew a disappointing twenty thousand at most—much fewer than the first day's rock 'n' roll extravaganza.

But that didn't stop co-promoter Louis Messina of Houston's Pace Concerts from claiming a new hold on the Picnic. "As far as I'm concerned, this was Year One of the 'Willie Nelson Picnic,'" Messina boldly told the *Austin American-Statesman*. "The days of going out in the fields are over."

Over the next two nights, Willie relaxed at the still-new seventeen-hundred-seat Austin Opry House he ran with Tim O'Connor. "It was the coolest Picnic we ever had," O'Connor told the *Statesman*.

Columnist Larry Besaw disagreed, saying the show—which started at 9 p.m. and didn't see Willie onstage until 1:30 a.m.—was marred by air conditioning that wasn't up to the task. The venue was like "Wichita Falls in August," he said.

The days of going out in the fields would return.

1979: Pedernales

SITE: *The golf course at Pedernales Country Club in the community of Briarcliff, about thirty miles west of downtown Austin*
ATTENDANCE: *As many as 25,000*
HEADLINERS: *Willie Nelson, Leon Russell, Ernest Tubb, the Geezinslaws, Steve Fromholz, Ray Wylie Hubbard, Johnny Rodriguez, Johnny Paycheck, Bobby Bare*

Willie Nelson had just purchased the vacant Pedernales Country Club and decided the nine-hole golf course would be the perfect setting for a return to Picnic glory. His new neighbors disagreed, of course.

A lawsuit filed in late June tried to halt the show, citing familiar mass-gathering problems. Picnic coordinator David Anderson was exasperated. "We figured if there was any opposition, they'd let us know before now. We've bought forty thousand dollars' worth of [portable toilets] for it. Willie's an entertainer; he's not in the porta can business."

The Picnic happened, of course, though a *Miami Herald* reporter spotted Willie associates wearing T-shirts that read "Willie's Seventh Annual Injunction Hearing."

Organizers admit the crowd estimate of twenty-five thousand was probably a bit high, blaming the lawsuit and the '79 oil crisis for the lower-than-expected ticket sales. Shuttle buses were even set up to bring in fans from Austin.

For once, a smaller crowd allowed organizers to not be overwhelmed by troubles. Medical personnel promptly treated injuries and overdoses. One man, revived via an injection of Narcan, cursed medics for "bringing him down from an eighty-dollar high." Several suffering medical emergencies ranging from heart attack to insulin shock were taken by helicopter to a hospital in Austin.

"I guess the fact that it went so smoothly is the biggest surprise," Anderson told the *Statesman*.

The stage was a little short on the star power that fueled earlier Picnics, but Leon Russell did return to the Picnic after being absent since '76, and Willie delighted in introducing one of his idols, Ernest Tubb, to his fans.

Willie didn't make any money and made a mess of his new place— photos after the Picnic showed the golf course covered in a sea of trash— but in the end, Willie decided he was going to lose less by cleaning up and repairing the golf course than by renting land and fighting rural townsfolk.

He told reporters that, yes, this was the Picnic's permanent home.

CHAPTER THREE

1980: Pedernales

SITE: *The golf course at Willie Nelson's Pedernales Country Club at Briarcliff*
ATTENDANCE: *Estimated at 60,000*
HEADLINERS: *Willie Nelson, Merle Haggard, Ray Price, Ernest Tubb, Leon Russell, Johnny Paycheck*

Picnic VIP Update
Willie Nelson: After the nationwide sensation of *Stardust*, Willie was one of America's most famous and recognizable musicians. He had homes in Texas, Colorado, and Hawaii and was friends with President Jimmy Carter. He had just released an album of duets with Ray Price.
Merle Haggard: Merle had enjoyed a string of number-one songs and released dozens of popular albums. He was considered one of country music's great artists. In the summer of 1980, he even brought Clint Eastwood to the top of the charts with the duet "Bar Room Buddies."
Ray Price: With a career beginning in the 1940s, Ray once had Willie, Johnny Paycheck, and Johnny Bush in his band. By 1980, he was in the late stages of his career as far as popular success goes, but he would be part of the Picnic off and on through the early 2010s.
Asleep at the Wheel: After a ten-year climb into the spotlight, the band was struggling with losing longtime members and finding major label success elusive. But Ray Benson and company still put on a hell of a show, earning praise from critics and crowds.

On July 3, 1980, twenty-seven Lincolns, Cadillacs, and chartered buses pulled up to Austin's Capital Plaza Cinema. A parade of movie stars, film and music industry VIPs, and press from across the country emerged for the world premiere of Willie Nelson's first starring role, in *Honeysuckle Rose*.

Dyan Cannon and Slim Pickens were there, as were director Jerry Schatzberg and producer Sydney Pollack. Even eleven-year-old Joey

Floyd, who portrayed Willie's son in the movie, greeted the enthusiastic crowd.

The *Austin American-Statesman* reported that Willie was in high spirits after the screening. "I was fantastic," he said. "Well, I was okay."

It wasn't all praise. A writer from the *New York Times* condescendingly presumed that Austin's first movie premiere would also be its last and noted that nearly everyone "looked like an extra from 'Urban Cowboy.'" (The *NYT* writer wasn't just condescending; he was wrong: Austin's first movie premiere was the 1966 *Batman* film.)

Pollack was optimistic about his film and his star. He was overheard telling a fan that Willie would soon be in high demand for leading roles—a movie star up there with Robert Redford. That would prove to be a little hasty, though it would have been hard to judge from *Honeysuckle Rose*. Willie was essentially playing himself on-screen, and the line wasn't always clear, to the point where Willie and costar Amy Irving's on-screen affair played out in real life for several years.

But there was no denying Willie was a superstar. His 1978 album *Stardust* was still a multiplatinum nationwide sensation. He was in the tabloids. He had his own country club and golf course. The man had his own jeans: A women's wear firm in Dallas had quickly sold half a million Willie Nelson jeans with "Willie" embroidered on a back pocket.

That night, thirty miles west of the premiere, workers were on the roads leading to Willie's country club in Briarcliff. Along FM 2322 and State Highway 71, they were installing two-foot-square white cardboard signs with large, bright lettering:

WILLIE NELSON'S

LAST
PICNIC

FRIDAY, JULY 4, 1980
AUSTIN, TEXAS

The Picnic had helped put Willie in the spotlight the past seven years. Now that he was Hollywood, who needed that kind of hassle?

"WILLIE BOUGHT THAT COUNTRY CLUB just to have Picnics." Freddy Fletcher said his uncle enjoyed having his own retreat and building his own recording studio, but the first focus was having a place for the annual Picnic. "It was kind of his compound," Freddy said.

Forty years later, head golf pro Fran Szal describes how the 1980 Picnic unfolded from the spot where the stage stood on the ninth green. Photo by Dave Dalton Thomas

In the beginning, the compound was kind of rough. Business hotshot Joel McQuade had owned the Pedernales Country Club, but he lived in Dallas, where he kept his eyes and his money focused on the Dallas Playboy Club he founded—until his fortune unraveled and he died young.

"[McQuade] never put any money into [Pedernales]," said Fran Szal, who was the head golf pro at the club at the time and later would run the course for Willie for years. "It was a tax write-off; he ended up abandoning it, basically."

When Willie took ownership of the property in 1979, the place was "a skeleton of a country club," artist Steve Brooks said, emptied of everything except for some rather large rats. "They'd scurry about everywhere," he said. Steve was among the Willie Family who spent the early part of the summer of '79 sleeping on the floor at Pedernales, trying to make the Picnic happen.

For Willie, a permanent home for the Picnic made a lot of sense. There would still be unhappy neighbors and prickly county officials, but overtures could be made and relationships could be built. And he could avoid any Texas Mass Gatherings Act showdowns by limiting the Picnics to under twelve hours.

After the 1979 Picnic brought in a smaller-than-expected crowd of under twenty-five thousand (and stretched into thirteen hours), Willie and Travis County Sheriff Raymond Frank were able to smooth over things with nearby homeowners upset about public nudity, unkept security promises, and lingering portable toilets.

By April 1980, everything was moving according to plan. The Picnic, which had long been a festival on the run from the upset communities it left behind, was on and it was going to stay at Pedernales.

By mid-May, however, there was a plot twist.

"After this year, we will no longer have a Picnic." David Anderson, Willie's longtime road manager who promoted the Pedernales Picnics, made the announcement to the media: "I think [Willie] feels it is time to go into something else."

Not that you could blame Willie. When this Picnic business started in 1973, he was playing Big G's in Round Rock and the Armadillo in Austin.

Artist Steve Brooks shows off one of the "Last Picnic" signs he had saved from the 1980 Picnic. Photo by Dave Dalton Thomas

Now he was playing for the president at the White House and speaking at the 1980 Democratic National Convention at Madison Square Garden.

The Picnic took way too much time and energy. Connie Nelson, Willie's wife from 1971 until 1988, said as soon as one Picnic was over, Willie would start planning for the next. "The Fourth of July Picnic for Willie was a constant work thing," she said. "Where to do it and how to do it? Was this the best place to do it or should we take it on the road? He was always working on it."

But if 1980 was gonna be the last, they had to do it right.

Willie hired professional security and a cleanup crew. He had the portable toilets already on hand and promised to remove them and the temporary fence within twenty-four hours. The show would last from noon to midnight, with fifteen-dollar tickets, three-dollar on-site parking, no pets, and no camping (although that would not be enforced).

That doesn't mean that Willie was a stickler on who would perform, though. Tim O'Connor shared a quick story on how Picnic planning went with Willie:

> So I'm out at the Pedernales. And Willie and I are sitting out by the pool or somewhere going over how much certain people get paid: "Well, they get ten grand, and no, those folks get four. . . ." And I would just write it down and as we got done, he said, "Oh, by the way. I met these guys, and they're really good people. I want you to give them a free apartment at the Opera House. And put 'em on the Picnic," and I said, "Well, how much are they gonna get paid?" He said, "Well, let's give them five hundred dollars; nah, make that one thousand dollars."

And that's how Willie worked. Make the right impression at the right time, and you were in.

The Picnic site would even have its own judge. After being overwhelmed with a crush of post-Picnic cases in 1979, Justice of the Peace Leslie Taylor planned to hold a right-now-court for misdemeanor offenses at the Picnic, drawing jurors from the crowd. Shortly before the Picnic, she abandoned that plan as impractical but still set up a field courthouse to let people post bond and pay fines instead of being taken to jail. It was a slow weekend: Taylor performed two marriages and saw fewer than a dozen offenders, collecting fines she said averaged about fifteen dollars.

Mike Simpson and his Ranger Security Systems were hired to secure the perimeter. He told the *Statesman* that, with two hundred men on the grounds, "we figure we can handle a crowd of 40,000." Then he hedged his bets. "If it gets a lot larger than that, I don't think anybody can handle it."

Fran Szal was standing on the ninth green on the nine-hole Pedernales course, pointing downhill at where the crowds would have been looking up at the stage forty years ago. The trees had grown a little over the decades, but it still was easy to recognize the scene from old photos. "[The Picnic] was on what we call 'the loop,' which is holes 7, 8, 9. The stage was set up on nine green, and then the crowd was dispersed all throughout the three holes."

Behind him was a large parking lot that would accommodate a fair number of tour buses and then the rest of the country club—swimming pool, condos, and all. The fans had to settle for the golf course, which was nice enough. For a while, at least. By mid-afternoon, the *New York Times* reported, the course looked like "a storage yard for a beer can recycling concern." And a prohibition on glass containers wasn't strictly enforced.

"For many years after that," Ray Benson said, "when we played there, you'd hit the ball and there'd be broken glass and stuff from where the audience was."

Szal was asked if it made a golf pro's skin crawl to see all those people tearing up the course, but as it turns out, he wasn't too worried at the time. "Yeah, it took some renovation to get it back as you would desire in a golf course," he said dryly. "But then again, it was quite an event. It was an absolute blast. I was too busy hitting on chicks and partying my ass off."

The 1980 Picnic drew an estimated sixty thousand fans to Willie's Pedernales Country Club. It took the golf course quite some time to recover from the 1979 and 1980 Picnics. Photo by Roger Collins

As it turns out, having fun was the key thing when it came to Willie and golf. Willie was hooked on the game by 1971, and by the end of the decade it was a crucial outlet for the no-longer-young Willie and Family. Not that their brand of golf was exactly sober or healthy, but sunshine, marijuana, and golf clubs were a hell of a lot healthier than nightlife, cocaine, and pistols.

"Golf saved our lives," longtime stage manager Poodie Locke told Willie biographer Joe Nick Patoski. "It got us out of the hotel room and our nose out of the bag."

That doesn't mean they took it *too* seriously.

When faced with a question about how well the boss can play, Szal doesn't hesitate. "The par here at this golf course is whatever Willie shoots," he laughed. Then he added that even in his late eighties, Willie can still drive the ball and is a good putter. "The main thing is here, it's all about the fun," Szal said. "We don't care as much about what our score is—our barometer is 'how much fun did we have for the day?'"

After decades at the Pedernales Country Club, Szal has seen an enormous amount of people show up, from the celebrities who play with Willie to everyday folks who want a glimpse of Willie heaven:

> The most interesting thing I would say is the simple fact that everyone loves Willie—the actors, actresses, musicians, people of all persuasions of all races of all music genres. But then I have people come to this pro shop from all over the world that don't even play golf. They just come because they want a piece of Willie memorabilia. And the main thing I hear from most people is, "I sure wish someday before I died, that I could smoke a joint with Willie Nelson." I'm talking about older people that come walking in who look like they never would even consider smoking. I've heard some of them say, "Well, I've never smoked a joint before, but I sure would smoke one with Willie."

"ONE OF MY FAVORITE stories about Larry is these guys shot him and put him in the trunk of a car and thought he was dead." Freddy Fletcher is talking about Larry Trader, who was very much alive in the trunk of that car. It was sometime in the 1960s and a dispute over money had gone wrong. Unfortunately, Freddy didn't know—or wouldn't tell—the rest of the story: What happened to the guys who shot Larry? Freddy simply said, "Trader was a tough old guy."

You can't talk about golf and Willie without talking about Larry, who grew up working at country clubs in Houston and San Antonio. He caddied for Lee Trevino and Tommy Bolt on the PGA Tour and ran the golf course at Pedernales for Willie until he retired. He was said to be an excellent golfer and something of a hustler.

But with Larry, golf doesn't remain the subject for long. He's also described as an old-school promoter, a grouch, a gangster, and someone you didn't want to cross. Larry met Willie through Ray Price in the 1960s, when Larry made his reputation as an imposing bagman, collecting the performance fee from club owners who often were various shades of less than honest.

"Larry grew up in the ranks of concert promoting and music promoting," said Roger Collins, former owner of the Austin dive the One Knite and a Willie associate. "He and Geno [McCoslin] were probably pretty much the last two" truly old-school promoters. "Everybody carried a gun, and you could really never trust anybody that was counting the gate at a concert."

And that included Larry, it seems. "Willie did, I don't know, countless shows for Larry," Connie Nelson said. "And I'd be willing to bet that Larry made more money than Willie did at any of them. And Willie knew it. And it was still, 'Well, that's Larry.'"

Larry Trader, shown with Willie in their later years, was one of Willie's closest friends. Photo by Rick Henson

It just shows that Larry and Willie were really close, for reasons that weren't spelled out for those who came along later. "People would say, 'Larry must have done something for Willie in the war, because Willie acts like Larry saved his life,'" photographer Scott Newton said. "And nobody knew exactly what it was that Larry had done."

Willie's loyalty to his friends was unshakeable, which often meant the closer you got to Willie, the more reluctant people were to talk about Larry.

Collins, retired and living in San Angelo, said, "He was a very confusing enigma. Trader could either be your best friend or your worst enemy."

Ray Benson, close friends with Willie, spent a long time searching for the right words: "He was just tough to deal with. We were friends; we were friends."

Szal, who said Willie's the best boss he ever had: "Larry was a character . . . quite an interesting person."

But Connie had a special relationship with Larry—one that acknowledged his tough reputation but was full of love nonetheless. "I'd call him every Mother's Day. Just to tell him 'Happy Mother's Day,' because there was a joke that he was the biggest mother of them all . . . the biggest motherfucker."

Larry, who died in 2007 from complications of a stroke, loved the joke. "When he got really sick, his wife told me that on Mother's Day, he'd sit by the phone or sit close to the phone because he knew I was going to call him," Connie said. "He'd wait for that call. I think of him every Mother's Day for that reason."

ROGER COLLINS WAS ONE of the lucky ones. After living it up at the Picnic headquarters hotel on July 3, he drove west to the community of Lago Vista and took a boat across Lake Travis to the Picnic site. "It was all a blur [after the *Honeysuckle Rose* premiere]. I think I partied right on through."

Some of the biggest stars took helicopters, but most performers went by boat, along with a sizable contingent of local and national press. By now, everyone knew that traffic was going to be a problem, but with sixty thousand picnickers on the way, it was considerably worse than officials predicted. Tommy Blackwell was a patrol sergeant at the time for the Travis County Sheriff's Department and was in charge of keeping FM 2322 open so that EMS could get in and out as needed. "There were some really, really long days," he said. "Really hot. Not much in the way of breaks, or sleep."

One of the more famous Willie Nelson Picnic photos shows Jerry Blundell with his cat "Precious" hitchhiking toward the Picnic along Highway 71. Photo by Stanley Farrar, Austin American-Statesman

He was out there from the morning of July 3 through July 5, zipping around on a Yamaha 250 dirt bike he had brought after 1979 taught him maneuvering a patrol car through traffic on 2322 was pretty difficult. Traffic was backed up for sixteen miles or more, all the way down 2322 and a good portion of Texas 71. Some picnickers spent five hours or more creeping along.

In her book *Heartworn Memories*, Susie Nelson describes the traffic as seen from her helicopter flying in: "It was bumper-to-bumper and hardly moving all the way. When we got to the country club itself, the place was covered with people—solid, swarming people, moving around like a fire ant mound you'd kicked the top off of."

"Our problems were mostly traffic blocking," Tommy said. "Somebody would just say, 'That's it, I've driven as far as I can drive, I'm stopping here. Let's get out and walk from here.' And they'd leave the car in the road. We'd get a wrecker, get it towed, and get the road back open."

Many picnickers arrived to find the three-dollar on-site parking full and had to park farther and farther away. This didn't bother local entrepreneurs, who charged up to twenty dollars a car for parking.

"A lot of people walked after parking a long way away, but once you got there, it was just the perfect Picnic scene," Scott Newton said. "The vibe was exactly what you want for Willie's Picnic."

Perception of the crowd differed depending on your vantage point. Scott, photographing the crowd from the stage, said, "Every bit as much as Gonzales was anarchy, this was peace in the valley. I just don't have a bad memory. Before the whole thing started, I went up to the center mike to take a crowd shot, which . . . it's just a beautiful shot. Everybody's grooving, though there's no music playing. It goes on and on forever. It just looks like I don't know how many tens of thousands of people communing with nature."

But Fran Szal, who spent the day in the crowd, remembers things were a bit wilder than that. "It was rowdy as hell. We have a pond on seven, and it happened to have water in it. People were just taking off their clothes and going into the water, naked and not worrying about a thing. People were having a blast, smoking weed, drinking, carrying on, and enjoying that show."

One stabbing was reported, as well as a fight in front of the stage, but in the end, only about sixty-five people were arrested, the *American-Statesman* reported, mostly for public intoxication.

Tommy Blackwell said getting arrested took some effort. "We weren't looking to make any arrests. We didn't want to have to try to make a jail transport. We just wanted people to settle down, behave, and move on."

"THE CRUEL, MURDEROUS, TEXAS SUN was relentless. Brains baked, bodies peeled and hundreds passed out." Much like the crowd, the heat was a matter of opinion. Sure, it was hot, but Bruce Kirkland, writing for Canada's *Ottawa Journal*, couldn't think of anything else, devoting almost all his story to the heat. "A team of medics patrolled the crowd with water canteens and salt tablets to revive people," he wrote. "Only when the sun went down . . . did the event begin to make any sense at all."

There was a heat wave going on in Texas that summer, and the high in Briarcliff that day was ninety-nine. Picnickers emptied two tanker trucks' worth of water, and medics treated more than three hundred people for heat-related issues. About half a dozen were taken to the hospital.

That said, most Texans took the heat in stride. When the gates had

Fans cheer on Ray Wylie Hubbard at the 1980 Picnic. While many Texans took the 1980 heat wave in stride, some out-of-state visitors were not as prepared. Photo by Phil Bannister, Austin American-Statesman

opened at 7 a.m., many rushed in to find shady spots near the stage or set up tents, beach umbrellas, or some other self-engineered shelter. The *Los Angeles Times* reported that the preferred remedy for the heat was "beer, tents, another beer, plastic canopies, more beer, minimal clothing and one last beer."

But it makes sense that some national and international visitors and press weren't quite prepared for the heat. Illinois journalist Vince Hoffard wrote in 2020 that he was determined to see "the Super Bowl of outlaw country music," but driving into Texas during the summer of 1980 was "like driving into an oven."

And longtime KUTX radio host Jay Trachtenburg, who covered the event for the University of Texas newspaper, the *Daily Texan*, recalls seeing a woman reporter for a national publication waiting for transportation to the Picnic with a sweater over her arm. "I just said she's obviously not from here. You're not gonna need a sweater 'til October."

The press who weren't overwhelmed by the heat seemed to think it was a pretty good time. Critics agreed that it was a more country-flavored Picnic than in years past, but everyone welcomed Delbert McClinton's raucous set.

"His sassy Texas roadhouse blues provided the perfect counterpart to the day's country styles," Rob Patterson wrote for the Newspaper Enterprise Association.

Trachtenburg praised the "pure honky-tonk" of Ray Price and the "feisty rascal" Johnny Paycheck but saved his biggest praise for Merle Haggard's western-swing-flavored set: "I was floored. It was just great."

Hoffard recalled Faron Young "stopping in the middle of his performance, taking out his wallet, and tossing all of his money to the crowd."

And the *American-Statesman* reviewers were impressed by Asleep at the Wheel: "Ray Benson imitated The Who's Roger Daltrey by swinging his microphone around his head like a lasso during 'Am I High?'"

Willie opened the show by bringing movie costar Dyan Cannon out for a duet on "Two Sides to Every Story" and adding Slim Pickens for a couple of hymns.

The day's lineup did not include star Charlie Daniels. Willie announced to the crowd that Charlie couldn't play because he was doing a show in Memphis. The real story is a little weirder.

Ed Ward of the *American-Statesman* explained in a July 9 story that Charlie Daniels and his band had flown in by private plane to the tiny Spicewood Airport (under normal circumstances, a twenty-minute drive from the Picnic site), but the helicopter that was supposed to pick them up didn't show. Ward wrote that after two hours of sitting in the sun waiting, they got on the plane and went back to Tennessee.

Tim O'Connor's memory of the incident is a little fuzzy but more interesting. He said they had a runner at the airport with two rental station wagons to transport Charlie Daniels, his band, and support crew to the show, but the kid ended up dropping one set of keys down the sewer. "What I heard is that we could have gotten Charlie there, because we had one of the vehicles," Tim said. "But his support would not have been there," and Charlie refused to go without them.

Tim said he's not positive on this one, since he was never able to clear it up. "I never got the opportunity to talk to Charlie Daniels on that specific event," he said. "Which I'm glad in a lot of ways."

Johnny Paycheck was mopping away the sweat while talking to the *Tennessean*'s Laura Eipper: "Singing in that heat—it just takes your breath away." The performers, of course, had the opportunity to get away from the heat in air-conditioned buses backstage, but they—and those working for Willie—had to spend plenty of time sweating under the sun, too.

That included Larry Trader, who was worried about how things were going. It was his golf course, and he had a lot of responsibility and

Willie's Honeysuckle Rose costar Dyan Cannon performs onstage alongside Willie Nelson guitarist Jody Payne. Photo by Roger Collins

worry weighing on him, not the least of which was making sure Willie was happy.

About 6 p.m., still well short of sundown, Larry blacked out while Ray Price was on stage and collapsed. It was said to be a heart attack. A helicopter swooped in and carried him to Austin's Brackenridge Hospital. That night, reporters were told he was in "serious but stable" condition at the hospital's coronary care unit.

"HE SAID, 'ROGER, I don't really care what you do. As long as you don't try to kill the president, counterfeit money, or run guns.' I said, 'I'm never gonna do any of those three things, so we're gonna have a great relationship.'"

Roger Collins is telling a story about the link between the Secret Service and Willie's Fourth of July Picnic. Not the US Secret Service officially, but a group of agents who had been a part of Lyndon B. Johnson's detail after he left office and came home to Texas.

"His detail were a bunch of hard-drinking guys that loved music, and they loved to be backstage," Roger said. "They became my best friends because they loved the One Knite. But they also became very good friends with Willie and all the stage crew. They wouldn't be doing drugs, but they would be drinking very heavily. "They took care of Willie, and Willie took care of them as far as giving them access, and he never had any problems."

Roger produces a couple of photos, one of a man he identifies as an agent in Texas flag running shorts posing onstage with stage manager Poodie Locke. Another of a man wearing a Secret Service ball cap who is reclining in a comfortable spot with two attractive women, a Willie Picnic pass affixed to his Hawaiian shirt and a can of Stroh's Light in his hand.

Backstage at Willie Nelson's Fourth of July Picnic was a different world, especially when the Picnic was in Austin. "The joke was, were there more people backstage or out front? How do we know?" Connie Nelson said. "From the early picnics on it was just a circus. . . . The backstage experience was wide open."

Steve Brooks let slip a mention of a special area backstage called "Fantasy Island," and Tim O'Connor carefully confirmed it, without getting into details: "At the [Austin] Opry House, with 218 apartments and Willie playing there often, we always had a 'Fantasy Island.' Meaning some of the closer-in artists could go to a specific [apartment], and it would turn into an all-night picking deal. And we'd have special guests, nonmusician folks, that we could invite into that area. That's how we treated a lot of people at the Picnic at Pedernales. There was a lot of [space] to be enjoyed and get out of the hot sun around the clubhouse."

Roger Collins remembers the backstage scene as just one giant family, where if you weren't in a band, you were likely in the music business, the drug business, or the press. And that was okay with him: "All of my friends pretty much in that period were either musicians or drug dealers."

And the drugs and vice were prevalent, at least at the early Picnics. "Pretty much in all the Picnics what was going on was a lot of a lot of marijuana smoking, a lot of cocaine use, a lot of drinking, and a lot of women," Roger said.

Ray Benson didn't disagree. "Mostly I remember, you'd smoke a lot of pot and do a lot of drugs and have a great time," he said. "All kinds of crazy stuff, you know. And we'd always jam with each other."

Connie Nelson was among those close to Willie to spill the secret. At some point during that first run of Picnics, the primary purpose became clear. It was an annual reunion for Willie and his closest friends. "That's pretty much what the picnics always were that I saw from Willie. It was a get-together of all of his closest friends," she said. This is why he kept doing them even though he struggled to make money on them—he loved the gathering too much to quit.

And if he could entertain fans, raise his profile, or get some money or attention for his friends, that was a bonus. "Willie, being so giving, if he was able to bring his friends out to a concert that he knew was going to be super successful and get them a good payday. That was a big draw for Willie to be able to do that," Connie said.

Ray Benson said that the Picnics were a homecoming for a lot of people. "For many years, you got to see a bunch of people that you knew very well and loved and didn't get to see very often. It was a gathering of the tribes."

Tim O'Connor said Willie's growing celebrity didn't affect how Willie saw his friends or how they interacted with each other. "Those are his friends. They grew up together musically and personally. And he got to see a bunch of them every year on the Fourth." He may occasionally tour with one or two, but "to have all his buddies around . . . it was a sight to see the joy on Willie's face and how happy he was."

In 1980, Ray Price and Merle Haggard joined the Picnic for the first time. Both would become regulars at the event, and having them there was a huge win for Willie. "Oh my gosh, I mean these were two of his best friends," Connie said. "He and Merle were super, super close. But he and Ray were like they were more like brothers, so that it meant the world to Willie for Ray to be there."

Willie Nelson at the 1980 Picnic on the golf course at his Pedernales Country Club. Photo by Bob Daemmrich, Austin American-Statesman

But it wasn't just the superstars who got the VIP treatment at the Picnics. Delbert McClinton praised the equality he saw between the artists: "The Willie Picnic quickly became the event nationwide and it had no boundaries. Everybody was equal; nobody had to wear a pass saying, 'you can't come in here' or 'only VIPs' or any of that stuff."

Willie would hang out onstage as much as possible, sometimes joining his friends, sometimes just watching. Connie said the other performers, even though they had their own spots to duck out of the heat, would mostly be hanging out as well, talking, sharing ideas and music.

"It was just one big reunion," she said. "I think for the fans too, not just the entertainers. By the time they rested the next day from all the hell they went through the day before, they were already looking toward, you know, forward to the next one. It's kind of like childbirth, you know; why would you ever go through that a second time? Because you kind of forget how bad it hurts the first time."

Roger Collins said he was always impressed by the fans in the crowd—he couldn't imagine being trapped in that heat for that length of time. "I wouldn't have done it. It was too damn hot, and too damn miserable. But every time there was a Picnic, everybody out there always looked, at least for the most part, like they were having the time of their lives, which I sort of never could figure out. It's two different worlds from the front and from the back."

"COME OVER HERE AND FIGHT ME, both of you. I want you two to kill me and put me out of my pain." This quote came from one of some three hundred campers that *American-Statesman* reporter Rick Smith found at the site on Saturday morning, possibly the most hungover. Or maybe it was the young man Security Chief Mike Simpson roused in the medical tent that morning—he wanted to know when the concert was going to start.

Among "heaps of crushed cans, ice chest shards and fragments of folding chairs," scavengers were either looking for things as necessary as their own clothes, as extravagant as diamond rings and watches, or as down-and-out as searching for unopened beers. "This is the fourth beer I've found so far this morning," one man said. "It's like hunting Easter eggs."

Talking to the Associated Press, Tommy Blackwell said reports of disaster would turn out to be exaggerated. "We'd get a report of a body, and it would turn out to be just another drunk sleeping under a tree," he said.

By all measures—at least compared to the Picnics in Dripping Springs

A fan sleeps on the Picnic grounds the morning after the 1980 Picnic. Photo by Zach Ryall, Austin American-Statesman

or Gonzales—this Picnic was an overwhelming success. An *American-Statesman* story about ten days after the Picnic said that Willie sold about thirty thousand tickets (although he somehow had sixty thousand at the show) and made about sixty-two thousand dollars after band fees, security, and cleanup—the first time a Willie-promoted Picnic had made a profit worth mentioning. A big reason is that Willie had held on to the fencing and portable toilets he had bought for the '79 Picnic.

The press seemed to believe it would be the final Picnic, and his neighbors seemed relieved. Jerry Bassler, president of Briarcliff Property Owners Association, said that "the Picnic has run its course. He no longer needs it. He's a star."

But did anyone close to Willie believe it was over?

Connie understood better than anyone Willie's frustration with the Picnic troubles. "Willie would go through stages of that anyway. He'd say, 'This is it, it's just too much trouble . . . I'm done.' I've seen him do that with playing music. I remember a lot of times, like after a tough show, or after a tough tour, he'd say, 'That's it, I'm gonna tell the band I'm done. I'm just off the road.' And then two days later, he'd be booking another forty shows."

But was the Picnic done? "No, no," Connie said. "I just knew Willie's passion for it."

Tim O'Connor: "When I started hearing that afterward, I would say exactly what I said to those folks that would ask me. I don't believe so. He never said anything to me."

"They may have advertised it that way. But I didn't believe it. Nobody else would have believed that either."

Ray Benson: "We figured it would last forever. I don't reckon we paid much attention to what was said even by Willie about it. We knew he was gonna do it again. He couldn't help himself."

Roger Collins snagged one of those "last Picnic" signs from the roadside and kept it for the next forty years. "I always thought it was very ironic because I knew that wasn't gonna be true," Roger said. "I just knew that he wasn't going to do that. I never in my wildest dreams thought that the Picnics were over, and neither did anybody else that I know."

For his part, Willie kept his options open. "We won't have one next year for sure because I'd like to leave the year open for other things I want to do," he told the *Tennessean* on the Fourth. "I'd like to rest for a while. But after that, well, we'll see."

"THE REASON HE DID IT was because Nashville's so full of shit and stupidity. Willie came in and started doing what Willie did. He changed all of that." Delbert McClinton is talking about the early years of the Willie Nelson Picnic. The Picnic wouldn't end in 1980. But it was the end of an era.

The legends were created in the first eight years of the Picnic—the wilderness of Dripping Springs, the anarchy of Gonzales. Nothing like that would happen again. When the Picnic would return to Texas in 1984, it would be a changed thing. With the exception of the Farm Aid II Picnic in 1986, future crowds would never be half as large as the sixty thousand people in 1980.

The early Picnics were visual representations of progressive country, redneck rock, and outlaw country. But for Delbert, the label wasn't as important; it was what Willie did for those who created the music. "The thing that is most important about those Picnics was that Willie ushered in the time of the songwriter. Willie made it clear to everybody that this was for and about performers and singers and songwriters. And that's pretty much what opened up the whole Texas music scene. It was a very, very important paradigm shift. Everybody was reverent to what Willie had brought about, and the reverence is what made it grow. It opened up a whole new avenue for music and songwriters. It was magic."

Many of those who attended described the Pedernales Picnics as "idyllic." Photo by Stanley Farrar, Austin American-Statesman

THE DAY AFTER the Picnic, the *Statesman* caught up with Larry Trader in his hospital bed. Apparently, he didn't have a heart attack at all, despite the collapse and the emergency helicopter flight. "My doctor said it might have just been hyperventilation. I guess it was just the anticipation of the picnic, trying to get everything just right. Maybe I just tried too hard this time."

Though there was much work to be done and a golf course to restore, Trader didn't seem to mind the rest. "That's okay that I'm here. As long as Willie's happy with the way the picnic turned out, I'm happy."

Tim O'Connor says that's not quite the end of the story. "We all thought he faked the heart attack."

Day was turning to evening at the Picnic, and several of the artists wanted to get paid and get on the road. "We all thought that Trader faked that because it was time for him to pay some artists. He had a reputation that once it was time to start to pay anybody, he would disappear."

Tim said that he ended up getting everyone paid and acknowledged that Larry, a longtime friend who would work with him on future Picnics, might have been at least somewhat ill. "But a helicopter landing right there? It was just like, really? It just felt weird. I'm not trying to be a shit toward him in any way. In fact, I had a lot of fun with him and a lot of laughs. But he did a lot of different things."

1981 and 1982

For the first time, there was no Picnic either year. Or, at least, not an official one. Willie Nelson, performing in early July at Caesar's Palace in Las Vegas, held a private July 4 party for five hundred VIP fans, including some of Houston and Dallas's social elite, as well as Jane Fonda and her husband Tom Hayden. A review said there were music, dancing, and a lavish spread but not a fistfight in sight. A brief *Rolling Stone* report said Willie performed "Up against the Wall Redneck Mother," among other hits, for the leisure-suit crowd.

With no Picnic in 1981, Mickey Gilley decided to hold his own three-day picnic at the rodeo grounds in Pasadena. Despite the *Urban Cowboy* connection to his famous club, Gilley's, the picnic was a bust, attracting a crowd generously estimated at one thousand. The Associated Press reported that Gilley postponed the opening act "when only 10 people had arrived by 11 a.m." Gilly said that he would try again next year: "We don't ever give up."

In a late July interview with the *American-Statesman*, Willie doesn't miss the Picnic at all: "That's one reason I stopped doing it. I started feeling guilty about inflicting unhappiness [on the Picnic neighbors]. When you move it inside, it's not the same thing, and when you move it into a stadium it's not the same thing. It had its own personality. It probably won't ever be duplicated."

Willie's whereabouts on July 4, 1982, are undocumented. To his credit, Mickey Gilley lowered his ticket prices to ten dollars; assembled some musicians, including David Allan Coe, Johnny Paycheck, Jerry Lee Lewis, and even Tiny Tim; and tried again. Media didn't cover the event.

1983: Syracuse, New Jersey, and Atlanta

SITE: *Carrier Dome in Syracuse on July 2; Giants Stadium in East Rutherford, New Jersey, on July 3; and Atlanta International Raceway on July 4*
ATTENDANCE: *From 55,000 at Giants Stadium to 30,000 in Atlanta to 25,000 in Syracuse*
HEADLINERS *(Syracuse): Willie Nelson, Merle Haggard, Linda Ronstadt, Emmylou Harris, Stray Cats*
HEADLINERS *(New Jersey): Willie Nelson, Merle Haggard, Waylon Jennings, Linda Ronstadt, Emmylou Harris, Jessi Colter, Stray Cats*
HEADLINERS *(Atlanta): Willie Nelson, Waylon Jennings, Merle Haggard, Hank Williams Jr., Linda Ronstadt, David Allan Coe, Stray Cats*

Willie couldn't stay away from the Picnic for more than two years. But before bringing it back home, he tried another first—a three-day running Picnic along the East Coast, including the then-hot Stray Cats on all three dates.

The Carrier Dome saw the smallest lineup and smallest crowd, about twenty-five thousand cooking inside what the *Syracuse Herald-American* dubbed the "Syracuse Sauna." The temperature inside the stadium was only eighty-five, but the humidity apparently was extraordinary. Reports also said fans had to wait in line an hour and a half for a $1.75 cup of beer or other concessions.

The next day, the field at Giants Stadium had been covered with a turquoise canvas, and fifty thousand showed up despite temperatures that were reported by the *Associated Press* to be as high as 115 degrees on the field. A more reasonable Reuters report said it was 103 degrees, but either way, hundreds were treated for heat exhaustion and other problems.

The real action happened in Atlanta on the Fourth, when Hank Williams Jr. and David Allan Coe were added to the lineup. At one point before the Picnic, a member of the press asked Willie if he was going to "control" what songs David Allan Coe performed. Was it going to be a family-friendly show? Willie laughed that one off.

Willie performed with Merle and Waylon, but a fired-up Hank Jr. nearly stole the evening, according to an *Atlanta Journal-Constitution* review. A full page of coverage inside the paper quoted a police officer from Memphis who "would do anything for David Allan Coe" and a fellow from North Carolina who loved Waylon so much "we'd give him all the beer in our cooler."

CHAPTER FOUR

1984: South Park Meadows

SITE: *South Park Meadows concert site alongside Interstate 35, south of Slaughter Lane in Austin*
ATTENDANCE: *Estimated at 18,000*
HEADLINERS: *Willie Nelson, Waylon Jennings, Jessi Colter, Kris Kristofferson, Leon Russell, Joe Ely, Jerry Jeff Walker, David Allan Coe, Billy Joe Shaver, Delbert McClinton*

Picnic VIP Update

Willie Nelson: At the peak of his popularity, Willie was a one-name icon. After an early-1980s string of duet albums, he had just released *City of New Orleans*, which would be his last platinum album.

Waylon Jennings: Past his popular peak, Waylon was still a dynamic performer. The Picnic would be one of his first big shows after quitting a serious cocaine habit a few months earlier.

Johnny Bush: He had struggled with the speech disorder spasmodic dysphonia for years, but by 1984, Johnny was newly divorced and dead broke. He didn't release another album until 1994.

The Geezinslaws: The comic duo were hot in the '60s but were in the middle of a decade gap between albums in '84. Sammy Allred was a longtime Austin radio personality and Willie friend.

"You can't do this, you can't do that—Jesus, what kind of deal is this?" An evolved Picnic had returned to Texas, and Dale Zurkirchen of Fort Worth was among those who weren't happy with the changes. The *Austin American-Statesman* noted he was drinking a $1.75 cup of beer while complaining that he and his friends weren't allowed to bring their cooler inside.

Pace Management Co. of Houston had recently acquired the —eleven-acre South Park Meadows concert site in far South Austin, and Pace Concerts was running a tight ship. Concertgoers today would be familiar with the blue-shirted employees searching purses and backpacks and blankets, but it was a new twist for veteran picnickers.

Just inside the gate, the *Statesman* reported, were big containers filled with unopened beers, fried chicken, liquor, chips, sandwiches, and pocketknives. Not even Frisbees were allowed.

Once picnickers made it in, what was ahead of them was fourteen hours of music in ninety-nine-degree heat. The eighteen thousand fans would drain one thousand kegs of beer—even at $1.75 a cup.

Letting Pace run the show definitely made it easier on Willie. "I think it was probably one of the better-organized Picnics," Freddy Fletcher said. "Everything was really kind of already there. Everything was pretty smooth."

The thinking was that although Willie enjoyed the Picnic, he was taking advantage of the opportunity to recast it as something that wasn't going to take up his time or hurt his now-international reputation. "I believe the intent was to allow Pace to do this," Roger Collins said. "So that it would tame it and remove it from the hands of all the yahoos and just make it into a well-run concert festival. It worked. But it was too tame. From a fun perspective, I think it was a little bit sterile."

A newly minted movie star at the 1980 Picnic, Willie hadn't quite become a Hollywood icon four years later, but he wasn't left wanting anywhere else. "He was just everywhere," said longtime music writer and author John T. Davis. "He showed up for every honor that he could qualify for. He was putting out four or five albums a year. He was on the cover of *Life* magazine."

However, the jet-set life of a one-name star didn't lend itself to writing songs with the same intensity that had brought him that fame. "He was doing tons of records, but they weren't totally career defining," Davis said generously. "His recorded output wasn't particularly distinguished."

Willie did a bunch of duet records during that era with friends and some of his mentors, the most memorable of which was *Pancho and Lefty*, with Merle Haggard. Yet his biggest single of 1984 was the oft-derided "To All the Girls I've Loved Before" duet with Julio Iglesias.

The country music scene had changed. "One of the things that changes between '80 and '84 in Nashville is they really milk everything they can out of that pop-country crossover thing," said Travis D. Stimeling, a country music historian and author. "This is when Alabama is hitting it big, Juice Newton and people who are doing lots of synthesizers and stuff in their country music. The *Urban Cowboy* sound was still big. But as far as record sales were concerned, the country industry was kind of struggling a little bit. If you listen to Willie's records in the early '80s, you see him kind of struggling with that, too. He and Waylon Jennings recorded some really terrible albums between 1980 and 1984. Just kind of wandering pop standard type stuff."

After Willie had taken the Texas-centric "outlaw country" surge to the top, Nashville had now stepped back into the country music spotlight. "I remember talking to Ray Wylie Hubbard about this," Stimeling said. "He basically said that when *Urban Cowboy* came, the life got sucked out of the Texas thing. There was a period there from about '80 to '85, where it was tough to get any traction as a Texas artist. Nashville had taken over."

By the late 1980s, Texas would be back in the spotlight with Steve Earle, Rodney Crowell, and George Strait hitting their peaks, but for now, Willie was a country superstar who was getting his first taste of moving past his popular prime.

Willie, of course, would not fade from the spotlight in the way contemporaries like Waylon Jennings or pre–*American Recordings* Johnny Cash did. Yet that didn't mean that coming home to Austin didn't have its appeal. "I think the fact that he had come back to Austin in '84," Davis said, "after that burst of national and even international celebrity was just to reacquaint himself with the locals, his hometown community; he'd been out of pocket for a long time."

Louis Messina of Pace Concerts was an old friend, having brought the Picnic to the inaugural Texxas Jam in 1978. So when Pace took over management of a concert venue in South Austin called the Meadows, it made sense to strike a deal with Willie.

On June 14, it was announced that the newly renamed "South Park Meadows" would be a permanent venue, hosting crowds of up to thirty thousand for seven months a year. Its first show would be the 1984 Fourth of July Picnic.

Willie held a press conference at the Austin Opera House and said he hoped South Park would be a permanent location. "The places we've had them in the past have not been the best places because we have had neighbors around," Willie told the *Statesman*. "People originally moved out to the country to get away from things and they have a right to be concerned when they wake up one morning and find 50,000 hippies on their front lawn."

Although, as always, there were neighbors who opposed the Picnic at South Park. An Associated Press story quoted ninety-year-old C. L. Fox, a retired chiropractor who lived nearby and was very much opposed to the concert. Fox thought the eighteen-dollar tickets were ridiculous. "People have gone crazy," he said.

This 1985 Picnic photo shows South Park Meadows as it looked in the mid-1980s. The site, along Interstate 35, is now one of the largest shopping centers in Central Texas. © Bob Daemmrich photo

South Park Meadows in 1984 wasn't quite all that rural. It was alongside Interstate 35 and easily accessible from Austin. And unlike at other sites, Pace Concerts had a good grip on traffic flow and parking. "Pace Concerts was the premier concert production company in the Southwest at the time," Davis said. "And they imposed a certain sort of structure and order that had been largely missing before."

The move to let Pace run the show doesn't seem strange to veteran Texas music journalists. For starters, Willie's original set of fans were no longer young hippies and rednecks. "They were getting older, and they wanted a certain amount of amenities beyond squatting in a muddy field and being frisked by bikers," Davis said. "There was a certain amount of amenities present at the South Park show that older concertgoers, which Willie's fans were turning into, had kind of come to expect."

And Willie no longer had the time to sort out the details before the Picnic or settle the lawsuits afterward. "The Picnics became more of a business," Joe Nick Patoski said. "Willie was paid to headline a big event. He no longer had skin in the game as a promoter; he had too much other shit going on. He was a one-name superstar, getting up to one hundred thousand K for a single gig. The Picnic at this point was a tradition, sort of, but for Willie, Inc., it was a distraction and a time suck."

One area where Willie was still running the show was the music lineup, something he found difficult to hold the line on. "Basically, if you were a Texas artist who could get Willie's phone number, you could probably be assured of a slot," Davis said. "He would add people up to the day of the show, come out and do twenty minutes or whatever."

"MICKEY MANTLE AND BOBBY LAYNE, they would always come to Lubbock to party. When they had a few days off, they'd come and just party for days."

Joe Ely is telling a story about the first time he felt indebted to Willie. "They knew that if they came to this old honky-tonk in Lubbock that the press would never find them. So they would come there and just spin yarns day after day."

It was sometime in the 1960s and Joe wasn't yet a Flatlander, just a struggling young performer. When the two sports stars requested that Joe play Willie's song "Night Life," Joe was happy to oblige—he had just learned the song the day before.

Joe Ely and his band perform at the 1984 Picnic at South Park Meadows. Photo by Scott Newton

CHAPTER FOUR \ 93

After he played it, Mickey Mantle slipped a hundred-dollar bill into the sound hole of Joe's guitar. "I felt really lucky to have learned that song of Willie's in order to make that hundred-dollar bill, which got me through the next year," Joe said. "I'd never seen a hundred-dollar bill before."

Sharon Ely said it was more than just good fortune: "The song and payment for singing the song gave Joe incentive to continue singing for a living instead of washing dishes at the Chicken Box."

Joe had gotten the opportunity to thank Willie a few years later, but he remained grateful. When the Picnic called in 1984, it didn't matter to Joe that he had just come in off the road after a years-long run. He was glad to say yes to Willie.

After the raucous 1970s, the reaction of Central Texans to the Picnic in 1984 was muted. "There was no buzz or vibe about it," Joe Nick Patoski said. Pace expected a sellout crowd and printed thirty thousand tickets, but the demand fell short.

Still, it was a Willie Nelson show, and the Picnic represented opportunity to all sorts of people.

Jerry White, a cops reporter for the *Austin American-Statesman*, was first to sign up to work on the Fourth of July and earn triple pay. Jerry, who usually worked nights, didn't know what kind of day he would have—he had never been to a Willie Picnic before.

Scott Newton, who had been onstage as a working photographer for several of the Picnics, wasn't working this Picnic and didn't have any intention of sitting out in the heat as a fan. Even when an old friend from high school asked him to accompany her and her boyfriend to the show, he told her the Picnics were "kind of a hassle." She wasn't deterred. "She goes, 'Well, I tell you what, I bought you a ticket. Why don't you come with us?'" Newton said. He told her he would go.

And Sandra Madrid, then only fourteen years old, perked up when her dad told her they needed people to work at the Picnic. She went down to Palmer Auditorium and filled out an application with Volume Services. "I lied about my age; yes I did," she said.

Probably the most iconic image to come out of the Picnics after the first era is Danny Garrett's "Uncle Willie" poster design—though even that had roots in the 1970s. Around the time Willie released *Stardust* in 1978, he had started wearing a top hat, a look that inspired the Austin artist. "It just reminded me of the James Montgomery Flagg recruiting poster. 'I Want You for the US Army,'" Garrett said. "The iconic American poster with Uncle Sam [pointing toward the viewer]. So when I saw Willie in the top hat, you know, it just seemed like a natural thing."

When a poster was needed in a hurry for the 1978 mini-Picnic at the Austin Opry House, Garrett sketched up a quick black-and-white version of "Uncle Willie" and added a few splashes of red and blue.

Garrett used a different design for the 1979 poster, and Steve Brooks did the poster for the 1980 Picnic, but by the time Willie's people returned to him for 1983's run of East Coast Picnics, Garrett had fully developed his idea. The "I Want You for Willie Nelson's Fourth of July Picnic" poster was born. Willie was so taken with the design that they used it again for the 1984, 1985, and 1987 Picnics.

Posters were a big part of advertising shows in the 1970s and 1980s, Garrett said, though how effective they were wasn't really possible to measure. Radio and TV advertising certainly had more impact on ticket sales.

Yet the posters became iconic in a way other means of advertising did not. They became prized by collectors, some for their beauty and others for their rarity. Pristine Picnic posters from Jim Franklin or Danny Garrett can sell for thousands of dollars at auction. And even the most beat-up, bent-up survivor is a tangible connection to a historic event. "The poster is a physical artifact of a concert, which—unless it was recorded—was not physical; it was ephemeral," Garrett said. "The sounds are produced, the concert happened, and then it was over. But the poster was always an artifact that remains."

DAWN BROKE AT SOUTH Park Meadows on July 4 with some fans already lined up outside the gate, hoping to secure the best spots. Whether they came early or late, picnickers would be searched for contraband—225 security officers would be at the box office, front gates, and entrances.

Jerry White, arriving early to seek out the Department of Public Safety and Emergency Medical Technician officials he would be in touch with throughout the day, remembers the containers of contraband and being surprised that so many Texans would give up their knives to get through the gate. People could bring their lawn chairs and blankets, but no umbrellas, pets, or any kind of food or beverage. The *Statesman* quoted security worker James Richards: "One lady told me she was a vegetarian, so I let her take in a couple of apples."

John Kolsburn of Houston may have offered the first version of the quote Picnic reporters would hear for years to come: "They call it a picnic, but you can't bring anything to eat. It's ridiculous."

Some fans set up on the concrete pad directly in front of the stage; others put their lawn chairs at strategic vantage points halfway up the hill or claimed a spot in the shade of a 60- by 210-foot red-and-green tent at the top.

Headed for her concessions job, Sandra Madrid remembers going through security early in the day. "I had my rainbow-colored Converse shoes on, I can remember. They put me in a little Coca-Cola trailer at the top of the hill."

Whether it was the security or just a new era, the crowds were not a problem at this Picnic. There were no stabbings or drug overdoses or anarchy of any note. "It's better than we thought it would be," Sue Schulz of St. Louis told the *Statesman*.

John T. Davis agreed it was fairly sedate. "I hesitate to say 'more grown-up,' but there wasn't the out-of-control sort of vibe that had been in some of the earlier ones."

Scott Newton recalls it was dusty, but not unpleasant. "People got exactly what they wanted. They got Willie; they got all those people doing all those songs; they got exactly what they came for. There's a certain legacy of fuzziness to memory, but all I get is warm fuzzies when I go back to that one."

The 1984 Picnic was fairly sedate, particularly when compared with the first era of the Picnic. There were few arrests and very little trouble. Photo by Scott Newton

That doesn't mean some people didn't get away with a little bit of trouble.

Country musician Michael Ballew attended the Picnic that year with his young daughter, who wanted to see Kris Kristofferson. "[The security] searched for booze, so I was surprised to see the guy next to us with a couple of bottles of tequila," he said. "I have no idea how he pulled that off."

The *Statesman*'s wrap-up reported that there were forty-five arrests, mostly for DWI and public intoxication. One of the more notable incidents was a man trying to push over a portable toilet while his friend was inside. "I just kept wondering when they were going to go really crazy," paramedic Mark Cook told the *Statesman*.

Within a few hours of beginning work in her trailer serving drinks, the concessions people brought fourteen-year-old Sandra Madrid a large box of wine and told her she was now selling wine coolers. "I honestly did not know how to make [the wine coolers] at all," she said. "They showed me one time, and I swear, I went through boxes of wine. And they were not cheap. I remember them being like $2.50, $3.00."

Sandra said the woman working alongside her did not ask questions about her age, though she's pretty sure she didn't appear to be the seventeen years she had claimed on her application. "I made wine coolers all evening long and had a blast," she said. "And people were just having a blast, eating big ol' turkey legs. The drunker they got, the more they danced. It was really a laid-back, kind of hippie situation. I mean, it was really cool."

Though the crowd was well behaved, the Texas heat remained a problem. More than four hundred were treated for heat problems, though none were sent to the hospital. Charles Tatom, who supervised a medical support crew of 180 people, said people weren't drinking enough water. "They just sit there in a lawn chair and suddenly they pass out," he told the *Statesman*. "You got to sweat and stink—that's what your body is supposed to do."

Jerry White said people were "plopping over" all day long, even though there were plenty of water stations. Michael Ballew recalled that at the hottest part of the day they turned firehoses on the front part of the crowd. "That felt good for a few minutes. Then we were hot and in the mud."

Willie opened his own show at 10 a.m., introducing the crowd to his old friend Johnny Bush: "He wrote 'Whiskey River' . . . and welcome to the twelfth annual Fourth of July Picnic." In his review of the show, John T. Davis wrote that "Nelson has always used these events to parade old and

Willie Nelson performs during his 1984 Picnic at South Park Meadows. Willie performed throughout the day and often introduced his friends. Photo by Bob Daemmrich, Austin American-Statesman

new musical friends before an appreciative audience." The opening hour included Bush, Floyd Tillman, Steve Fromholz, the Geezinslaws, and, possibly, Gary Busey, with whom he had just filmed the movie *Barbarosa*. Busey was on the schedule, but his appearance hasn't been verified.

Davis later agreed that the presence of classic country stars at the Picnic was testament to Willie's loyalty. "He never forgot the guys that helped mentor him coming up," he said. A common element to all the Picnics is Willie's "loyalty to the people that he admired or that helped him or that he was contemporary with when he was a nobody."

Johnny Rodriguez, Billy Joe Shaver, Faron Young, Jackie King, Jerry Jeff Walker, and Moe Bandy filled the early-afternoon hours. Davis's review noted that Jackie King seemed to be having more fun than even Willie, Jerry Jeff played all the anthems, and Moe Bandy "turned South Park Meadows into an open air beer joint" with his honky-tonk songs, although the song that got the biggest applause was the Culture Club parody "Where's the Dress?"

Things turned interesting during the late afternoon with David Allan Coe, Joe Ely, and a surprise performance by Townes Van Zandt during the set change before Leon Russell.

Tyler Mahan Coe remembers the family story of his father's set at the '84 show: "My dad thought that it would be cool to take his rhinestone jacket off and throw it in the audience. You know, just like some big rock star thing to do." The crowd apparently thought so, too. They surged forward and ripped it to pieces. "They all tore it up, everyone trying to get a piece of it, like a Jimi Hendrix smashed guitar or something like that," Tyler said.

When David Allan got offstage, he called home to describe the incident, only to find out that famed clothes tailor Nudie Cohn had died a couple months earlier. "My dad had just thrown his Nudie jacket out into the audience and watched it get torn to shreds and then couldn't get another one," Tyler said. "It's kind of a sad story."

David Allan told the *Fort Worth Star-Telegram* that playing the Picnic was a family tradition. "We're the Willie Nelson Family and this is our tradition."

If it feels odd to hear noted rebel David Allan Coe place himself in Willie's shadow, Tyler described his father's relationship with Willie as "full hero worship": "It wouldn't matter what Willie Nelson told David Allan Coe to do, he would do it."

Several remember Joe Ely's set as the best of the day. Scott Newton said, "Joey really ripped it up," and Davis praised it in his review and noted Kris Kristofferson being stunned: "Great #$%* band!" is Kris' reaction as it appeared in Davis's column.

"I've pretty much always had kind words for Joe," Davis said. "He is one of the strongest live performers I've ever experienced." For his part, Joe said he felt like he put on a good show, but he can't really recall. "I remember how much fun I had. It was the first one of the Picnics that I played and was quite a ball."

Backstage, the fun was subdued, compared to the bacchanalia of Pedernales. "There was more hierarchy," Davis said. "A lot of people had their own buses or their own RVs. Leon Russell was not hobnobbing with Joe Ely, for instance, or anything."

Not that Ely had any less fun. "It was a party going on in every room," he said. "I can't remember who all was there because we'd been on the road for a long time and every day was Saturday night. It was memorable, and it's hard to remember at the same time."

One thing that was notable about the 1984 Picnic was that there weren't a lot of people hanging out on the stage. "Usually, there are so many people that are somebody that even if you have a stage rule that says you can't get onstage unless you're somebody, there's just too many somebodies," Collins said. "And it's just hard to manage it. But not that one."

Collins had a personal advantage at this Picnic. His home was just a mile or so away from the rear gate of South Park's backstage area. "I could literally drive back and forth to my house and roll joints and eat and enjoy some air conditioning. We used my house is an extra backstage area for me and a lot of my friends."

When he wasn't joining his friends onstage, Willie spent his time on his bus, where he would meet with friends, other musicians, and journalists. Davis said he was always first in line to get a quick interview with Willie, mostly because he was efficient about it and quickly made room for the next person.

The efficiency wasn't part of his personality; it was a lesson learned through experience. "I found out early on [interviewing Willie on his bus] I had to do that because he was blowing that polio weed in your face the whole time," John T. said. "And if I didn't get my three questions out within ten minutes, I would just turn into a cigar store Indian."

The final stretch of the Picnic featured Kris Kristofferson, Jessi Colter, Waylon Jennings, and Willie himself, playing just after a fireworks show. Michael Ballew remembered hoisting his daughter onto his shoulders and moving toward the front of the crowd so she could see the movie star. She didn't make it to Willie. "She was exhausted and getting grumpy, so we left as soon as the fireworks started."

The *Statesman* noted that many other exhausted fans headed toward the exits as Willie came on. Sandra Madrid, however, now off work and watching alongside her father, stayed until the end. "I remember him doing 'Pancho and Lefty.' And my dad loved that song. To see him just smiling . . . it was really great."

For first-time Picnic-goer Jerry White, it all made for an amazing day: "Just being back by the fancy buses and seeing the people who were performing, that was neat, but the absolute best memory was at the very end of the day." Coworkers White and Davis were backstage watching the fireworks after an exhausting dozen or more hours of work. "We both just leaned back on the hood of a car, there were these fireworks going off, and we could hear the music. It was just the coolest ending of any assignment I ever had," White said.

Davis remembered it as well: "The fireworks went off just after dark and were chased all over the sky by the lightning. That was a fairly amazing spectacle."

Willie Nelson and Kris Kristofferson spend time together at the 1985 Picnic at South Park. Spending time with old friends was a big part of why Willie continued to do the Picnics. © Bob Daemmrich photo

Roger Collins recalls being surprised that the Picnic ended so early and without incident, compared to past events: "I think we might have even been out of there and back home by 11 o'clock or so. It was just sort of a flat deal. Like you left with 'well, is that all there is to it?'"

WHEN THE DUST CLEARED and the trash was picked up at South Park Meadows, Willie was looking at a Picnic that fell far short of the expected attendance of thirty thousand. Pace Management told the *Statesman* it happened because they got a late start on the Picnic; however, John T. Davis later wrote that it was a "crisis of indecision" by Pace. The promoter didn't tell people tickets would be available at the gate until the day before the show.

The smaller crowd may very well have been the result of changing tastes in country music and older fans, though some people involved in the Picnic during its 1970s heyday think a tamer Picnic just wasn't that appealing. "When you transition from an open field out in the middle of nowhere to a more formal outdoor facility that regularly hosts concerts, something's lost," Joe Nick Patoski said.

Travis D. Stimeling doesn't necessarily buy into that. The historian said it's easy to mythologize the early days, though there's something to be said for turning the Picnic into a civilized event. "That 1973 picnic has an awfully good myth around it, and that paints a nice picture of just how energetic that progressive country thing was. Truth be told, it was also the Fourth of July, and hot and dusty, and there weren't enough toilets and all that sort of thing. What you lose in the freewheelingness of it, you build a more pleasant experience for the concertgoers."

The fact is, even with easy access to parking and toilets, the Picnic still provided plenty of challenge to Texans, and eighteen thousand of them were okay with that.

"If you're going to go to one of those things, you're going to be walking; you're going to be standing in lines; you better have brought some money, because you're going to be paying for shit," Scott Newton said. "You're probably going to be hot and miserable. But the bottom line is . . . they think that's fun in Texas."

And, of course, the reunion of friends was still fun for Willie. Tim O'Connor said performing alongside his friends and family is one of Willie's favorite pleasures. "He loved [performing on his own]; don't misunderstand it, but Waylon wasn't standing next to him. And there wasn't a crescendo at the end of the show. And there wasn't a lot of bullshitting when they all arrived and partied a bit. That was kind of the feeling we loved. We were a family."

John T. Davis saw that Willie enjoyed the ritual of the Picnic and how they kept him connected with the people he came up with. "Yeah, it's a little bit self-indulgent on his part. He doesn't have to do 'em. He did them because he wants to keep some constancy going in a life that has really been kind of all over the map. They were a touchstone back through the whole of his career."

GO TO SOUTHPARK (now one word) Meadows today and you'll find one of the largest shopping centers in Central Texas. Thousands of shoppers a day visit Southpark businesses, most having no idea that thirty-one thousand people came to see the Police in 1983. Or that in 1985 the Highwaymen stood on a stage that was once in front of where Marshalls is now. Or that a mid-1990s revival brought in bands and artists such as Metallica, Pearl Jam, R.E.M., Alanis Morrissette, and David Bowie.

When development began in 2004, the future shopping center was an open field where cattle grazed and Slaughter Lane was on the far southern edge of Austin. In 1984, the site seemed far enough removed from Austin that the *Statesman* referred to it as "south Travis County." The nearby historic D. E. Crumley Grocery completed the rural Texas feel. The antique-festooned country store lasted until the end of 1984.

"Every time I drive past that mall, my heart sinks a little bit," Joe Ely said of the new shopping center. "It's a massive, massive structure. It was hard to see it change so quickly from just an open field where you would feel like you were one thousand miles away with great music and all."

1985: South Park Meadows

SITE: *South Park Meadows concert site alongside Interstate 35, south of Slaughter Lane in Austin*
ATTENDANCE: *Estimated at 12,000*
HEADLINERS: *Willie Nelson, Johnny Cash, Waylon Jennings, Kris Kristofferson, Neil Young, Jerry Jeff Walker, David Allan Coe, Ray Wylie Hubbard, Hank Snow, June Carter Cash*

After the 1984 Picnic ticket sales were lower than expected, the 1985 show upped the ante by adding some star power to the bill—but attendance at the rain-soaked South Park Meadows fell further still.

Pace was forced to close its soggy ten-thousand-car parking field and had picnickers park alongside Interstate 35. Those who made it inside found one of the coolest Picnics, with a high of seventy-nine degrees and lots and lots of mud. "[The Picnic in] 1985 was so much more of a bigger deal," Roger Collins said. "Even though there were fantastic performers in '84, they were mostly people who we saw all the time and played in my club and local clubs."

The addition of the Highwaymen, Neil Young, and Johnny and June Carter Cash was much more exciting, Roger said. "It was much more of a festival type of atmosphere. It seemed to me like everybody that was performing was in a really good mood. It almost was like there was electricity in the air."

American-Statesman reviewer John T. Davis noted that Willie "was seldom absent from the stage" and that Asleep at the Wheel and Johnny and June Carter Cash had particularly powerful sets, though it was the inaugural Austin appearance of the Highwaymen that had everyone riveted.

The Picnic itself was a peaceful affair; by nightfall only seven people had been arrested. Not everything went just right, though.

"The funny thing was, there was a concrete slab where the stage set. Literally at the bottom of the damn hill, you walked on concrete. And O'Connor got this great idea." Tim O'Connor is self-deprecatingly describing one of his Picnic mistakes, although it seemed reasonable at the time. He decided to have the concrete area in front of the stage cordoned off and set up picnic tables so he could charge for VIP tickets. It's an idea that the Picnics in Fort Worth and at the Circuit of the Americas would later successfully pull off.

"After the show, Willie is sitting on the bus and he called me over there and said, 'O'Connor, were you the brilliant guy who did all that in front of the stage?'"

Tim spoke up quickly, "Yes, sir." After all, he had sold a good number of tickets at twice the price.

"And Willie goes, 'Don't do that again. Because the entire night I played to picnic tables. I couldn't see the damn crowd,'" Tim said. "I'll never forget; he was pissed off."

1986: Farm Aid II at Manor Downs

SITE: *Manor Downs, a horse racetrack near the town of Manor, northeast of Austin*
ATTENDANCE: *More than 40,000*
HEADLINERS: *Too many to name but included the usual Picnic suspects, the Beach Boys, Julio Iglesias, Neil Young, Stevie Ray Vaughan, Rick James, Jon Bon Jovi, Steppenwolf, Bonnie Raitt, Don Johnson, the Reverend Jesse Jackson*

If you're prone to dividing things by category, this hybrid event was technically Farm Aid II rather than a Fourth of July Picnic, but it was a hit either way you count it. The eighteen-hour extravaganza drew more than forty thousand fans (a number the Picnic would not approach again), was broadcast on VH-1, featured more than seventy-five acts, and raised $1.3 million for American farmers.

The event was originally set for the University of Texas Memorial Stadium, but the university remembered ruefully the 1974 ZZ Top Rompin' Stompin' Barndance and Bar B.Q., where concessionaires had run out of food and drink and hot and thirsty fans ended up tearing water fountains from the walls. Negotiations finally broke down over insurance concerns and left Farm Aid II homeless. A brief move to South Park Meadows didn't work out either.

With days to go, Woody Roberts, who was now producing special events at a horse-racing track in nearby Manor, called Larry Trader and Tim O'Connor to let them know Manor Downs was available, and a deal was quickly made.

Willie opened the show shortly after dawn, sitting in with Cherokee Rose, and many early performers got to perform only one song. Most would be limited to two or three songs throughout the day. A revolving stage was used to minimize setup delays.

It was a day for the unusual—Willie performing alongside Jon Bon Jovi and Vince Neil, or Minnie Mouse following Roy Head—and the sublime—Bonnie Raitt playing "Angel from Montgomery" alongside John Prine and Kris Kristofferson, and Stevie Ray Vaughan bringing the crowd to their feet.

There were problems, traffic was a disaster, hundreds were treated for heat problems, forged tickets were an issue, and the $1.3 million raised was disappointing next to the previous year's $9 million. But the event unfurled as planned, and Willie closed the show just after 1 a.m. with an all-star sing-along, including "Amazing Grace" and Woody Guthrie's "This Land Is Your Land."

CHAPTER FIVE

1987: Carl's Corner

SITE: *Carl's Corner, a few miles north of Hillsboro on Interstate 35E, across the highway from the truck stop at the intersection of 35E and Ranch Road 2959*
ATTENDANCE: *Estimated at 10,000*
HEADLINERS: *Willie Nelson, Bruce Hornsby and the Range, Kris Kristofferson, Roger Miller, Joe Walsh, the Fabulous Thunderbirds, Eric Johnson, Joe Ely, Asleep at the Wheel, Billy Joe Shaver*

Picnic VIP Update

Willie Nelson: Willie was leaning on duet albums with pop-flavored productions and his artistic collaborations with the Highwaymen. While filming a made-for-TV remake of *Stagecoach* a year earlier, Willie had met future wife Annie D'Angelo and was separated from wife Connie.

Kris Kristofferson: His acting career had dwindled to TV movies after the *Heaven's Gate* fiasco, and his music career wasn't doing much better. His 1986 album, *Repossessed*, was fueled by his political activism and was not a commercial success.

Asleep at the Wheel: The western swing band had just released their tenth record—*10*—and had found their way back to critical and commercial success. Among the four charting hits was one of their signature tunes, "House of Blue Lights."

Billy Joe Shaver: Billy Joe was still a songwriter's songwriter but otherwise relatively unknown. He had gotten sober and had a big payday when John Anderson covered "I'm Just an Old Chunk of Coal," but he was still looking for the recognition he was due.

Carl Cornelius brought one of his town's police officers with him when he came to confront Tim O'Connor after the 1987 Picnic at Carl's Corner. "Where's the money?" Carl asked.

"Well, we didn't make any money," Tim said. "We lost money, Carl." Tim had what cash there was, but the gate receipts were slim. That money was going to the artists, not Carl.

"You stay right here, Tim," Carl said. He walked off, maybe looking for Willie or maybe for more backup.

Reflecting on it thirty-four years later, Tim said he had no choice but to defuse the standoff. "I took off," he said. "Because—and I don't want to overdramatize this—it was getting to a point where the next move would be pistols."

It's not an empty boast. Had the scene occurred a decade earlier, it likely would have ended differently. "I don't believe that you would let somebody piss on your boots," Tim said. "That's where I came from. Fortunately for Carl, at that time, I was in the midst of trying to learn a different way."

The bad blood between the guy who ran the town and the guy who ran Willie Nelson's Fourth of July Picnic had been brewing for a month or so.

If the Picnic had brought in the eighty thousand to one hundred thousand fans from across the state that they had expected, the hard feelings might have dissolved amid the money. However, the Picnic had attracted only about 10 percent of the people they had prepared for, and everybody was angry.

Other Picnics have had smaller-than-expected crowds. Other Picnics have been plagued by traffic and trouble and chaos. But no Picnic was really a full-scale bust . . . except 1987.

IN 1984, CARL CORNELIUS opened his truck stop on the west side of Interstate 35 East, just north of Hillsboro and about sixty miles south of Dallas. Everyone noticed—primarily because of the ten-foot-tall dancing frogs cavorting above the gas pumps. The sculptures, created by Austin-based artist Bob "Daddy-O" Wade, had originally lived above a nightclub in Dallas.

Monk White, a Dallas businessman, owned seventeen hundred acres just north of the I-35 split and said that Carl came into his office one day wanting to buy the property. Monk agreed to sell it for two million dollars, though Carl didn't have a down payment or even "a pot to piss in."

Carl started selling ten- and twenty-acre tracts. and "within ninety days, he already had enough sales to give me a down payment," Monk said. "Next thing you know, he had a truck stop and a little bar."

Carl was in the truck stop business, but he wanted to be in the empire business. He added a small motel, a swimming pool and spa, a chapel, and

Carl's Corner was essentially just a truck stop before Carl Cornelius bought the place and established his own small town. © Bob Wade, from Daddy-O's Book of Big Ass Art

even a catfish pond to his truck stop and restaurant. Then he started dividing up the ranchland he had bought in 1979 and bringing in residents.

The two-hundred-odd residents voted to incorporate the town in 1986, and suddenly Carl was mayor, judge, fire chief, and Texas celebrity. "You go by Carl's now, and it's just another generic truck stop, but back in the day you had the giant billboard shaped like a semi truck and the frogs on the roof," author John T. Davis said. "That whole thing had a really funky, Texas amusement park feel to it."

Monk said the circus was fueled by Carl himself. "Carl was a character, God rest his soul. He was a hell of a character."

During the truck stop's first few years, Carl became friends with Zeke Varnon, a fellow beer-bellied, white-haired local who had grown up with Willie Nelson in Abbott, about twenty miles south. In the spring of 1987, Zeke brought Willie to Carl's Corner and Carl made his pitch.

After being surprised by a giant billboard of himself, Carl, and Zeke alongside I-35E, Willie walked into the truck stop and was approached by Carl. Willie described the moment in his first autobiography:

> A burly fellow with a big, open country face approached me, his cheeks blooming with whiskey flush, a straw cowboy hat pushed to the back of his head, his belly hanging over his silver belt buckle, crumpled jeans, and ostrich-skin boots. He had a wide, yellow-toothed grin and eyes that looked like they had just been through a sandstorm.
>
>   Carl is not bashful. He cut straight to the meat of the matter.

"Hi, Willie," Carl said. "Let's have your 1987 picnic right here in my town this Fourth of July. Carl's Corner is ideal. There is not a single tree to block the view of the stage."

The legend goes that Willie, Carl, and Zeke stayed up all night, drinking beer and tequila and playing dominoes. At some point, Willie, intoxicated and impressed by Carl's audacity, agreed to have the Picnic at Carl's Corner.

While not entirely out of character for Willie, who at fifty-three was recently separated from third wife, Connie, the legend does seem more like good storytelling. However, when asked if it really happened that way, Tim O'Connor just nodded.

The Picnic would be held across the interstate from Carl's Corner, in an empty field Carl owned at the intersection of I-35E and Ranch Road 2959. Once the crew got a look at the site, they knew it would be a rough one. "It was just a bad place to have one," said Budrock Prewitt, longtime lighting director for Willie. "But when Willie picks a place to do a Picnic, you know we don't question it. We just go and do it."

Tim said he tried to let Willie know it wasn't a good location, but "Will was determined that he'd already made a deal."

"This is what we're doing," Tim said, quoting Willie. "Do the best you can."

Willie, Zeke, and Carl envisioned tens of thousands of fans coming down from the Metroplex and up from Austin and Waco. Carl was naturally suited to drumming up publicity, and by mid-May, newspapers nationwide were running an Associated Press story that said up to one hundred thousand were expected. "I think it will be one of the biggest events Hill County ever had," Carl told the AP. "And who knows, if it goes well, we may have it again here next year. Maybe it'll have a permanent home." A month or so into his friendship with Willie, Carl didn't hesitate to hypothetically steer the future of the Picnic.

Carl knew how to help his truck stop—the Picnic was dedicated to America's truckers, and Carl gave away tickets to those who bought at least fifty gallons of diesel from him. His ideas about concert promotion weren't quite as keen.

He wanted the stage as close as possible to the interstate, giving the event a roadside carnival feel. Carl may have felt that people driving by were going to stop for the fourteen-hour show. What really happened is that everybody driving by in the month before the show got a good look at the desolate and exposed site.

Janis Tillerson, a longtime Willie superfan (across the fifty-year life span of the Picnic, she says she missed only two of them) and photographer, drove down from Greenville daily for several weeks to document the site preparations. "My husband told me it was kinda stupid, that I didn't need to do that," Tillerson said. "But I thought I did."

The Hard Rock Cafe in Dallas joined in as a sponsor, and a substantial number of vendors signed up. The Picnic did advertise that people would be allowed to bring in their coolers—as long as they didn't bring in alcohol. The Texas Alcoholic Beverage Commission was now keeping a close eye on the Picnic. If the promoters were selling beer (and they planned to), then people weren't allowed to bring it in.

"We're calling this the 'can-do' picnic, because we're trying to make it as comfortable and uncomplicated as we can," Tim told the *Austin American-Statesman* before the show. "People can do stuff; bring in food, non-alcoholic beverages, umbrellas and stuff. I've never yet seen anybody impaled on an umbrella."

Tickets were twenty-one dollars, with free parking opening up at 4 a.m. on the day of the show.

Asked how difficult it was to set up in an empty field, Budrock was dismissive. "Well, all we need is a stage. The rest is up to the promoter to provide the amenities for the crowd: the pissers and the places to eat." By that point, the crew had set up so many stages in empty rural fields that it didn't seem like a challenge worth commenting on.

Carl's Corner did have one advantage over the other Picnics: Dr. Red Duke, the famous folksy surgeon from nearby Ennis, was in charge of the two hundred medical personnel on-site.

As late as July 3, Tim was quoted by the UPI as saying up to ninety thousand were expected, but the *Statesman* and the *Fort Worth Star-Telegram* had dialed back their estimates to forty thousand and fifty thousand, respectively.

In truth, Tim already knew the attendance wasn't going to be there. The lineup was packed with small-time artists such as Mack Abernathy and Bennie Kirby and the Country Dummies. And some of the bigger names had already bowed out: Emmylou Harris, Merle Haggard, David Allan Coe, and Jerry Jeff Walker had all said they couldn't make it.

"You're getting feedback if you're smart," Tim said. "And Jerry Jeff, God bless him, had connections. . . . They were getting feedback. And it was troubled. 'I don't need to go up there and stand in 105-degree heat and not get paid.'"

Carl Cornelius didn't see it coming. "I think this will be the biggest

Picnic ever," he told the *Star-Telegram*. "There's the interstate; there's traffic in the area. It's going to be wonderful."

JANIS TILLERSON and her husband were among the first on-site on Independence Day. They had camped out in a nearby field the night before and were at the gate when it opened, blankets and ice chest in tow. They were among the lucky ones who managed to sneak some beer in their cooler. Many other picnickers were well stocked with beer and were surprised when they weren't allowed to bring it in.

Bob Wishoff, then a new member of the Willie Nelson Family, says one of his prime memories of the 1987 Picnic is seeing people standing outside the gate, chugging down beer as fast as they could. "They told everybody to finish all their beers in the parking lot," he said. "So they got pretty wasted. It was kind of like an English pub—you know right before they close, people get like five [pints] of beer and then chug them all down at once."

Tim O'Connor grimaced at the description. "[The fans] were so happy with us," he said sarcastically. "They haven't even gotten in, and they're shit-faced and they're angry."

Once inside the gate, though, there was little to excite the senses. The water stations were PVC pipes coming out of the muddy ground. There were plenty of food concessions and Porta Potties, but for the most part, it was the stage, the pasture, and the people. "There was nothing to look at and nowhere to hide," said John T. Davis, who covered the event for the *American-Statesman* and recalled a hot and dusty day.

Tillerson agreed: "There were no bushes, no barns, no nothing out there."

Yet, from a fan's perspective, Tillerson didn't think it was a bad Picnic at all. "I'm going to say that was the last free-feeling Picnic. You could come and put your blanket out in the middle of wherever, and you could leave everything at your blanket and wander around all day, and you could go up to the front of the stage anytime during the day."

Tillerson recalled water-gun fights in the crowd, a lot of room to roam, and plenty of things to spend money on. Vendors had prepared for the expected crowd of more than ninety thousand and quickly began dropping prices.

Davis called the Picnic "the last of the old school. You know, 'Let's fence off a cotton patch and put on a show out in the dirt.' It hearkened back to the early ones like Liberty Hill and Dripping Springs."

Bob Wishoff, a longtime Willie associate known as "Computer Bob," recalled the 1987 Picnic as pretty wild despite the low attendance. Photo by Dave Dalton Thomas

There was still a distinctive 1980s feel, though. "Spuds Mackenzie was big then," Tillerson said, recalling the Bud Light advertising mascot. "And there were *several* Spuds there."

Also wandering around was Jim Kimmel. "The Reverend Jim Kimmel, as he was calling himself then, was one of the original strange San Francisco characters," Bob Wishoff said. He said Kimmel would carry *The Urantia Book* as if it were a Bible . . . a Bible loaded with tabs of LSD. "I mean, I was pretty high most of that show, too, I have to say. I think it was hash that was floating around that year, but who can tell you? There are many people who might have been doing some tabs. I can't imagine being at a Picnic and not being intoxicated."

Wishoff wasn't alone. Jeff Guinn, who covered the Picnic for the *Fort Worth Star-Telegram* and later became a best-selling author, said that pro wrestler Kerry von Erich "staggered onstage at one point and rambled incoherently. Like all the other Willie Nelson events I ever covered, the people attending had laid-back attitudes. The only complaining I heard was about a very largish biker chick who kept pulling her top off. People around her repeatedly screamed for her to 'put it back on!' This was, of course, before body-shaming was frowned upon."

The drunkenness was par for the course, Tim said. "If you weren't fall-down drunk, you weren't going to be harmed. If you didn't start a fight, you're not gonna be harmed."

Drunken driving, however, was another matter entirely. Tim said security would do their best to discourage drunks from getting in their car after the show, admitting that sometimes it was difficult. To be sure, law enforcement was keeping a close watch on picnickers leaving the show, and Tim said he never heard complaints from law enforcement about excessive DWI cases after a Picnic. (The *Hillsboro Reporter* said that eighty-seven were arrested by the Hill County Sheriff's Department from 5 p.m. July 3 to 5 a.m. July 5, including forty-nine for DWI.)

Even with the drinking and the drugs, the casualty list for the Carl's Corner Picnic was exceedingly light. There were some cases of dehydration and heat exhaustion, but Dr. Red Duke told the UPI that the biggest problem—at least early in the day—occurred when a little girl picked up a field mouse and it bit her. He said the high winds were helping keep picnickers from overheating, along with free Gatorade.

Tillerson said that in those days, the Willie fans helped take care of their own—from soaking towels in ice chests to cool down those who were passed out to giving water to those who looked like they were in trouble. "People really looked after each other," she said. "And you didn't know each other. You may or may not see them at the next Picnic."

"WELCOME TO WILLIE What's-his-name's Picnic," shouted Willie as he started the show ten minutes early. The short opening set included a prayer and a recitation of the Pledge of Allegiance with Brother Wayne Johnson, Willie's old pastor from Abbott. The *Star-Telegram* reported that during the prayer, "the names 'Jesus Christ,' 'America' and 'Willie Nelson' received equal cheers from the crowd-turned-congregation."

One of the more notable musical aspects of the Picnic was the multitude of unknown artists. More than half of the acts on the bill were virtually unknown to the average fan—then and now. "I think that also didn't help in the attendance," Tim O'Connor said. "Nothing against those musicians, but they weren't some of the well-known artists."

One of those artists was Rattlesnake Annie, who at the time was as close as she would come to being a household name. "I didn't notice any-

Willie performs at the 1987 Picnic. Willie was genuinely excited to have the Picnic at Carl's Corner, close to his hometown of Abbott, but the crowds didn't come. Photo by Tom Lankes, Austin American-Statesman

thing about [the small crowd]," she said. "Because I just felt really satisfied. I had just signed with CBS, and they showed up with my new guitar and my new amplifier. Everything was going my way, and I didn't have any complaints."

Rattlesnake (as she still called herself thirty-four years later) was one of just a handful of female artists onstage. Asked about the Picnic being a "boys' club," she was quick to answer. "Honey, I damn sure know what you mean. You think I hadn't lived in the middle of the boys' club for the sixty-five years I've been on the road? I never feel uncomfortable around guys. You got to be thick-skinned to be in the music business and last as long as I have."

Willie joined Rattlesnake onstage for a duet on "Long Black Limousine," and she got to enjoy seeing a lot of Texas friends. "It was just a day full of great joy and love for me," she said.

Not everyone was quite as happy playing to a half-empty barren field beside the highway.

John T. Davis said he imagines some of the artists such as Bruce Hornsby and rock guitarist Eric Johnson were "used to a little bit more cosmopolitan sort of setting. . . . I think they were probably a little bit taken aback by it."

Johnson said when he was asked to come play, he was excited. "I grew up on country music. It's kind of maybe not so evident, but it's, it's a part of my DNA." When he arrived, however, Johnson wasn't so impressed with the aesthetics. "It was a little like, 'I don't know about this . . . this doesn't quite work.' It just wasn't like the big Fourth of July Picnic that Willie usually has. It was still cool to do it. But yeah, it didn't seem like it went over that well."

Without naming names, Tim O'Connor said he got several "Who chose this fucking place? Are you kidding, Tim? Does Willie know about this? What it's like?" He said a lot of people were frustrated but went ahead and performed. "The cloud was over them; you can't spread your abilities. It was kind of a damper. And it was very obvious. There wasn't the normal joy and happiness."

Davis said the blowing dust didn't help the camaraderie. "There weren't a lot of musicians hanging around onstage watching each other since they mostly were staying in their respective buses."

Still, some artists really did connect. Davis praised the Fabulous Thunderbirds as "really on top of their game." Bob Wishoff was blown away by Eric Johnson. Jeff Guinn said Joe Ely stole the show.

One of the more intriguing additions to the lineup was Bruce Hornsby and the Range. Even at an event known for including unusual performers, Hornsby seemed to be an odd fit for the Picnic. At the time of the '87 Picnic, Bruce had won a Grammy for Best New Artist and had big hits with the mellow pop singles "The Way It Is" and "Mandolin Rain."

Both Davis and Tim couldn't quite recall how Bruce became part of the show. Bruce was kind enough to spell it out in an email:

> We played the picnic . . . having just had two very enjoyable, memorable experiences with Willie the previous spring; we had recorded with Willie at his studio, with Ray Benson producing, a song I had written with the late, great jazz bass player Charlie Haden and my brother Jon entitled "Nobody There But Me" while in Austin making a video. Then we were part of a TV special [with Willie]. So it seemed very natural that we were asked to play the legendary picnic, and we said yes to the request instantly.
>
> The most memorable part of the gig was the very beginning. . . . We started our set, probably with our song "Jacob's Ladder," and just seconds into the song the power went out and we were left there standing around

while engineers feverishly worked to restore it. We weren't really too thrown by this because we had experienced a crazy year of emerging from obscurity fairly rapidly on the strength of our first album and first singles becoming widely known around the world, and this was just another nutty thing that happened.

"THERE ARE CERTAIN LOYALISTS who will eat the toast. They don't see any of the mistakes." Tim O'Connor is praising the Willie fans who remember the 1987 Picnic fondly. "They've been waiting a year [for the Picnic]. 'So let's go see Willie.'"

Janis Tillerson accepted the praise: "Yeah, we always have a good time. No matter what."

It's not just the fans who feel that way.

Jimmie Vaughan, who played in the Fabulous Thunderbirds during the 1987 show, knew Carl's Corner only as "where the frogs were" on the drive up to his hometown of Dallas. But the T-Birds didn't hesitate to take the gig. "We just played for Willie whenever he called," Jimmie said. "It was Willie Nelson. It was like the president in Texas."

So how many people did show up at the 1987 Picnic? It's hard to nail down. The promoters announced forty thousand from the stage. At the time, newspapers were reporting crowds of between twelve thousand and thirty thousand. Tim O'Connor said he thinks it was about ten thousand. Willie said it was eight thousand in his first autobiography. Budrock says, no, that number is still too high.

Publicly unfazed, Willie was telling people he was satisfied. "It's a great site," Willie told the *American-Statesman*. "I'd put this up with the best of them."

Monk White said the crowd seemed large to him, "but remember, I'm backstage drinking my whiskey and onstage watching these guys perform. So, to me, it was fabulous."

As late as Farm Aid III that September, Willie was telling reporters that he intended for the Picnic to return to Carl's Corner. It was the latest "permanent site," as Willie was fond of saying.

Even in his autobiography, Willie admitted to losing six hundred thousand dollars on the Picnic, dismissing the loss in Zen-like fashion. The music was great, Willie said, and he felt comforted playing so close to where he grew up.

Behind the scenes, Tim said, Willie was pissed off. "Extremely," he said.

For the hard-core Willie fans who did come to Carl's Corner, the '87 Picnic was a good time. Photo by Tom Lankes, Austin American-Statesman

The Picnic was dead once again . . . at least for a few years. Instead of going out with a celebration like it did in 1980, it went out with a wheeze. "Yeah, that's probably going to kill it," Tim remembers thinking.

TIM O'CONNOR CALLED the 1987 Picnic a "major failure," no doubt thinking about the lost money and sparse crowd. John T. Davis, working with a different scorecard, sees it as somewhere in the middle on the Picnic disaster rankings. "If you look at the big successful ones, like South Park Meadows and College Station, and the ones that were just kind of a clusterfuck, like Dripping Springs, and you know, maybe Gonzales or something. I think it's about midway on the spectrum of real success versus a real bust."

There's no debate, however, that the Picnic did not live up to expectations. If you start asking why, you'll uncover multiple reasons.

Remote location with no suitable camping: When asked where the expected crowd of ninety thousand was going to stay after the fourteen-hour show, Davis said, "I don't think they ever thought that through comprehensively." The bands took the available hotel rooms in nearby Hillsboro, and what camping was available was as primitive as could be. "I would not have wanted to camp by any stretch of the imagination out there," Davis said. "That would have been a little slice of hell as far as I'm concerned."

The crowds were peaceful at the 1987 Picnic, but law enforcement was on the lookout for trouble. © Bob Wade

The roadside location worked against them: "The people we're trying to get there are driving by the place; it's not like it's hidden," Tim O'Connor said. "It's not like you have to get on a dirt road and go four miles west." Tim argued that a little mystery is a key part of the Picnic—walking in and discovering a new world. Putting the Picnic right alongside Interstate 35E like a carnival had the opposite effect. "I've driven by there a thousand times, and it's a piece of shit," Tim said, channeling potential fans. "I don't need to stand in a field."

The Beach Boys had a competing show in Austin: On July 4, the Beach Boys put on a show in Austin's Zilker Park, drawing at least fifty thousand to their family-friendly show. Tim and Davis agreed that the competition had an impact on the Picnic. Willie had performed on the Fourth of July in Austin the past three years, and the casual fans likely had little trouble deciding between staying for the local show or driving several hours north for the Picnic.

The original Willie Picnic fan base had aged out: The twenty-something picnickers who walked for miles in Dripping Springs or stayed stoned in Gonzales were now pushing forty years old. Even though parking was nearby and there was less lawlessness at Carl's Corner, the idea of a shadeless field in some remote spot was more and more tiresome. "Yeah, they grew up," Tim said.

Those closest to the show, however, said that Carl Cornelius's interference is ultimately what wrecked the show.

Tim was still hung up about a *Dallas Morning News* photo that shows Carl posing with a rifle in front of his truck stop. He said that image, as much as anything, hurt ticket sales. "That's the last piece of visual promotion," Tim said. "And it certainly wasn't about the Picnic. It was more about Carl."

In Tim's mind, Carl should have been grateful for the publicity and content to let the professionals do their jobs. But that wasn't how the man was cut out. "He wasn't gonna be told what to do with his town and how to do it," Budrock said. "It was gonna be his way. And I think Willie maybe kinda helped him with that."

It's true that Willie's relationship with Carl was a problem. While Budrock says he thinks Carl just saw Willie as a gold mine, Tim says Willie didn't necessarily see the negative in Carl: "Carl didn't act like God with Will. He was kind to him. He was polite to his ability."

And Willie, who didn't have much interest in refereeing conflict, wasn't the sort to settle the feud between Tim and Carl. "Willie being Willie doesn't really help," Bob Wishoff said. "He's not going to be one that says 'so-and-so's in charge,' right? 'Don't come to me with your problems' would be more likely. 'You guys have to work this out.'"

Tim said what hurt him the most was that he didn't go up there to fight with Carl; they went up there to have a good time, put on a show, and help him. "I just don't understand . . . I never have . . . how you can have that many megastars coming in a few days and not recognize that we *do* this," Tim said. "We know what we're doing. We're not asking you for anything."

If anything, Tim was even more annoyed that Carl was a tough, shrewd guy with a little shady history and he might have fit in with the Willie Family's kind of crazy. "He could have been in our family," Tim said. "In a distant way."

WILLIE AND CARL DREAMED big and came up short . . . this time. In his autobiography, Willie wrote that he shrugged off the financial loss and got lost in the music—and that Carl picked up the tequila bottle and got drunk.

The artists who didn't pull out played for the fans who did show up. The fans didn't care about the attendance; they were mostly intoxicated and happy.

And the crew? It was just part of the up-and-down life on the road. Asked if they were upset about the poor turnout, Budrock was direct. "Well, from my point of view, I don't think any of us gave a shit. We thought it was a piece of shit place to have a show. You know, a Picnic's a Picnic. They're never easy. It's never easy."

1988 and 1989

These are the missing years of Willie's Picnic. After Carl's Corner, the Picnic may or may not have been dead, but it certainly was on life support. "We were all pretty exhausted, so we let it ride," Tim O'Connor said. "And that came from Willie. In other words, 'let's just wait.'"

A July 4, 1988, story in the *Austin American-Statesman* led its Fourth of July roundup with "Willie Nelson has closed up his Independence Day tent" and quoted Tim as saying "the days of the big concert out in the middle of a field" may be coming to an end.

But there was no word on what Willie was doing instead of performing. During at least a portion of July 1988, he was filming the movie *Where the Hell's That Gold?*—a made-for-TV western starring Delta Burke.

Willie's whereabouts on the Fourth in 1989 are unknown.

1990: Zilker Park, Austin

SITE: *Zilker Park in downtown Austin*
ATTENDANCE: *About 15,000*
HEADLINERS: *Willie Nelson, Johnny Cash, Waylon Jennings, Kris Kristofferson, the Highwaymen, David Allan Coe, Kimmie Rhodes, Little Joe y la Familia, Billy Joe Shaver, Shelby Lynne, Kinky Friedman, Asleep at the Wheel*

The July 4 concert at Zilker Park three years earlier by the Beach Boys had drawn a crowd of fifty thousand, and organizers were expecting up to thirty-five thousand, so there must have been a sense of disappointment when fewer than fifteen thousand showed up at the 1990 Picnic for country music's most awesome foursome: Willie, Waylon, Johnny, and Kris.

But reviews of the show don't reveal any hard feelings, just a sense of relief over the smoothness of an efficiently run, city-embraced, well-behaved Picnic. "The smoothest Picnic ever," Willie told the *Austin American-Statesman*. And who could argue with thirty shuttle buses, free drinking water, and entertainment for the kids?

Tickets were an incredible seven to nine dollars, and Willie agreed to donate one dollar for every ticket sold to the fund to build a new playscape in the park. Ultimately, he donated $13,155.

There were only about a half dozen arrests, and despite the 101-degree temperature, an EMS technician said the problems with heat exhaustion were minimal, noting that "the crowd had good sense and wore light clothing and drank a lot of water." About fifty were treated for heat-related problems, but there were no serious issues.

Still, the heat took its toll. Turk Pipkin remembered that his wife, Christy, was supervising the filming of the Picnic for Willie's Cowboy Television Network. "It was hot as firecrackers," Turk said. "Christy had camera crew and audio crew and everything out there on cranes and towers, and they were dropping like flies from the heat."

The outlaw image that had lingered after Gonzales was thoroughly gone—Thom Steinbeck, son of author John Steinbeck, attended and said of the Picnic: "These are good, gentle people." Yet the Picnic hadn't lost any credibility in the transformation.

The Highwaymen would erase any doubts about the authenticity of the evening. It might have been Willie's Picnic, but it was Cash's show. The Man in Black got roars for "Folsom Prison Blues" and "A Boy Named Sue" and patriotic approval for his spoken-word "Ragged Old Flag."

The Highwaymen turned in a nineteen-song set, ending with "Luckenbach, Texas" and "On the Road Again." If you wanted to rank Picnics on a dollars-to-awesomeness ratio, this would seem like a good place to start.

Tim O'Connor told the *Statesman* a few days later that the Picnic either broke even or lost less than ten thousand dollars . . . and that Zilker Park *could* be a permanent site.

1991–1994

Life started coming apart for Willie in late 1990 when the IRS cracked down on him for nonpayment of taxes, surrounding him on his golf course and raiding his properties in Briarcliff. In 1991, several auctions were held, though friends purchased and returned most of his property and belongings.

After the IRS bust, Willie had to make some money, and the Picnic couldn't even be counted on to break even. In 1991, Willie spent the week of July 4 playing sold-out shows at the Paul Masson Mountain Winery in Saratoga, California.

Thanks in large part to the release of *The IRS Tapes: Who'll Buy My Memories?*, Willie eventually settled his tax fight with the IRS a few years later.

Then on Christmas Day 1991, Willie's oldest son, Billy, was found dead in his Nashville home. Willie was deeply wounded by Billy's suicide. He didn't discuss the tragedy publicly but stayed in the public eye. Onstage was where he felt sheltered.

He spent six months of 1992 performing at a theater in Branson. Instead of being on the road again and again, Willie and Family were quietly going mad playing to bus tours day in and day out. July 4 was just another day in the grind. When his contract expired, Willie left and didn't look back.

July 4, 1993, saw a mini-Picnic that drew fewer than two thousand people to Tim O'Connor's newly opened venue in Bee Cave, the Backyard. Originally billed as "The First Annual Geezinslaw Family Fourth of July Picnic," sanity ultimately prevailed and it was made clear that Willie would be closing the show. Asleep at the Wheel and Kimmie Rhodes were among the other performers for the show that started at 5 p.m.

Willie's whereabouts on the Fourth in 1994 are unknown.

CHAPTER SIX

1995: Luckenbach

SITE: *Luckenbach on FM 1376, southeast of Fredericksburg*
ATTENDANCE: *Estimated at 12,000*
HEADLINERS: *Willie Nelson, Kris Kristofferson, Leon Russell, Ray Price, Robert Earl Keen, Little Joe y la Familia, David Allan Coe, Jesse Dayton, Ray Wylie Hubbard, Gary P. Nunn*

Picnic VIP Update

Willie Nelson: Willie had been through hell and had emerged on the other side, ready to record and perform exactly what he wanted. On July 4, 1995, he released *Just One Love*, an album of cover tunes, including the title track by Kimmie Rhodes.

Ray Price: Ray's career had slowed to a crawl, but his performances were as fine as ever. A year after the Picnic, Ray would be inducted into the Country Music Hall of Fame. "It's about time," he said.

David Allan Coe: The country outlaw was a popular touring performer and had released three new albums in 1994, each including rerecordings of popular songs from his past and new material.

The Geezinslaws: Seeing a bit of a career renaissance, the Geezinslaws had released five albums between 1989 and 1994. *Feelin' Good, Gittin' Up, Gittin' Down* in 1992 included their first hit single in decades: "Help, I'm White and I Can't Get Down."

As Robert Earl Keen launched into his newly revved-up version of "The Road Goes On Forever," the first empty beer can flew into the air. Then another. Then a dozen more. Then hundreds at once, all rising and falling until the area in front of the stage looked like an old-fashioned popcorn popper. A not-quite empty can flew over the stage, leaking Shiner beer.

"I remember the police talking about how Robert was about to whip the crowd into a frenzy," said Doc Mason, the Picnic's chief medical officer.

VelAnne Clifton, Luckenbach's manager at the time, remembered it well: "About three or four thousand Aggies went apeshit."

Reflecting on it twenty-five years later, Keen still sounded a little awestruck. "I don't know what's really happening at this point."

In the months before Willie Nelson's Fourth of July Picnic first came to historic Luckenbach, the community had feared that it would be too rowdy. Gillespie County Sheriff Milton Jung had diplomatically handled neighbors' concerns, given notice to Picnic producers on what he expected, and worked with Luckenbach to make sure they were ready.

So far, the Picnic had unfolded with little drama. But as Jung watched the crowd react to Keen, his own deep-seated fears came back. "Yeah, I figured that's when all hell was gonna break loose."

"THE MID-'90s were the great transition." Joe Nick Patoski was talking about Willie, but he also could have been talking about the Picnic, the Texas music scene, or even Luckenbach. They all took new paths around that time, and they all converged on July 4, 1995.

Willie Nelson spends a reflective moment backstage at the 1995 Picnic. Willie's life had changed dramatically in the previous half decade, but his passion for the Picnic was undiminished. Photo by Rick Henson

For Willie, he was a man in a different place. He had suffered the tragedy of losing his son, the stress of the IRS fight, and the ignominy of doing what he had to for a steady paycheck—including spending a season off the road in Branson.

Then, after eighteen years with Columbia/Sony, Willie was dropped by his record label. Many artists would have been shaken, but secure in his new marriage to Annie and settled with the IRS, Willie was free. Not feeling the pressure to maintain old sounds, meet old album sales marks, or have hits on radio, Willie could explore different musical avenues.

"Classic Willie was morphing into the Living Legend Willie and—most significantly with *Spirit*—the band's sound changed," Patoski said. "Paul switched to brushes. Bobbie's piano and Willie's guitar came up in the mix, and subtlety replaced power. Django swing becomes part of the show. This period introduces the Willie you hear today."

John T. Davis agreed that the pressure was off and noted that Willie was enjoying recording such departures as *Six Hours at Pedernales* or *Healing Hands of Time*. "I think musically, he was at the point of just indulging himself," Davis said. "He was doing whatever he wanted for whoever was interested in the product. And I think he's still indulging himself to this day."

It would have been understandable at the time to think leaving "Classic Willie" behind also meant the end of the Fourth of July Picnic. If you had missed the tiny 1993 Picnic originally billed as a Geezinslaws event, the 1990 Picnic seemed like a last gasp for a show fatally wounded in 1987.

Since then, a new scene had started taking shape. By the end of the '80s, Robert Earl Keen had released three albums and was a celebrated songwriter and charismatic performer. As the '90s unfolded, however, his live shows started to take on a life of their own, bringing in college kids who sang along to every word and sometimes left the venues and themselves a little worse for wear.

Keen said he never had an expectation that his shows would get so rowdy. "There was a little bit of like, 'Okay, okay, fine, I get it. I get it. I certainly didn't ever egg it on. Those kinds of things I never could quite get totally comfortable with."

If Willie brought together the hippies and the rednecks, Keen's shows brought together the frat boys and everyone else—whether or not everyone else liked it. And there were some who saw the party and thought, "Hell, I can do that."

The Texas music scene still featured Willie, Jerry Jeff Walker, Gary P. Nunn, and the other survivors of the '70s. Joe Ely was still rocking. Ray

Wylie Hubbard was newly sober and serious. But when Keen blazed his own trail, a new crop of musicians sprang up along that path.

Jack Ingram, Pat Green, and Cory Morrow were among the new guys, writing songs and playing parties. By the middle of the decade the scene was coming to a boil. "That was the year that all these guys just kind of like exploded out," said Richard Skanse, longtime editor for *Texas Music Magazine* and prolific music journalist. "Their biggest hits came within two years after that, but 1995, that was the starting point. A lot of these guys were still in college before that, wanting to be Robert Earl Keen, but '95 was the year a lot of them started making records."

Jesse Dayton, who performed at the 1995 Picnic, recalled that year as the "tail end of the real deal Texas outlaw thing." Before Pat Green and the rest took over the state, Dayton saw Texas music as less accessible and more edgy. "I think in '96 and '97, everything changed. That's when that whole scene started to kind of take over and these Texas music guys were selling out the Astrodome. You know, it was huge. It was really big business."

Former Luckenbach city manager VelAnne Clifton poses with a 1995 poster at her home in Brenham. Luckenbach hired her to be the manager in 1993, and she made a big difference in connecting the Luckenbach of the 1970s to what Luckenbach is today. Photo by Dave Dalton Thomas

WHEN TEXAS ICON HONDO CROUCH died in 1976, Luckenbach couldn't possibly remain the same. At the beginning of the decade, Hondo and actor Guich Koock had purchased what was left of a small German community and, with Jerry Jeff Walker's help, turned it into a honky-tonk fantasyland. After Hondo's death, his share of Luckenbach was left to his daughters, Becky and Cris.

By the late 1980s, however, Luckenbach was a far piece from Hondo's dream. It was decidedly not whimsical. There were few events, and the bar often served as a hangout for rough characters. "We were all scared to go there because it was guns and speed," said VelAnne Clifton, who came of age in the Austin music scene of the '70s. "We would only go for Jerry Jeff's birthday, when he rented the place and kind of shut it down." In fact, it was Jerry Jeff's annual celebrations that kept Luckenbach afloat. Cheap beer and cheap music tickets the rest of the year just didn't pay the bills.

As the 1990s rolled around, Luckenbach's owners decided to make a change and fired the manager. Cris had married John Graham, an Air Force colonel who would make the unlikely transition from working at the Pentagon to being president of the board at Luckenbach.

Jerry Jeff suggested that VelAnne (who had once been a nanny to his kids) would be a good manager, and John Graham hired her in 1993. Bringing change to Luckenbach always carried a lot of emotion. In a place where "everybody's somebody," a lot of those somebodies felt as if they owned the place, paid for one afternoon at a time at the bar. "People would come into my office," VelAnne said, "and they would try to tell me how it was going to be."

But Luckenbach was not a democracy. It was a business—a business with a lot of potential. Soon enough, rougher characters found they weren't welcome, and Luckenbach became increasingly tourist-friendly.

VelAnne, with her deep connections to the Texas music industry and high-energy promotional skills, started putting on shows in the dance hall on a frequent basis and supercharging special events such as the annual Hug-In and the Mud Dauber Fest.

The 1970s were put on a pedestal—Luckenbach and Jerry Jeff celebrated the twentieth anniversary of the recording of *Viva Terlingua!*, and VelAnne brought Gary P. and Ray Wylie to the dance hall often—but the place wasn't a time capsule.

Luckenbach was suddenly a destination for up-and-coming artists and a favorite venue for young fans. Robert Earl Keen played the dance hall at least three times in 1994, including a March show that brought a horde of overenthusiastic supporters from Texas A&M, Keen's alma mater. That night would give the Aggies a reputation in Luckenbach.

By early 1995, it was clear to John Graham that they had made the right call in hiring VelAnne. "VelAnne started us on the road to recovery, financially and in the news. She knew all the histories, all the players—she played a major role in the resurgence of Luckenbach."

There's no consensus on how exactly the Picnic came to Luckenbach in 1995, but this is how VelAnne remembered it: She came up with the idea and made her pitch to Austin attorney Peggy Underwood, who in turn pitched it to her good friend Lana Nelson, Willie's oldest daughter.

Cris Graham said that the original plan was not a Picnic but a Willie concert and recalled that VelAnne called up Lana directly.

And Jimmy Lee Jones, Luckenbach's singing bartender, said he got the ball rolling when he and fellow Luckenbach employee Maggie Montgomery went to visit his old friend Poodie Locke, Willie's stage manager. They ended up on the bus, telling Willie that Luckenbach would "love to have him play there."

"So the next week he sent Larry Trader and Poodie to look at the place," Jimmy Lee said. "And Larry said, 'Hell, we can do the Picnic here.'"

What's certain is that one day early in the spring, VelAnne was in her office in the "Egg House," a stone's throw south of the bar, along with Maggie and John Graham, when her phone rang.

"Hi, could I speak to VelAnne?" The voice was dizzyingly familiar.

"This is she."

"Hi, VelAnne, this is Willie Nelson. I hear you want to have a Picnic."

VelAnne paused.

"And I went, 'Well hi, Willie!' And Maggie stopped what she was doing. And John was in the back, and he stopped what he was doing. And everybody looked at me. The world kind of went into slow motion. It was like God was on the phone."

Jalapeno Sam Lewis, a friend of Luckenbach and a friend of Willie, had already caught wind of the impending Picnic. Lewis owned property down the road from Luckenbach called the Armadillo Farm and was often at special events where he held armadillo races. He was an armadillo expert, promoter, salesman, entrepreneur, and all-time Texas character.

In the days before Willie called, Lewis approached VelAnne with some advice: "If you do the Picnic, you just do whatever Willie wants," VelAnne remembered him saying. "You don't put any demand on Willie or anything."

VelAnne told Willie on the phone that, yes, they did want to have a Picnic and Willie responded, "What do you want? Part of the gate, the concessions, or what?"

Thanks to Sam Lewis, VelAnne said she responded with "the smartest thing I've ever said in my life: 'You tell me; I've never done this before.'"

Willie said, okay, his people would take the money from the gate; Luckenbach would get the money from the concessions.

The Willie Nelson Fourth of July Picnic and Luckenbach were a pair of Texas icons, both exploding into popularity in the 1970s and both anointed with legend and myth. Now they were joining forces.

Larry Trader, one of Willie's oldest friends, would be in charge of producing the Picnic. "Maybe I'm the only one that'll say it but dealing with Trader . . . was not easy." Years later, VelAnne Clifton was still weighing her words carefully.

John and Cris Graham were just as cautious in choosing what to say. "We had trouble coming to an agreement on stuff," John said diplomatically. "Larry was from the old school for Willie. Back when they would travel around and play behind chicken wire." (An example of one dispute was Trader not wanting to pay the little bit more to fence off the creek along the back of the property. VelAnne had been to enough Picnics to know that giving that many drunks access to the creek on a hot July day was a significant safety issue.)

Age had not mellowed Trader's negotiating style, but neither Colonel Graham nor VelAnne was going to be bullied into a bad deal. A standoff ensued, and Willie ultimately sent Tim O'Connor to save the Picnic.

Tim was friends with Trader and knew what this meant. "At [Larry's] age and his friendship with Will, he wanted one of the badge of honors [to produce the Picnic]," he said. "But I don't believe it would have come off if the people that I gathered hadn't been there to help."

In mid-April, the contract was finalized. VelAnne and Maggie Montgomery danced in the street as Willie's people drove away. "I thought it was a cool town," Tim said. "And honestly, I thought we were going to have just a skate. It was going to be great."

"I WAS LIKE THE DEMON witch woman, and it was just going to be the worst thing that ever happened to Gillespie County." VelAnne's babysitter worked at one of the peach stands in nearby Stonewall, and she told VelAnne that all the women talked about was how awful the Picnic was going to be. "Everybody's gonna get raped and murdered and cut up into little pieces," VelAnne said.

Gillespie County was a deeply conservative place, populated by descendants of German pioneers who believed in law and order. The Hill

Country tourism business hadn't yet exploded, and many of the surrounding communities were still wary of anything that would draw too many outsiders at once.

Production manager Jack Yoder said he didn't blame them. "There's a lot of [people who hadn't been] exposed to something like this. They weren't too excited about us coming the first year."

VelAnne said people would come to her office and cuss her out, saying she was going to ruin Luckenbach. "I'd shut the door and get out a bottle of bourbon and take a few shots and cry a little bit. And then I'd get over it."

The opponents included Luckenbach's closest neighbor: Elizabeth Engel, who lived on Luckenbach Town Loop, just a hundred yards or so from the bar. Her late husband, Benno, had sold Luckenbach to Hondo.

Elizabeth Engel lived with her son, John, who testified against the Picnic before the Gillespie County Commissioners Court in late April, saying Luckenbach neighbors had been told to "get a motel room if they didn't like the noise."

Yoder was a large, burly, bearded man with a gentle nature. He made a point to visit the neighbors and help smooth things over, starting with Elizabeth Engel. "The first year she met me at the door, she wouldn't let me in the house. Which is kind of to be expected; we don't look like

The Luckenbach crowd of about twelve thousand represented a new era of the Fourth of July Picnic, whether the locals liked it or not. Luckenbach Texas Inc.

bankers, most of us. But anything she wanted, I tried to do for her, and the second year she invited me in for coffee and doughnuts."

Tim O'Connor said the Picnic had encountered resistance before, and they knew how to ease concerns. Sometimes it was as simple as giving a family a handful of tickets and telling them that Willie would like them to come.

For the ranchers along FM 1376, Tim pushed the idea of offering parking in their fields, telling them the money would be all theirs and even sending crews to show them how to park cars to maximize profits and minimize problems. "I think there was more respect for Willie than there was hate for the idea of a Picnic," Tim said.

Matthew Carinhas, who owned what was then called the Luckenbach Inn, a bed-and-breakfast about a mile up the road where Yoder, Trader, and Tim would stay, was definitely on the side of the Picnic. "Look, it pumped millions of dollars into the economy of Fredericksburg. Millions of dollars. If anybody complained, it was someone who wasn't directly involved and didn't have a clue of the ramifications of a big event like that."

Except for the county sheriff. Milton Jung knew full well what the Picnic could bring. When he first found out about the Picnic coming, he started checking around with law enforcement in counties where the Picnic had been held before. "We found that the last ones weren't quite as bad as the first ones," he said.

That doesn't mean that Jung wasn't concerned: "Of course, I put them on notice right off."

VelAnne remembered that Jung was "pretty stern" about the first Picnic. But the Picnic had a built-in advantage: Ray Price was on the lineup. And Milton Jung was a huge Ray Price fan.

Still, Jung was going to do his job: "I told them the people of Gillespie County are for enforcement of the narcotics laws." If he saw someone smoking weed, the person was going to be arrested, no matter who. "You can tell Willie he's not to come out onstage with a joint in his mouth or something because he's going to get arrested," Jung said. "I will promise you that." But there was a line he wouldn't cross. "What they did in the buses, I don't know. I didn't get into buses; that was not my place to go."

Jack Yoder said it was only normal that Willie's bus was a sanctuary. "Well, there's a certain amount of respect for Willie. That's his house. He would rather be in the bus than a two-thousand-dollar-a-night hotel room. Most people respect that."

Yoder said the crew also respected Jung's ultimatum, but he couldn't resist a joke at one early meeting where he and Larry Trader were sitting next to the sheriff in the dance hall. "Milton said, 'We're not going to put up with anything; if I see any dope or pot, they're gone,'" Yoder said. "So I grabbed Larry's arm, and I said, 'Well hell, take him now!' Milton and Larry didn't think it was too funny, but everyone else did."

When the deal was struck, Luckenbach was in charge of preparing everything from the stage forward, which was no small task for a slice of the Hill Country that had hardly changed since electricity had arrived. VelAnne's first priority when she was hired as manager was to rewire the bar/general store and the dance hall. The wires were still cloth-covered, she said, and hot to the touch. The historic buildings were at risk of burning down.

But now the entire electrical system had to be overhauled to meet the upcoming demand. VelAnne said Luckenbach invested seventy-five thousand dollars in infrastructure, including electricity and water for the vendors.

Just as important was recruiting all the volunteers who would be needed. John and Cris Graham praised VelAnne's ability to bring in members of the community on the promise of a free concert and T-shirt. "All of our friends were running Gatorade tents and Dr Pepper booths," VelAnne said. "We got the PTA to do one. Boy Scouts and Habitat for Humanity. We got all the community involved."

Luckenbach would also need a few professionals to oversee key areas, starting with medical services. VelAnne knew the perfect candidate. Doc Mason was not just an emergency room physician in Kerrville but also a singer-songwriter who had played Luckenbach a few times—and a longtime fan who said Willie's music had helped him make it through medical school.

Mason didn't hesitate to make a deal. He would oversee the medical tent throughout the day, but he and his band would get to perform early in the day, and his daughter Ava would get to sing the national anthem at the opening of the Picnic. Picnic fans got a little unexpected culture in Ava Mason—though this was her first music gig, she would later become an opera sensation under the stage name Ava Pine.

David Anderson, a local who had served as "bier meister" for Fredericksburg's Oktoberfest celebration for the last few years, was recruited to oversee the outdoor bars. Anderson helped build a bar in the shady vendor area and another between the Egg House and the General Store, just off the main field in front of the stage. To speed things up at the bars, fans would have to buy tickets and then exchange the tickets for beer or water.

Security was another area of concern. The Gillespie County Fairgrounds had long held horse racing on the Fourth of July and already had local security under contract. Not only had Luckenbach promised neighbors that they would provide security at their homes, but VelAnne felt they needed a team to protect Luckenbach. "We had people watch the store to make sure it wasn't damaged. We didn't want people pulling off the signs and stuff."

The team was mostly local, under the supervision of Zip Zimmerman, a longtime Luckenbach regular. VelAnne was able to recruit a few neighboring county sheriff's deputies who would watch over the crowd on horseback.

"They estimated that they were going to have nine hundred arrests. That was what the captain of DPS said. And we all kind of looked at each other and shook our heads." Zip Zimmerman didn't believe what the DPS was telling him at the pre-Picnic security meeting. But Sheriff Jung wasn't taking any chances.

"We only had a fifteen-bed jail at that time," Jung said. "But I knew the guy that was in charge of the buses [at the Texas Department of Criminal Justice] that transported prisoners around. So they sent me three buses." They would end up parking the buses at the site to hold the arrestees. When a bus was full, they would send it to Fredericksburg. "We had a [justice of the peace] on hand that magistrated them, and if it was [a misdemeanor charge], they processed them, made them make bond, and let them go," Jung said. "Hell, there was just no way we could keep them all."

Most of all, Jung said, he was worried about people getting on the road after drinking too much. Luckenbach's agreement with Gillespie County was that the show would open at 11 a.m. and end no later than 11 p.m. And one more thing . . .

"We needed to cut everybody off an hour before they left," VelAnne said. "So at 10 o'clock, on the Fourth of July, we had to tell ten thousand people that they couldn't have another beer. That was a little tough."

Shaping the lineup required some effort—and offered an opportunity. "When we stood back from it, we really did feel that there was a possibility to get a new group [of fans] that just wanted to come party," Tim O'Connor said. "We really tried to shape [the Picnic] so that it wasn't the old man's club."

Willie oversaw the lineup, so old friends like Ray Price and Leon Russell weren't going to lose their spots, but he took an interest in the artists at the bottom of the lineup as well. "Every one of the artists who showed up was invited by him," Jack Yoder said. "If not personally, he would call me and say, well, I want this guy here. It was very personal to him."

The Geezinslaws salute the crowd in Luckenbach after their set at the 1995 Picnic. Willie and his people definitely wanted some new players at the Picnic but not at the expense of old friends. Photo by Rick Henson

VelAnne said Willie called her to ask if she had anyone she wanted to add to the bill. "We wanted to get Waylon [Jennings] to Luckenbach," VelAnne said. "We had this big dream of getting Waylon and Willie here to sing 'Luckenbach, Texas.'"

But that first year, Waylon was already booked. Instead, Luckenbach got some local talent on the lineup, taking the fifteen- to twenty-minute spots at the beginning of the day that more prominent artists didn't want.

A few days before the Picnic began, the crew started constructing the stage at the far end of an open field. In addition to "historic," one of the key descriptions of Luckenbach is "small." "Population 3," the signs and bumper stickers boasted.

This offered a new challenge to the crew assembling the stage, sound, and lights. "It was a strange setup," said lighting director Budrock Prewitt. "We were used to working in bigger, larger areas. Very tight, I guess would be a good word for it. Getting a truck in there was tight, and you couldn't get multiple trucks."

On the eve of the Picnic, John Graham was in the Egg House paying bills. Luckenbach had gone all in. "We pretty much wiped out our bank account, if not gone over," he said. "And about that time this big storm comes up, a really heavy thunderstorm. And it knocked over some of the big light towers."

John Graham could just picture Luckenbach being left with hundreds of thousands of dollars in new infrastructure, beer, and T-shirts, but no Picnic.

Up the road, at the Luckenbach Inn, Jack Yoder, Tim O'Connor, and Larry Trader were just as concerned. "It was a gully washer," Yoder said. He and Tim drove the mile into Luckenbach in the lightning and rain to see if their work had washed away.

THE DAWN OF THE PICNIC came warm, bright, and humid. The storm the night before had moved through the Hill Country and left nothing damaged that couldn't be quickly fixed. Sheriff Jung was among those who had to leap into action early. "When it started off, I said 'Oh, God.' . . . I thought it would be a pretty rough day. This was eight o'clock in the morning." Jung and his staff were just finishing up an early breakfast meeting when the call came in that there were some teenagers already at the gate outside Luckenbach, drinking heavily and wanting in. The highway patrol zoomed off to get them.

"It was four or five kids from Mason, drinking beer. They thought they could go down there." Jung laughed at the memory. "They got arrested and their parents called to come get them."

Cris Graham woke up concerned that picnickers zooming west on US 290 would miss the turn at FM 1376. In traditional Luckenbach fashion, she had gotten some poster board at Walmart and drawn a big arrow with the word "concert," with plans to nail it to the fence. When she arrived at the intersection, however, she found that the highway department had put up enormous signs, flashing "concert" in large, glowing lights. This was the big time.

And nothing said big time like Willie's bus rolling into Luckenbach. "He was here," Cris said. "It was like Santa Claus had come, it really was."

At the main outdoor bar, David Anderson was feeling the pressure. "I was really a nervous wreck. They started passing the word, 'the gates are open, the gates are open, here they come.' Man, what can I do?" VelAnne told him to just relax, there was nothing else to do.

At the front gate, Zip Zimmerman sensed an opportunity to ward off trouble before it could happen. "We put up a big sign that said 'drug dogs on premises.' There wasn't no drug dogs out there, but they didn't know that."

"WE DROVE ALL NIGHT after playing the Troubadour in L.A. I walked backstage, and then Sammy Allred and Billy Joe Shaver took me in this RV and fired up a joint."

Jesse Dayton is telling a story about his first performance at Willie's Picnic. He'd been to Picnics before as a spectator, and to Luckenbach as a motorcyclist. This was different.

"I just got totally ripped," he said. "I wasn't prepared for it, you know what I mean? I was like, 'Yeah, I'm here; sure, I'll take a hit.' And I went up onstage and played, and I remember thinking the whole time, 'I wish I wouldn't have done that.' Right before I went onstage, Billy Joe Shaver said, 'Man, your eyes look like a frog on the highway in the middle of the night.' I can remember being onstage and looking over at Billy and him just smiling at me like he did it on purpose."

Welcome to the Picnic.

The gates opened at a fenced-off Luckenbach about 10 a.m., and the people just poured in throughout the morning. The main field in front of the stage was about the size of a football field, and Sheriff Jung was concerned about whether it could hold everyone. It turned out, some people had no intention of sitting in the sun and stayed in the shadier spots.

"Some of them weren't even close to the stage," Jung said. "They were back over there along the creek. The music was loud enough, they could enjoy it back under the trees."

Luckenbach's own Jimmy Lee Jones and his Texas Hill Country Band opened the show at 11 a.m. From the stage, the crowd looked almost like a religious meeting—so many dressed in white shirts and wearing white hats.

For John and Cris Graham, it had, incredibly, all come together. "We literally cried," Cris said. "We were just so emotionally excited and drained that first morning. And by 1 or 2 p.m., you could barely move. We were just all packed in like sardines."

In her star-spangled outfit, Luckenbach "Mare" [mayor] VelAnne got onstage to have everyone take a pledge to take care of Luckenbach. "I made everybody honorary Luckenbach citizens," she said, trying to recall her speech from that day. "Raise your right hand! Repeat after me! 'On my honor, I will try to be a good Luckenbach citizen, drink lots of beer, and be somebody, because everybody is somebody in Luckenbach.'"

Bob Wishoff was printing passes as needed from his RV backstage. He seldom had a hard time finding a good time at the Picnics, but this one seemed special. "That was my first time at Luckenbach. I think a lot of people who went had never been to Luckenbach. They'd heard of

Luckenbach, but they'd never been there. I was one of them. I just thought it was cool as shit."

Paula Nelson had grown up going to the Picnic and remembered the crazier days through the eyes of a child. "I remember seeing dad sign so many boobs and thinking, 'I wonder if Mom knows about this?' Paula said. "I'm like, 'Oh, yep, she's right over there.' So the '70s were definitely a different kind of feeling."

Paula was the first of Willie's children to play the Picnic, something she found entirely different from just watching from the stage. She had recently started performing, and it was important to her to be seen as "Paula Nelson" and not "Willie Nelson's daughter."

Still, at the Picnic, a dad's pride wasn't so easily contained. "I'd be in the middle of singing a song, and all of a sudden the crowd went crazy," Paula said. "And I'm thinking, 'Wow, they're digging this, they really like me.' And then I turned around and Dad had come onstage. Like, 'Oh, yeah, *that guy*.' But I loved it, and they loved him and who can blame them?"

Bob Wishoff was among the Picnic veterans who had to work a little harder to smoke a little marijuana at the show: "As far as the Picnic goes, you know, it was really one of the more mannered ones in a lot of ways. There wasn't a lot of trouble. But then there was a lot of cops." Wishoff

Though there was plenty of shade across the creek where the concessions were, there weren't a lot of shady spots with a view of the stage. Those few spots were quickly claimed. Luckenbach Texas Inc.

didn't mind so much, but some of the others backstage were at least annoyed about it, calling the show a "Pig-nic."

"It's just Gillespie County, you know?" VelAnne said. "They kind of had it in for everybody the first year."

John T. Davis recalled the police presence in '95 as being rather heavy-handed but said nobody knew what to expect. "I don't really blame them. But, yeah, they certainly erred on the side of overcompensation."

Asked about the law enforcement presence, Sheriff Jung appeared stung for a moment. "We didn't have a whole lot of extra help except for the highway patrol," he said. He did have most of his staff out there, but he "didn't really have all that many people."

To his relief, Jung didn't see very many serious problems that day. If he ran into someone using drugs, the person was arrested. But for the most part, the problem was people drinking too much. "I was up on the stage, and there were some guys pretty drunk and some gals pretty damn drunk, and they started pulling up their blouses and stuff," Jung said. "I got the [deputies] to get them and told them to just take them off the grounds."

It was better to be caught by Zip Zimmerman's Luckenbach security team. In some instances, people seen smoking marijuana were told, discreetly but firmly, to put it away, that they couldn't do that here. "I told my guys, I said, we're not bouncers, we're ambassadors," Zip said. "We're not here to bust any heads—none of that."

Zip had sixteen guys working for him, and before the show they all prepared for the worst, but he said they spent most of their day separating the crowd so EMTs could get to people who were falling out from the heat. "That first year, I remember there was just one fight in the crowd," Zip said. "That was because somebody was throwing a football and hit somebody in the back of the head."

And of course there were drunks. Some of them partied harder than they were used to. Some of them started too early. "There was a lot of 'em who were down and out when the party started," Zip said. At Luckenbach, this was something he was used to handling. "I'd tell them, 'Drink a beer, drink a water, drink a beer, drink a water.'"

The Picnic had always mixed rock 'n' roll in with the country but had seen very little Tejano music. That didn't concern Little Joe Hernandez. "Willie had a lot to do with educating his fan base about different styles and genres of music that turned out that they liked or maybe didn't know about. It was really important," Little Joe said. Performing as Little Joe y la Familia, he had long been friends with Willie and didn't hesitate to play a run of Picnics between 1990 and 2000.

Little Joe Hernandez poses backstage at the Luckenbach Picnic with Willie Nelson and Ray Price. Photo courtesy of La Familia Enterprises archives

"It would bore me to death if I just played one style of music," he said. "Because of the variety of music that I grew up playing, playing Willie's crowd, you know, there's not that much difference; it's all about feeling; it's not so much language."

Having Little Joe y la Familia perform wasn't a bid to draw in Tejano fans. The 1995 Picnic, like all others, was overwhelmingly white. Instead, it was Willie introducing his fan base to a different style of music, which has long been an underrecognized virtue of the Picnic.

From the Pointer Sisters in 1975 to Clarence "Gatemouth" Brown in 2004, fans usually came away with something they hadn't experienced before. "I'm sure that Little Joe made some fans, if they weren't there already," John T. Davis said.

For Little Joe, working with Willie was a "learning experience" and a chance for him to do a little something different as well. "I remember Ray Price called me to his bus. He was wanting to record an album in Spanish, and [he wanted to sing and record with me]. Ray being one of my all-time, big-time heroes . . . that was so special for me. I just felt really privileged and proud."

The same goes for Sheriff Jung. He got to meet Ray Price and struck up a friendship—visiting Ray's hometown a few years later. VelAnne said the sheriff was "just beaming" when Ray played. "Well, I thought it was pretty dadgum good," Jung said. "That was my kind of music."

VelAnne had to put out a lot of small fires the day of the Picnic, including a particular bit of country spite. When one Luckenbach neighbor was getting more cars parked on his ranch—and making more money—the neighbor down the road wasn't happy. She had decided to chain off a part of her property that was being used as a bus turnaround.

It was simply a matter of geography. One property was catching people coming down FM 1376 from US 290. The other got people coming up 1376 from Interstate 10 in Boerne. More people were coming from Austin. "John Graham said I had to take her to meet Willie. So here I am back there with this German Queen Elizabeth in her therapeutic shoes," VelAnne said. "That was not my fondest moment." But it worked. The upset neighbor decided that having the bragging rights of having met Willie backstage made up for the indignity of the other neighbor making more money. Saint Willie played his part—a moment of undivided attention from Willie goes a long way—and she went home satisfied, the turnaround unchained.

Willie Nelson performs at the 1995 Picnic. Willie performed alongside friends throughout the day, but he was also in high demand backstage. © Bob Daemmrich photo

At the medical tent, Doc Mason had finished his early-afternoon performance and was fairly busy overseeing people who had had too much beer and too much heat. "I had a good team," he said. "We basically had an ER out there, so we took good care of 'em."

The Kerrville hospital where he worked had provided the equipment he needed, and he found volunteer nurses from there as well. He said he didn't see a lot of drug problems, mostly just heat exhaustion. "There was one guy that came in complaining of chest pain, and he went out by ambulance," Mason said. "One fellow who fell out [from dehydration], he probably had at least three bags of fluids. They carried him in, and at the end of the night he walked out. If his friends wouldn't have brought him in, it could've been bad."

It wasn't hard to drink yourself dry in the July sun. Beer was a serious business. Refrigerated trucks were staged in the parking lot. More were waiting on the road to Luckenbach to restock as needed. And the beer tickets were selling as fast as they could be handed out.

"I remember we were making so much money so fast that I was stuffing it into a little zipper bank bag and sitting on it because there was nobody coming by to get our money from us," said volunteer Monica Andrews, who was selling beer tickets from a makeshift stand along with her mother. "At one point I think it was sitting on about four grand, and I'm like, 'Somebody needs to take this bag.'"

After a little while, Monica said her mother told her she had the college kids figured out. "She said, 'I know the kids from Baylor because they only buy one beer ticket. And I know which kids are from Texas A&M because they buy a whole string of tickets.'"

"ROBERT EARL . . . that was really before there was such a thing as 'Americana' of course, but he was a huge star in Texas already." John T. Davis agreed that Robert Earl Keen's performance was one of the biggest moments of the day, and the inevitable closing song was a moment of sheer insanity.

"'The Road Goes On Forever' was practically the national anthem of Texas for a while, maybe still is," he said. "When he sang that, people just went apeshit. They were pouring beer on each other and drowning out Robert singing on the chorus. It almost upstaged Willie."

Keen was singing a newly revved-up version of the song that most of the fans hadn't yet heard. "We did do it kind of just pretty much like the record [*West Textures*] for a long time," he said. "At one point, I went over to Rich [Brotherton], and everybody and said, 'Man, we've got to beef this

Robert Earl Keen jokes around with Sammy Allred of the Geezinslaws backstage at the 1995 Picnic. Though Keen was already a big deal at his Luckenbach shows, he called the raucous response at the '95 Picnic a "coming-out party." Photo by Rick Henson

up.' So we beefed it up." Keen said the 1995 Picnic was pretty close to the debut of the new version.

The flying beer cans were certainly a concern at the time—Larry Trader grumbled about the safety of those onstage—but nobody ended up getting hurt, and a quarter of a century later, Picnic VIPs were charitable.

"We felt 'wild' was a compliment," Tim O'Connor said.

"To watch twelve thousand people sing with [Keen] was pretty awe-inspiring," John Graham said.

Keen himself was surprised at the response. A *San Angelo Standard-Times* reporter intercepted him as he climbed down from the stage, but Keen paused only long enough for a single quote: "Did you see that?!"

Twenty-five years later Keen called the experience a big blessing. "It was a huge thing, and it was very exciting, and you could feel it. We had the crowd with us from the minute we stepped onstage. That was probably almost like a coming-out party for us."

Kimmie Rhodes had the unenviable task of following Keen. Fortunately, Willie came out and joined her on her first two songs, keeping the crowd from chanting "Robert Earl Keen" through her set. "The crowd was always [riled up] when Willie hit the stage regardless of who went before that," Kimmie said. "Willie would always come on and sing a couple of my songs with me. And of course, the crowds would go crazy."

They started with "Just One Love," the title track to the album Willie had released that day. A video from the day shows Willie, his braids mostly red, but his beard mostly gray—playing Trigger and harmonizing with Kimmie as the crowd slowly quieted enough to listen.

"It was always wonderful to be able to sing with Willie," Kimmie said. "It was a very exciting time for me because Willie had recorded my songs, and we've done some recording together. There was a lot of anticipation. It was a very, very special time."

Dahr Jamail's band, Titty Bingo, took a different sonic approach. Budrock Prewitt was visiting the soundboard when Titty Bingo's sound guy came over. He was asked how Titty Bingo wanted the sound. "He said, 'Turn everything up and bury the vocal.' I cracked up over that because Dahr is the vocalist and leader of the band. I think [those were Dahr's] instructions, by the way."

And with Ray Price watching, who wouldn't be nervous about the vocal? "Ray Price was a motherfucker," Dahr said. He meant that in a good way. "Fucking unbelievable. He had Johnny Gimble and Jimmy Day playing with him."

Leon Russell was just as good, standing out among his old friends. "I was busy doing something, you know, walking from the store to the dance hall or something. And I go, 'Oh, my gosh, who is playing the piano?'" Cris Graham said. "So I walk closer to the stage, and here's Leon Russell with the hair and the whole regalia, and from that moment on, I was a huge fan."

Cris wasn't familiar with Leon, but the performance stood out for Dahr as well, and he had been watching Leon for decades. "Leon had a fucking smoking show," Dahr said. "They never stopped. It was blowing. I mean, it was one of those shows where he was just on fire."

If the depressing scenery of Carl's Corner had dampened the "reunion" aspect of the Picnic in 1987, the charm of Luckenbach definitely reinforced it. "I remember standing there watching Ray," Dahr said. "And looking around and Leon's standing there and Willie's standing there and everybody's watching. We're all friends, you know, and they were hanging out more."

Paula Nelson said the Picnic has always been a family thing, meaning the extended family of musicians who loved Willie and whom Willie loved in return. "Because of the tour scheduling, it was like buses passing in the

Luckenbach city manager VelAnne Clifton onstage with Willie Nelson at the 1995 Picnic. Luckenbach Texas Inc.

night," Paula said. The Picnic was "a place where everyone really got to hang out and Dad would play with them."

Jack Yoder said so many of the artists had such a personal connection with Willie that he would have to encourage Willie to stay offstage a little so he didn't tire himself out before his own performance at the end of the night.

It was hard to resist what Ray Wylie Hubbard called "that down-home vibe of friends getting together." "It was real laid back," Hubbard said. "It wasn't like '48 Hours at Atoka,' where you got David Allan Coe and Jerry Lee Lewis comparing guns. It was just naturally cool."

Bob Wishoff said the Luckenbach mystique helped get the Picnic back in the spotlight. "It's such a mythical place, I think it helped the Picnics enormously." Both institutions stood on their own, but the Picnic and Luckenbach helped each other and 1995 marked a new era.

When asked if this was a reinvention of the Picnic, a revived event with revised expectations, Tim O'Connor couldn't say yes fast enough. "Yes, sir. Absolutely. We needed to get all the dust out of the closet and all the bullshit away from us. And so we took real care of our actions."

John T. Davis agreed it was a reimagining of the Picnic. The physical location limited the crowd and the chaos. The Picnic was well produced, but there was still room for a surprise or two. "It was really family-friendly," Davis said. "People didn't come there to get drunk and crazy. So I remembered it as being a really pleasant kind of reinvention of the whole idea—it's probably closer to what Willie intended when he first got the idea for it."

"THIS PLACE WAS JUST SO FULL. And to me, it was amazing to see just that swarm and flood of people . . . just to see Luckenbach transformed like that." Monica Andrews had seen crowds at Luckenbach in the 1970s, but nothing like this. And through it all, Luckenbach saw to the details as if it had hosted a dozen Picnics. Trash was picked up during the show. Porta Potties were emptied to keep them operational.

For the Grahams, the relief was enormous. "It worked!" Cris Graham said. "We had never done anything that size at Luckenbach. It worked

Ray Price was a favorite of Gillespie County Sheriff Milton Jung, perhaps easing dealings between Luckenbach and law enforcement. Luckenbach Texas Inc.

with no tragedies, no knifings or overdoses. It was all positive. I think everybody went away happy."

That included Luckenbach, which made enough money to redo the septic system, provide insurance and retirement funds for its employees, and give back to law enforcement and the community.

"It gave us a lot of confidence for the future and bigger concerts," John Graham said.

A lot of the locals walked away happy as well. Singing bartender Jimmy Lee Jones ended up going on the road with Willie to play a series of shows.

Doc Mason didn't get paid but got to perform at the Picnic alongside his daughter. "I did it for Willie," he said. "He's a good man."

David Anderson said he enjoyed the "crazy-ass experience." "I'm glad I got to do it. Nothing like that will ever come down the pike again."

Zip Zimmerman said the first year saw ninety arrests, most for public drunkenness. Sheriff Jung said his memory was fuzzy, but he thought there were "about 130" arrests at the 1995 Picnic and much fewer at the subsequent ones.

"It was pretty dadgum good," Jung said.

Asked what his favorite Picnic was, Tim O'Connor didn't hesitate to say it was the first couple years in Luckenbach—and not just because the Luckenbach Picnics were financially successful. "It was the perfect match. We were in an incredible spot. It had a good country feel to it. It was just right for what we were trying to accomplish."

During the five years the Picnic was in Luckenbach, Tim enjoyed building relationships with Luckenbach's neighbors. He would meet with everyone after each show and listen to their concerns and promise to make improvements. In turn, he built a small army of Willie supporters.

"Every place I went after maybe a short or a long conversation, they were excited," he said. "So if I needed something on a local basis, they provided it." For Tim, after the Picnic had spent years on the run from angry locals, getting compliments from the people who lived next to it was a rare joy.

Picnic veterans, as well, were impressed with the show. Dahr Jamail said Luckenbach didn't have the intensity of the early Picnics, but it was fun in a relaxed way.

Bob Wishoff recalled it as "plum wonderful." "Nobody was too drunk. Nobody was too fucked up. It just was idyllic. That particular show set off a groove that we kind of expected every year thereafter."

John T. Davis said he had every bit of confidence in Tim O'Connor producing the show and VelAnne Clifton promoting Luckenbach. "I thought it would come off pretty smooth. And in retrospect, I think it did."

As far as Willie goes, Wishoff pointed to the fact that the boss kept joining everyone onstage, something he didn't always do with such frequency. "That's a sign that he was having a good time, too. He didn't want to hang out in the back and just get stoned."

A quarter century later, VelAnne's pride was undiminished. "It was magic. Don't you think it was magical? Except for that one couple that was getting it on behind the Porta Potties. But other than that, it was magical."

Sometimes all the planning didn't work out.

While cleaning up, crews found rolls of the same type of tickets that were used for beer. It didn't take much detective work to figure people would buy several different colors of tickets, stash them in backpacks, and then break them out once they saw what color Luckenbach was using. "So we said, 'Okay, that's a lesson we learned,'" John Graham admitted. "We have specially marked tickets now."

But then sometimes a plan made up on the spot worked out just right.

That sign outside the gate that said, "Drug dogs on site": "The first two Porta Potties there [by the gate], the guy that emptied them said, 'Zip, come look at this,'" Zip Zimmerman said. "There was probably two or three pounds of pot in there."

Bartender and "Sheriff" Marge Mueller was a Luckenbach icon. She didn't let the Picnic impress her too much. Photo by Dave Dalton Thomas

"Sheriff" Marge Mueller was a Luckenbach icon, known for her rattlesnake earrings and no-nonsense German demeanor. A direct link to Luckenbach's 1970s heyday, she had attended the Luckenbach School that had been just down the road. She was a bartender by trade but carried more than enough authority to be Luckenbach's unofficial law officer.

In her sixties during the Luckenbach Picnic era, Marge was not expected to do more than man her spot behind the famous bar. But that was plenty. She opened beers all day long, constantly yelling at her husband, James, and her grandsons to keep restocking beers from the walk-in cooler.

It was a hard day. Nobody would have blamed her if she had called in sick the next day. But the sun came up on July 5 and Marge came to Luckenbach. "She had one of those minivans that looked like a Dustbuster," Cris Graham said. "She comes barreling in the next day, ready to work. She had rubbed her legs and James's legs and her grandson's legs with this horse liniment so they would be able to walk."

VelAnne Clifton, more than a little wobbly and weary herself, asked Marge what she thought of her first Willie Nelson Fourth of July Picnic. "It was just like any other day in Luckenbach," Marge replied.

More than twenty-five years later, VelAnne still laughed about it. "Hell yes, that's what she said. I wanted to kill her."

1996: Luckenbach

SITE: *Luckenbach on FM 1376, southeast of Fredericksburg*
ATTENDANCE: *Estimated at 12,000*
HEADLINERS: *Willie Nelson, Waylon Jennings, Leon Russell, Ray Price, Little Joe y la Familia, Robert Earl Keen, Billy Joe Shaver, Ray Wylie Hubbard, Jesse Dayton, Kinky Friedman, Supersuckers, Tenderloin*

Not only was this Picnic unusually hot—the official high in nearby Fredericksburg was ninety-nine degrees as recorded by NOAA—but there had been a drought all year. The withered vegetation, hot winds, and dust made the day feel even more parched. The crowd drank about sixty thousand beers and still bought up all the water Luckenbach could find.

Willie had announced that proceeds from the Picnic that year would go to Farm Aid to help struggling farmers in Texas.

But what everyone remembers is that Waylon Jennings was there. If you had wanted to go to Luckenbach with Willie, Waylon, and the boys, this was your first and only chance.

The day had unfolded with little drama. Billy Joe Shaver was up early to record a music video. When asked how many Picnics he had been to, Shaver (who lost a couple digits in a sawmill accident as a young man) said, "Hell, I don't know. I can't count 'em all on my fingers."

Kinky Friedman seemed to have been looking for reporters, holding forth about himself in the third person. "I had my first gig here in '73— Kinky and the Texas Jewboys," he told the *San Angelo Standard-Times*. It was "mostly German immigrants, which caused Kinky to be just a bit nervous."

Robert Earl Keen's set was just as popular with the fans. Willie continued to sit in with his friends frequently through the day. But as the afternoon stretched on, people kept asking, "Where is Waylon?"

The rumor was that he was holed up in a restaurant bar on the far side of Fredericksburg, drinking heavily and saying he wouldn't play. But Grant Alden, cofounder of *No Depression* magazine, was there when Waylon's bus arrived about 8 p.m. and he just saw a man "who didn't particularly want to be there."

"I didn't pick up on any of that at all," said Alden of the drinking rumors. "He just seemed really tired." During a thirty-minute interview, Alden saw Waylon as a man already in poor health who would rather have been playing with his grandson on his bus than standing on a hot stage in Luckenbach.

Waylon had said for years that he didn't particularly like the song "Luckenbach, Texas," which was a monster hit for him in 1977. He had never been to Luckenbach and neither had songwriters Chips Moman and Bobby Emmons—they were working off a description of the place from Guy Clark.

VelAnne Clifton recalled seeing Waylon at a recording of the *Austin City Limits* TV show a few years earlier, saying, "I hate this song, and I'm never gonna go there." "When I started running Luckenbach, I thought I'm gonna get that son of a bitch there if it's the last thing I do," she said.

And she did, though Waylon didn't pretend to like it. Sometime after his scheduled appearance, Waylon showed up onstage and peered into the darkness. "It's the first time I've ever been here. And I still ain't seen Luckenbach."

He did a handful of songs and began to walk offstage. Nancy Coplin, a longtime Austin music authority, was standing right there. "Everybody was really disappointed when he started to walk off," she said. And Willie said to him, 'Hey, aren't you gonna do that song that made you about eight million dollars?'"

Waylon stepped back up to the mic and, along with Willie, ran through a quick and disjointed "Luckenbach, Texas." Ten thousand fans sang along. It wasn't great, but it was historic.

1997–1999: Luckenbach

SITE: *Luckenbach on FM 1376, southeast of Fredericksburg*
ATTENDANCE: *Estimated at 10,000–12,000 each year*
HEADLINERS: *Willie Nelson, Leon Russell, Ray Price, Little Joe y la Familia, Asleep at the Wheel, David Allan Coe (1997), Joe Ely (1997), Emmylou Harris (1998), Robert Earl Keen (1998), Larry Gatlin (1999), Pat Green (1999)*

The Picnic spent an unprecedented third year in a row in Luckenbach, then a fourth and a fifth. By this time, everything was in place, the crowds were consistent, and the challenges were minimal.

In 1997, Joe Ely brought out surprise guest Dwight Yoakam for a couple of Buddy Holly songs. Yoakam had been filming the movie *The Newton Boys* nearby.

In 1998, Emmylou Harris brought a little beauty to the boys' club that was the Picnic, and fans enjoyed cooler temperatures and a little afternoon rain.

In 1999, Willie is asked if the Picnic is staying in Luckenbach forever, and he jinxes it: "This is the spot."

Were Luckenbach and the Picnic a partnership that could have lasted longer? Budrock Prewitt offered the crew's perspective: "At the end, we were glad to get the hell out of there. Because Luckenbach had decided that they were about as important as the Picnic."

2000: Southpark Meadows

SITE: *Southpark Meadows concert site alongside I-35, south of Slaughter Lane in Austin*
ATTENDANCE: *Estimated at 11,000*
HEADLINERS: *Willie Nelson, Leon Russell, Ray Price, Pat Green, Joe Ely, David Allan Coe, Shelby Lynne, Susan Tedeschi and Francine Reed, Willie K*

The Picnic was setting up at the new Stone Mountain venue in Dripping Springs when someone learned that the 76th Texas legislature had revised the Mass Gatherings Act the year before. Now, instead of being able to hold a twelve-hour show without a county permit, the cutoff was five hours. Organizers scrambled to put together the permit application—and missed the state-mandated deadline by a week. They asked Hays County for some leeway and to approve the permit anyway, but the county refused.

Direct Events and ownership of the new concert facility then blamed the county, accusing officials of wanting to rid Dripping Springs of the Picnic. "The bottom line is that county politics did this event in," Walter Biel, co-owner of Stone Mountain, told the *Austin American-Statesman*. The *Statesman* reached out to a handful of officials and found no reason to believe the state law could be stretched. The law "is not permissive," Hays County District Attorney Michael Wenk said. "It's black and white."

Ultimately, a month ahead of July 4, the Picnic was moved to Southpark Meadows, where it had spent 1984 and 1985. House of Blues Concerts of Los Angeles now operated the amphitheater and was planning a fifteen-million-dollar renovation to make Southpark one of the premier venues in Texas. In truth, the 2000 Picnic was Southpark's grand finale, the renovation never happened, and within five years the property was on the way to becoming a giant shopping center.

The show itself was a hit, with Pat Green rising to stardom, more female artists performing than usual, and Willie throwing the schedule into chaos by coming out to jam with his friends frequently and lengthily. Otherwise, the Picnic ran smoothly, with little trouble.

"I think everything happens for a reason," Willie told the *Statesman* of the Picnic's move from Dripping Springs. "In this case, the positive side is we got to bring it to Austin and see everything turn out great. It looks like they still enjoy a good party."

2001 and 2002

Tim O'Connor and Willie wanted to bring the Picnic back to Luckenbach, and both years they clashed with new Gillespie County judge Mark Stroeher. Negotiations didn't get far in 2001, but in 2002 Stroeher issued the permit now required under the Mass Gatherings Act. However, he did so with the warning that he could revoke the permit at any time.

"I thought we were actually moving forward until he said, 'Mr. O'Connor, you do realize that we have the right to shut the whole thing down the day before?'" Tim said. "And I said, 'That's really good to tell me that.' I went outside and sat in my car and called Willie. He said, 'How's it going? What do you think?' I said, 'Nope, this ain't the place. It really has changed.'"

Tim and Willie decided not to invest $250,000 in a Luckenbach Picnic subject to the judge's whim. Years later it was still upsetting to Tim because, for once, the neighbors of the Picnic and many other citizens were standing in the courtroom showing their support for the Picnic. "All of them wanted it back," Tim said.

Matthew Carinhas, who had owned a bed-and-breakfast near Luckenbach, said the loss of the Picnic was an economic blow to the community. "It wasn't just the hotels. It was the trickle-down effect. Everything from taxicabs, restaurants, hotels, suppliers, landowners, mechanics, the fencing people. I mean, it just goes on and on and on. I think it's a shame that the politics ended up pissing Willie off. And he said forget it."

In 2001, the *Shreveport Times* reported that Willie spent the Fourth of July playing golf, swimming, hanging out with friends, and watching fireworks. "I've never been off on the Fourth," he told the *Times*.

In 2002, it turns out that the cancellation of the Picnic was likely a good thing. "On July 2 that year we had the hundred-year flood in Luckenbach," owner Cris Graham said. "The water came up to the middle of the store, through the dance hall, and wiped out the cotton gin and blacksmith shop."

Anything that would have been set up along the creek by July 2—vendor stands, ticket booths, fencing—would have been gone. "It would have been a real scramble," Cris said. "It wasn't gonna dry out by the Fourth."

CHAPTER SEVEN

2003: Two River Canyon

SITE: *Just east of the town of Spicewood on Texas 71, fifteen miles west of RM 620*
ATTENDANCE: *Estimated at 22,000 on July 4 and 17,000 on July 5*
HEADLINERS: *Willie Nelson, the Dead, Neil Young, Ray Price, Toby Keith, Pat Green, Merle Haggard, Billy Bob Thornton, Patty Griffin, Leon Russell*

Picnic VIP Update
Willie Nelson: At the time of the Picnic, he had released a half-dozen albums in the last three years, including *The Great Divide*, which included duets with Lee Ann Womack and Kid Rock.
Leon Russell: The rock legend had a busy streak in the early 2000s, releasing four albums and stretching across genres by recording with the Nashville Symphony and New Grass Revival.
Johnny Bush: Botox helped him defeat spasmodic dysphonia, which had derailed his career. Enjoying his comeback, he was inducted into the Texas Country Music Hall of Fame in 2003.
Ray Wylie Hubbard: His journey from outlaw to the patron saint of Texas songwriters was picking up speed. No longer country-tinged folk, his sound had grown grittier and bluesier.

"We're not doing all this just to do it once." Tim O'Connor was showing off the still-under-construction Two River Canyon amphitheater to *Austin American-Statesman* music writer Michael Corcoran and talking about having seven or eight shows a year. He was thinking big. The place might even be known one day as the Red Rocks of Texas.

There would be no test runs. It was going to open with a one-million-dollar, two-day production of Willie Nelson's Fourth of July Picnic. The thirtieth anniversary show would feature Willie, Neil Young, and the Dead—the newest incarnation of the Grateful Dead after Jerry Garcia's death in 1995.

The landowners, siblings James and Deana Hebert, invested as much as seventy thousand dollars in creating a venue out of the Hill Country ranch they had inherited from their grandfather.

But when thousands of Deadheads joined Picnic fans driving the thirty-five miles west of Austin on July 4, it created a traffic jam stretching more than ten miles and lasting for hours. Some fans turned around and went home. Some parked alongside the road and walked. Others smoldered in their cars and showed up really pissed off.

After the Picnic ended, Two River Canyon never hosted another event.

For twenty years, the conventional wisdom has been that the traffic jam on the first day of the Picnic killed the venue. It turns out that's not the whole truth. "We were let down," Deana Hebert Gideon said eighteen years later. "It was a horrible situation. I mean, our lawyer wanted to go after them for it."

When James and Deana Hebert first inherited the family land near Spicewood, they had big plans. Maybe it could be a ranch for mountain bikers. Perhaps it could have a rodeo arena. But the first and foremost idea was to have an amphitheater. "We started heading toward trying to do it," Deana said. "And we did not have lots of money. We got involved with lots of big boys that did have money."

One of these was Tim O'Connor, who lived nearby. One afternoon in 2002, Tim crossed the fence and walked through the ranch. "I had heard that they were thinking of building some sort of live music venue out here," Tim told the *Statesman* in 2003.

There might not have been anyone in Texas more experienced at building something out of nothing in the middle of nowhere. Tim saw the potential immediately. "When I stood there overlooking the land, I could see where the stage would go, where the grass would be laid out, where the fans would come in from," he told the *Statesman*. "I saw it all."

Soon there were talks to have the thirtieth-anniversary Picnic at the site—and not the smaller version that had been held since 1995. This was going to be big. The Heberts were pleased to be working with a music industry legend, though they didn't have the deep pockets needed to fund the improvements to the land the Picnic required. "We were very young, and we didn't have money to back us or put us where we needed to be," Deana said. "So anything we did, we had to take out a loan to do."

As Two River Canyon amphitheater was getting started, so were several acts that were going to get their first big-time exposure at the site.

Alex Ruiz of the band Del Castillo said the band had been talking with Tim. "We were trying to get some gigs in town and kind of mingle with the big boys," he said. Brothers Mark and Rick del Castillo both said that maybe it was manager Bill Ham or maybe Ray Benson who got them on the Picnic. Either way, it felt huge. "It was our first big, big deal, playing that," Mark said. "We had just started."

In 2002, Stephanie Urbina Jones mortgaged her house for the first of three times to make her debut album, and one of the singles, "Shakin' Things Up," went to number one on the Texas Music Chart. "That was how I got the invitation [to play the Picnic]," Stephanie said. "It was just a really big deal, to be recognized by Willie. And to be on that bill was just . . . when you look at that bill, it's like 'what?' It's insane."

James Hyland of the South Austin Jug Band still isn't sure how the band managed to get on the bill, though he had been friends with Willie stage manager Poodie Locke for some time. Still, they were happy enough to be there. "It doesn't get any better than getting to play on anything involving Willie Nelson," James said. "Period. Full stop."

Asked about the 2003 Picnic eighteen years later, O'Connor's first reaction was to grimace at the painful memory. He explained he shouldn't have been involved. "That's on me. I had been in the hospital, and I had no business whatsoever trying to do anything."

Dahr Jamail isn't sure why, after a run of successful, smaller Picnics, that Willie decided to go for such a large production but said it was likely just cooked up one night on the bus. "These don't get put together by concert promoters. It gets put together in a cloud of smoke on Willie's bus. So if the Dead showed up with a couple of good joints . . .

"[Willie, Neil, and the Dead] might have all been somewhere together in California talking about [the Picnic]; I'm just telling you how that happens. It's totally organic; it's not a bunch of bean counters figuring out 'how can we make the most money?'"

With two major costarring acts, 2003 would join 1976 and 1974 as the only multiday Picnics. (There had been other back-to-back Picnics, the last one in 2008, but they were separate events in different cities.) The Picnic would even allow camping one last time.

Production manager Jack Yoder recalls that he had to charter a jet to fly Neil Young in from the East Coast, which wasn't the sort of treatment afforded Ray Wylie Hubbard or Ray Price. "[The Picnic has] never been that big as far as artists before. We always had a good bill but never as big as that."

Dahr said having a two-day Picnic might have been as simple as avoiding the conversation of who played second to last, Neil Young or the

Dead. "I've been doing this a pretty long time. But that isn't a minefield I'd want to go wander through."

NEAR SPICEWOOD, James and Deana Hebert were trying to turn their eight hundred acres into a twenty-five-thousand-capacity amphitheater. They had hired former radio programmer Willobee Carlan to manage the venue and were scrambling to get everything done. Carlan talked a good game to the *Statesman*. For the four thousand fans who would be camping, there was to be a twenty-four-hour convenience store, and the campgrounds would be supervised by experienced camp rangers. "We've had hundreds of strategy and planning meetings with the sheriff's department and county officials," Carlan said.

One of those officials, Burnet County Commissioner James Oakley, approved the mass-gathering permit. "We were all pretty green," Oakley

More than twenty-two thousand came on day one of the 2003 Picnic at Two River Canyon amphitheater. The venue was hastily constructed but had an enormous amount of promise. Photo by Gary Miller

said eighteen years later. "We weren't used to having mass gatherings. What we were really concerned about is having that many people in an area that didn't have emergency services built into it."

At the time, however, Oakley told the *Statesman* that his big fear was traffic congestion: "There will probably be a bit of a learning curve this first event."

The idea was to preserve the site's natural beauty, but Hill Country beauty is in the eye of the beholder. "It was a nice piece of land with possibilities," said former *Statesman* entertainment editor Ed Crowell. "But it looked like it had been overgrazed a lot in the past."

"The venue wasn't finished," said Willie lighting director Budrock Prewitt. "It was really rocky. It had the concept of an amphitheater, but it was a little rough."

Tim O'Connor, who had signed a long-term operating agreement with the Heberts, looked back at the preparations with regret. He said he didn't have the control he usually did and left much of the work to James Hebert and Willobee Carlan. "The boys, their naïveté showed because of their age," he said. "They hadn't been in the business. . . . It was thrown together rather than put together. And it had that laissez-faire attitude, which bled on to the event."

In 2003, however, Tim was still optimistic that if they could just get through this show, Two River Canyon was going to be huge. "I remember talking to Tim about it at length," friend Roger Collins said. "And he was telling me this was going to be the site—the holy grail that we had been looking for for thirty years."

"I HAVE BEEN SEEN as a man that could walk into a field and within a couple hours know if it was going to work or if it wasn't going to work. It's just vision."

This is not ego, Tim O'Connor said, but the lessons learned from decades of experience in the music business doing everything from loading trucks to producing high-profile shows.

Tim was fifty-eight years old when he produced the Two River Canyon Picnic and had spent most of his adult life closely associated with Willie, but not beholden to him. He made and lost multiple fortunes on his own.

After a youth of juvenile crime, failed efforts at going to college and starting a family, and various legal and illegal enterprises in Kansas, California, and Colorado, Tim O'Connor came to Austin in 1970 to help Doug Moyes run the Castle Creek Club.

Tim O'Connor, a daunting and determined figure, was often Willie's right-hand man when it came to making the Picnic happen. Photo by Dave Dalton Thomas

It was there he ran into Willie Nelson and started going on the road with him, including producing the 1974 Picnic in College Station. After an incident involving a stray bullet and a CBS Records executive, Tim left Austin for a while, honing his show production skills in New Mexico and surviving his first battle with cancer.

He returned to Austin in the late 1970s to run the Austin Opera House for Willie. The Opera House was the king of the Austin scene through the 1980s, and Tim built a powerful empire through his connections with music industry professionals of all sorts. All the while, he worked directly with Willie whenever possible, including promoting the 1984 and 1985 Picnics at South Park Meadows, the 1986 Farm Aid II/Picnic at Manor Downs, and the ill-fated 1987 Picnic at Carl's Corner.

The Opera House crumbled as Tim's IRS troubles mirrored Willie's in the early 1990s, but it wasn't long before he built a new empire, starting Direct Events and owning the Backyard in Bee Cave, Austin Music Hall, and La Zona Rosa. He continued producing Picnics, including 1995–2000, 2003, and 2010.

Eventually, his music venues all went the way of the Opera House. Development claimed the Backyard as well as a newer version that opened in 2010. Tim retired to an isolated home near Spicewood with a handful of beloved dogs and a broken front gate—though he stayed in close contact with some of the friends he had made over the years. By 2020, his continuing battles with cancer had left him much thinner and more reflective.

"I'm really emotional about it, because I love music," he said of his career. "I didn't give a shit if I got paid or not; I'm being very upfront here. It was those moments of energy and love—I was standing right there. So as the bucket was being poured out, I got some splashed on me. I'm not kidding. I just went up and down the road and did this and had a great time."

Over the years, Tim has made a big impression on a wide range of people. James Oakley described him as "a bit of legend," and John T. Davis said that while he could be gruff and hard-nosed, "he was a stickler for putting on quality events."

Charlie Jones, who was a third of the promotion company C3 Presents that ruled Austin after Tim's heyday, said Tim was indeed a visionary. "He was very hardheaded in his ways, but a lot of times his ways were right. He taught me a lot about how to do some things right. And some things, you know, I don't want to do it that way. Because sometimes the Tim O'Connor way was a little bit messy. But he got the job done. And he was very powerful in the way that he commanded his staff to follow through on his vision."

Tim was well respected within the Willie Family as well. "He is one of my favorite human beings on this planet," Paula Nelson said. "I grew up with some really good folks that were pretty much all about just taking care of Dad and the Family. Tim O'Connor was and still is one of those. He's my Papa Tim."

As far as Tim's relationship with the Fourth of July Picnic, Bob Wishoff said what Tim wouldn't. "I think the Picnics were painful for Tim. Because he knew they weren't going to make a lot of money, they're going to be a big hassle, Willie was going to do whatever he wanted, [and] it wasn't going to be particularly well organized. They could completely decompose. For a promoter, that's kind of hard to deal with."

But Tim kept doing it, probably because he knew nobody could do it better. And because Willie wanted him to.

WHEN THE FOURTH ARRIVED, Dahr Jamail found humor in the chaos that was the traffic on Texas 71 leading to the 2003 Picnic site: "Maybe it was a little crazy. There was a lot of traffic. But it was funny stuff. . . . There was a stream of naked people on bicycles. I mean, that alone would tell you this was an event." Many, many others weren't amused at all.

The forecast for July 4 was relatively cool for a Picnic, a high in the upper eighties and a little bit of rain in the early afternoon. The gates would open at 11 a.m. for a noon-to-midnight show, but most fans weren't in any hurry to get out there and get rained on just to see the opening acts.

And the Deadheads, in particular, weren't going out there to see the Geezinslaws or James Hand or Johnny Bush. It was easy to presume the Dead would play just before Willie closed the show, so why hurry? Fueling the Texas Deadhead fervor was the fact it had been decades since they had seen their heroes in their home state. The Grateful Dead had last played at Manor Downs, near Austin, in 1985 and hadn't played in Texas at all since 1988.

By 2 p.m. the traffic started stacking up on Texas 71. It got worse quickly.

"When it started raining, I decided to go back to the office and I'd file my story and then I'd come back, even though it was about thirty miles away," music writer Michael Corcoran said. Seeing the line of cars as he was exiting, he checked his odometer. "There was eleven miles of cars backed up, waiting to get in. It looked like Woodstock; people were ditching their cars on the side of the road, walking."

James Oakley said people would even get out of their cars and leave them in the road. "I found myself getting in vehicles that were still running, or the keys were in them. Some people weren't even looking to pull off the road; they just stopped."

Oakley moved cars that he could, brought in tow trucks for others, and called local radio stations to urge them to tell their listeners to take the backroads and avoid 71.

Those who decided to wait it out sat in their cars for two, three hours, or more. Those coming from the west had no problems. Roger Collins, driving in from San Angelo, said he could see cars lined up for miles to the east as he drove right up to the site.

W. T. Smith, chief deputy for the Burnet County Sheriff's Department, played defense with the *Statesman*, saying that officials had hired a traffic engineer to develop a traffic plan that had been approved by the Texas Department of Transportation. And Travis County Sheriff's Department spokesman Roger Wade said there was little they could do: "It's just a lot of cars trying to get into one place."

That didn't help those who waited angrily in their cars, missing acts they wanted to see, and having to pee on the side of the road. When they reached the entrance, Tim O'Connor was there, trying to help. "There was a lot of anger, and I don't blame them," he said. "I was standing right there in the little median that we had, and you wouldn't believe some of the things they said."

The root of the traffic problem appeared to be the parking process. The gravel parking lot had only one entrance from Texas 71, the *Statesman* reported, and everyone coming in had to stop and pay five dollars.

Even before the traffic started piling up, the disorganization showed. "I got there really early, and they really weren't prepared even then," Corcoran said. "They had no real system for parking cars. Drive to one person who'd tell you to go to that person or that person . . . so you just kinda had to park on your own."

Oakley agreed that the venue wasn't processing cars fast enough but said it wasn't entirely their fault. The excitement over the new amphitheater, the camping, the timing of the arrivals all contributed to the problem, he said.

Deana Hebert Gideon was more straightforward: "We weren't really prepared for the amount of people coming through. I don't think anybody was prepared for the amount of people and the amount of parking we needed."

Roger Collins, who had been part of the backstage craziness in the 1970s and 1980s, had brought his children to see a "real" Willie Picnic, though he wasn't sure this one counted. "The women were not there that had always been there for the Picnics; the booze, the drugs weren't there. I felt like an observer. You know, like a UN observer during a war."

The first thing he observed was that everyone seemed to be big-time now. "Everybody was in a bus. That really impressed me. Because, you know, we had come a long way from being the grungy hippies in '73 to now everybody's basking in air conditioning."

But sober and without a job to do, he sought the camaraderie of the old days . . . and found it lacking. "At least for me, it wasn't there. Everybody was having their own private little party inside their bus."

In front of the stage, the *Austin Chronicle* noted the VIP area had a "tent the size of a football field erected to placate sponsors and other guest-listers with free booze and a big-screen TV with no sound."

In contrast, the crowd sat on the rocky hillside, and the parking lot was crowded with Deadheads, many illegally hawking alcohol and hippie treasures.

The rain came down at about 2 p.m., cooling the crowd and easing the workload in the medical tent, which still treated minor injuries but had much fewer cases of dehydration and heat exhaustion.

With the March 2003 invasion of Iraq still fresh, Austin music fan Alfredo Tomas Garcia noted that the Picnic climate seemed a little different. "There were people who were walking around with yard signs, 'Stop the War' and things like that. It was sort of like hanging in suspension over this holiday weekend, but this was also an opportunity to kind of take a break from whatever else was going on outside of Two River Canyon."

For his part, Willie brought his new friends Dennis Kucinich, an antiwar Democratic congressman who would run for president in 2004, and Toby Keith, who sang his "we'll put a boot in your ass" hit song "Courtesy of the Red, White and Blue."

"WHEN IT'S YOUR TIME to take the stage, Poodie would lead you out. And, you know, it's like the backstage is really packed, right? When Poodie headed toward the stage, that big packed crowd would just part like the sea."

James Hyland of the South Austin Jug Band is telling a story about performing at the Picnic. "We're right behind him. And I remember looking out, and it was just like an ocean of people. I'd never played in front of a crowd that big. I couldn't possibly estimate how many people were there."

Poodie Locke had explained to the young band that there was a countdown clock on the side of the stage. It started at ten minutes and counted down. When it hit zero, it was time to get offstage to make way for the next band. As it turns out, the clock wasn't the most distracting part of the setup. "Willie Nelson's guitar was onstage like . . . it was *right there*, man," Hyland said. "It's like the holy fucking grail. It's more impressive than the ocean of people, to turn around and actually see that guitar right there. It was so amazing. It's like that scene from *Pulp Fiction* when they open up the briefcase. You don't know what's in there, but it's something special. It's like an extended part of Willie. To be that close to history is moving. It's really cool. It goes by so fast. It's the fastest ten minutes of your life."

Stephanie Urbina Jones sang the national anthem to open the Picnic and took the stage later that afternoon. She recalled the area in front of the stage was pretty empty, not surprising for a new artist early in the day. "I'd like to think I knew that I had a gift of communion with an audience, but I did not know what to do with that big open field."

James Hyland of the South Austin Jug Band remembered being highly distracted by Willie's guitar sharing the stage with him—when Trigger is on the stage, you know Willie isn't far away. Photo by Gary Miller

But when she started playing "Crazy," Willie came out to join her. It was nearly an overwhelming moment. "People talk about him and his presence. But it is something I will never forget. It's kind of transcendent. I just felt his love and his great heart and spirit. And when I kind of came out of that moment, I looked out and people had come forward to be a part of it.... I remember feeling the energy of this audience coming to be with us."

After his band played, James Hyland was still coming down from his big moment. He decided to sneak off under the stage, which stood far enough off the ground that he could stand up underneath it. "I remember lighting up a joint and just listening to Merle Haggard. And you could kind of see out across this ocean of people. It started raining right when he was singing 'Silver Wings' and Willie Nelson [came on] stage. It was the greatest country music by two of the greatest country artists of all time."

Onstage, Poodie was jubilant. "I think the Picnic's found a new home," he said. Not all of Willie's crew was so pleased.

"It was awful, it was terrible, I hated it," Budrock Prewitt said. "My lighting console was much higher than the stage, way up high. I couldn't see the stage and couldn't see the lights at all." He had a point. It's hard to be the lighting director when you can't see the lights on the stage. All he could see was the top of the roof and the front part of the stage.

At the end of the day, with Toby Keith performing with Willie, Budrock recalled that Willie was basically standing in the dark. "It really sucked. It was killing me. I had no communication [with the stage], and they couldn't hear me anyway. It was horrible."

Willie Nelson and Merle Haggard shared the stage on the first day of the two-day 2003 Picnic. Photo by Gary Miller

The night was supposed to end with Pat Green, Toby Keith, the Dead, and Willie. But when Green's bus got stuck in traffic, the Dead moved up ahead of Green and Keith—adding to the disappointment of those Deadheads still stuck in traffic.

Alfredo Tomas Garcia recalled that the band was already onstage, playing "Cumberland Blues," when he finally made it to the amphitheater. "It was just great; I mean, they were just on point." But the part of the night that stands out to him was when Willie joined the Dead to perform a cover of "El Paso." "The crowd singing along—'wild as the West Texas wind'—was a moment I'm not bound to forget," he said. "Everybody's kind of drinking and smoking and carrying on. It was raucous. To hear Trigger and the Dead share the stage like that. It lit up the crowd."

The Dead did nearly eighteen songs, hitting fan favorites such as "Truckin'," "Ripple," "Jack Straw," and "China Cat Sunflower" and ending with the inspired cover "Not Fade Away."

The Deadheads who made it to the show got what they wanted. But for Dahr Jamail, it was a long three hours. "I mean the Grateful Dead, I never could figure out when they were playing or tuning. I think it's just a state

The Dead were a powerful draw the first day of the 2003 Picnic. The Grateful Dead had not performed in Texas since 1988. Photo by Gary Miller

of mind. You can see part of the Dead and probably get it as much as you're going to get it. But if you're not in love with it, you really don't get it."

James Hyland said he stayed "until they kicked us out," even going out front to watch the Dead from a fan's perspective. "The thing I remember about them is when they left, I remember every band member had their own bus. I can't imagine how expensive that is. I mean, that's rock 'n' roll, man."

For the four thousand picnickers who camped out on the ridge, the scene was mostly chaos. Whether it was happy chaos or not depended on how high-strung you were and how many intoxicants you had brought with you.

"The website had all those crazy rules for camping—exact dimensions for spaces and all this stuff," said San Angelo music fan Josh Spurgers. "We had a pretty big group going, and we went a day early to try to save room and sort out the rules. When we got there, you could just go wherever and do whatever. They weren't enforcing anything."

The campsite at least, was easy to approach. Campers could drive right up to their site with as many supplies as they could fit in their vehicle. Those with a two-day wristband and a camping wristband could go to and from the concert site as they wished.

But it was primitive. Darren Morrison, a musician from San Angelo, called it "a goat track, something they had run a skid steer over." He didn't recall if there was water or not but didn't worry because his cooler was loaded.

Deana Hebert Gideon admitted that "it was not the most ideal camping." We didn't have anything but just ground and some Porta Potties. It was just basically in the pasture, set up as quick as I could get it together."

But it did work for those who wanted to tie one on and not risk driving back home. "I do remember Deadheads walking up with a beer or two," Spurgers said. "They'd hand them to you and then sit down in your campsite and try to drink your beer all night long."

SINGER-SONGWRITER PATTY GRIFFIN was among those headed to Two River Canyon on July 5 and wasn't taking any chances after the July 4 traffic jam. "We're hearing stories about people getting stuck in traffic and not being able to get to the gig. So I remember we left Austin really, really early and got out there."

Some came early, some took circuitous backroads, but the end result was there were zero traffic problems the second day. Part of that was the absence of the Deadheads. The Picnic drew about seventeen thousand fans on Saturday after drawing about twenty-two thousand on Friday.

Law enforcement presence was much less obvious than it had been during the Luckenbach Picnics. Alfredo Tomas Garcia said he didn't recall seeing officers walking through the crowd, and people enjoyed, perhaps discreetly, their freedom. "You could smell what people were smoking. But it was Willie's Picnic. It was fine."

In 2021, James Oakley said there were no arrests at the 2003 Picnic. "Crime was not a component of the event."

Asked if there weren't even a few arrests for smoking pot, the Burnet County judge said no. "I'm not gonna say that there wasn't a lot of that going on. But I think what happened in Spicewood stayed in Spicewood." The *Statesman* did report that ten people were arrested on July 4 and fewer the next day.

Griffin, who arrived with her band in a van, said they spent most of the day hanging out in Jack Ingram's RV. "He kind of took us in and gave us a little beer to drink. It was fun."

Deanna Herbert Gideon said that up to that point, hosting the Picnic was a great experience. "I had a great time. I mean, we stood up on the hilltop and saw the crowd; we got to meet Willie when they came in the buses. We got to do some live interviews on TV, which was fun. The show was great. It was just unbelievable. I got to see all our dreams come true. We couldn't believe how big it was and how many people were there and all the entertainers that were there. And we're just small-town Spicewood folks. So it was pretty amazing."

Rick del Castillo and his Del Castillo bandmates were not ashamed to admit they were a little starstruck backstage at Willie's Picnic. "It was just a laid-back kind of vibe. With that lineup of great musicians playing, it was just one of those perfect days."

Alex Ruiz remembered hanging out with Los Lonely Boys and watching the celebrities: "Matthew McConaughey was there, and we got to say hi. And Billy Bob Thornton was there. Just the passing by and hanging out felt like a great time."

Mark del Castillo said that when they went on to perform early that afternoon, he wondered why he hadn't seen Willie yet. "We started playing, and I turned to my right, and there's Willie standing there watching. I was like 'wow! He came out!' It was so awesome. And he was paying attention. He was having a good time. That was a great moment for me to see Willie just really digging what we're doing."

Willie Nelson and Ray Wylie Hubbard perform at the 2003 Picnic. Photo by John Carrico

Rick said the band's sound was a "flamenco Gypsy, South Texas blues combination. Honestly, we never really thought about what we wanted it to be. We just started creating, and that was what was so magical about that time."

The band definitely hit their mark that day: off-center, but exactly where they wanted to be. "We stuck out like a sore thumb," Mark said. "But in a good way . . . it's like throwing Santana in the middle of all these country artists and people were shocked, but they loved it. It was just a different flavor for the day."

Alfredo Tomas Garcia said that Del Castillo had been just a name on the lineup to him, but they turned out to be an awesome surprise. "It was just a great choice to have them on; they were great. Everybody seemed to really enjoy the dueling flamenco guitar at that volume. It was so good to hear songs going back and forth in English and Spanish like that and then to see a crowd that large enjoying it."

If the 2003 Picnic was aiming to be an old-school Picnic, then there ought to be a Billy Joe Shaver story and Patty Griffin had one: "We were about to go on, and I got to see Billy Joe Shaver's set. He was amazing. He came offstage, and he was soaking wet with sweat, and I was standing there and we've never met. He said, 'Do you mind if I hug you?' He gave me a big hug and I was so honored. But then somebody else told me he did that to them, so it wasn't a unique situation . . . but it was still special."

By this point, the Picnic was running far behind, but Griffin didn't mind at all. The timing meant that she performed as the sun went down. "That's the best time to get to play in a festival," she said. Playing without drums or bass meant they were limited in terms of volume, but it worked out. "People were feeling a little worn out. We were a nice little transition into the evening. It was magical."

Hours later, the next woman artist faced a tougher crowd. By this time, picnickers were pretty eager to hear Neil Young and not quite as excited for Shawn Colvin. "She began by saying something like, 'Hey, folks, I'm looking forward to seeing Neil, too,'" Alfredo said. She ended up cutting her set a bit short. It was past 11 p.m. and the Picnic was supposed to end at midnight.

It didn't. Neil Young wasn't going to give any ground.

"When Neil took the stage, you heard those opening chords of 'Down by the River,' and the lights went dark. Everybody just sort of perked up." Alfredo was blown away by Neil Young: "The amphitheater was full of sound. It was just loud as bombs."

Patty Griffin agreed: "I just remember thinking how loud it was. I was like, 'man, no one plays this loud anymore.' It was like old-school rock concert loud."

Dahr Jamail was impressed by the sound as well, but in a more technical sense. "His guitar sound blew me away. He just sounded fantastic.

Neil Young played the second night of the Picnic, impressing the hell out of everyone who saw him. Photo by John Carrico

I remember going up to his tech and specifically asking him about his guitar sound because it was that great. I thought he had one of the best guitar sounds I'd ever heard."

Willie came out to jam with Neil for a while, and Dahr said the 2003 Picnic is a fine example of their friendship. "When Neil comes to do something like that, he's just basically doing it because he loves Willie. Neil can go sell out a stadium; he doesn't have to do [the Picnic]. But that tells you that it's just out of love; he just wants to be with Willie, just like Willie would do the same thing for him. "

Jack Yoder said Neil Young felt relaxed because they had made sure that his family was well taken care of. "He was great. It went great."

Despite the lengthy jams and late hour, when Neil came offstage, he and the band started talking about an encore and what they were going to do. "But they waited too long," Yoder said. "When they started to go back onstage, they realized the audience thought they weren't coming back and it just kind of killed the energy."

Willie and Family closed out the night, bringing whatever artists were left onstage for the gospel sing-along finale.

"IT HAD BIG POTENTIAL; it just never reached it. Maybe another year or two later, they might have had a great Picnic out there." Budrock Prewitt was one of many who said Two River Canyon could have been something special.

James Oakley said the county wasn't fazed by the first day's traffic and would have allowed the Picnic to return.

So what happened?

"We took loans against the property to make the improvements [that Willie's people wanted] and were promised to get certain amounts of money [from the Picnic]," Deana Hebert Gideon said. "And we were let down. We didn't have enough to pay off our loans. We had to sell our property. I'm sure somebody made a profit, but it wasn't me. It wasn't my brother."

Deana didn't say what they were paid but that it was "probably a fifth of what we were promised." She said Tim O'Connor offered various reasons why, but the bottom line was that it wasn't enough. "I feel like we were taken advantage of. "It was horrible."

Tim O'Connor conducted his final interview by phone from hospice care in early July 2021. By the end of the month, cancer, a decades-long adversary, would finally claim him.

His immediate response was that it was the first he had heard of Deana's complaints. Then he regained a little fire and said the Heberts got 100 percent of the money from camping and parking and did "a piss poor job" of organizing both. "They wouldn't listen to anybody else. I would be totally shocked if they didn't make any money. They controlled money that nothing came out of."

In a previous interview, Tim had said he didn't have his normal crew helping run things, and because of his health at the time of the Picnic, he wasn't able to be the controlling presence he should have been.

Deana said it was their first year and they were kind of thrown into it. "We threw it together the best we could, and I think we did okay for what we were given. We were given a large, large event, and we tried our hardest."

But the music business cares little for how hard you try. "As far as the show was concerned, I think the gross was somewhere in the neighborhood of $170,000," Tim said. "I think people ought to stop and think about who the artists were onstage and what they charged."

The Dead and Neil Young definitely got their money. But not Willie. "I remember Willie finding out at the end of the day he was the only one that didn't get paid," Budrock said. "He wasn't too happy about it."

With Tim O'Connor unable to talk in more detail and Willobee Carlan and James Hebert unwilling to be interviewed (Deana said her brother was still bitter about the Picnic), the full accounting of the 2003 Picnic's finances remains elusive.

The key question is, Was it bad luck, a misunderstanding, or did Tim O'Connor take advantage of the young landowners? It can't be said definitively, but it's fair to mention that Tim was often linked to lawsuits and unhappy business partners.

Deana said the disappointment really stung because she loved Willie Nelson. "I grew up in Spicewood; Willie's our neighbor. He's like family. You don't think someone like that would do that to you. I'm not saying it's directly his fault. He may not have even known."

She said they faced a tough situation, debating about what to do. "I guess we were too young and too poor. We had lawyers telling us which way to go. But the problem is, when you have people that have money versus people that don't have money, you know who wins—the lawyers win. And we walked away."

James Oakley said with a little more law enforcement and today's smartphone technology allowing people to communicate about conditions and backroads, the event could have been problem-free as far as traffic goes. "Unlike a lot of venues that kind of start small and work their way up, this thing started out with the Super Bowl, right? So obviously, you're going to find things that could be done better."

Both Deana and Oakley still feel the loss of what could have been. "I think we could have had a great venue; we could have had a great relationship with all of them," Deana said. "And it would've been awesome to have the Willie show from there on out."

Deana almost quit her day job in Austin during the production of the Picnic. "I really thought we were going to have something big. And it didn't happen that way. I'm not trying to be ugly or rude, and I'm not misrepresenting anything. I'm just telling you, we were not done fairly."

That said, Deana said she still considers the whole thing a great experience. "A quick roller coaster ride is what it was. There was a high and a large low."

"IT DEFINITELY WAS ONE OF THE BEST days of my life. It's like getting to play a Super Bowl for a football player. There's no other gig like it." James Hyland of the South Austin Jug Band said playing the Picnic was a life-changing moment, something the other younger artists agreed with.

Rick del Castillo said it was an honor to be part of the Picnic's history, but it was the relationship they built with Willie that changed the trajectory of the band. Del Castillo recorded with Willie and ended up performing at multiple Picnics.

Bandmate Alex Ruiz said they were initially nervous about bringing their Latin-based sound to the Picnic but were reassured quickly. "We felt embraced for the first time in the music world." Only later did they recognize that Willie had long been a supporter of music of all types. "He had been with Little Joe and helped him out," Alex said. "There was a lot of stuff that we got to see along the way that helped us realize that Willie was special."

Stephanie Urbina Jones said her performance that day held deeply personal meaning, changing what she believed was possible, opening doors in the music business, and giving her more faith in herself. "It's one of the top moments of my life. As long as I'm here, it will always be. I feel as if I touched heaven on Earth in Texas, that day."

CHAPTER EIGHT

2004: Fort Worth Stockyards

SITE: *In the "North Forty" field adjacent to Billy Bob's Texas in the Fort Worth Stockyards*
ATTENDANCE: *Estimated at 20,000*
HEADLINERS: *Willie Nelson, Merle Haggard, Ray Price, Kris Kristofferson, Clarence "Gatemouth" Brown, Los Lonely Boys*

Picnic VIP Update

Willie Nelson: Willie was on cruise control, in between releasing his jazz-flavored album *Nacogdoches* and beginning to film his role as Uncle Jesse in the remake of *The Dukes of Hazzard*. Within a month of the Picnic, he would launch his first joint concert tour with Bob Dylan.

David Allan Coe: The notorious David Allan had released a trio of cover albums (including his takes on classic cowboy songs) in the years leading up to 2004 but was also getting attention from his own *Live at Billy Bob's Texas* album, released a month before Willie's.

Ray Price: Ray had released his final solo studio album, *Time*, in 2002 and had released a collaboration with Willie, *Run That by Me One More Time*, a year later. Though he was known to be conservative, he had made national news in 1999 with an arrest for marijuana possession.

Asleep at the Wheel: The band was still riding high on the success of the 1999 album *Ride with Bob: A Tribute to Bob Wills and the Texas Playboys*, which had been nominated for six Grammys and won two. "We were on a roll," Ray Benson said. "It was our second coming."

Rick Smith was born in 1956 in Haltom City, a suburb just immediately east of "Where the West Begins." By 1998, he had gone a pretty far piece. Rick was living on a boat in Florida, getting his start in the music business after a career in retail. He wanted to step up his game and, through a mutual friend, arranged a meeting with Billy Bob's co-owner Billy Minick.

"Rick Smith walked into my office," Billy said. "He had hair down to his shoulders, John Denver glasses, an Armani suit, and tasseled loafers. And he said, 'I want to do recordings at Billy Bob's.'"

Rick pitched the idea of *Live at Billy Bob's Texas* to the longtime rodeo cowboy, and Billy immediately saw the value of the idea—though he wasn't going to compromise on Fort Worth's western self-image. "I basically said, 'Let's get it on.' But I've got one request. It's not a request; it's mandatory. You go across the street and get some jeans and boots and a pickup.' He did. And he never got out of 'em."

Eventually there would be more than fifty *Live at Billy Bob's Texas* albums. The idea was to work with up-and-coming Texas artists who didn't have labels—such as Pat Green, who recorded the first *Live at Billy Bob's* album in December 1998—and legendary artists who were between labels, such as Willie Nelson in late 2003.

"Rick was a crazy sumbitch but a borderline genius," Billy said. "He became my best friend. And every morning he would call me and say, 'What are you doing, motherfucker?'"

Pam Minick, retired marketing director for Billy Bob's, said Rick's creativity and energy kept her husband young and inspired him to think creatively as well. "Rick was always thinking outside the box. And he wasn't afraid of trying anything. In his mind, there was no stupid idea; it's just how do you do it?"

While recording Willie's live album in December 2003, Rick had a new vision. Pam said it was likely January 2004 when Rick approached Billy with a new pitch. "What if we do Willie's Picnic here?"

WHAT IF A CITY HOSTED WILLIE'S PICNIC and everyone loved it? In mid-April, Willie was standing on the steps of the historic Livestock Exchange Building in the Fort Worth Stockyards, alongside Mayor Mike Moncrief under a giant banner announcing the Picnic.

Willie had already leaked the news, telling the crowd about the Picnic during a show at Fort Worth's historic Ridglea Theater in late February. On Texas Independence Day, *Fort Worth Star-Telegram* columnist Bud Kennedy had confirmed the show, quoting fellow writer Joe Nick Patoski: "His career was really launched in Fort Worth. It's like bringing Willie back home."

At the press conference, enthusiasm for the show was still growing.

Mario Tarradell, who spent nearly twenty years as the music critic at the *Dallas Morning News*, was one of those allowed on Willie's bus after the press conference for a brief interview. He remembered that "Willie in

Willie Nelson held a press conference at the Livestock Exchange Building in the Fort Worth Stockyards to formally announce the 2004 Picnic. Joining Willie onstage are, from left, Pam Minick, Rick Smith, Fort Worth mayor Mike Moncrief, and Rosie Moncrief. Billy Bob's Texas

person was a whole lot like Willie on the phone: super calm, super chill, making sly jokes, laughing at his own jokes." It wasn't hard to be charmed by Willie. "It was a huge deal," Tarradell said. "There was a lot of buzz about it. It was a pretty hefty lineup with some serious legendary names."

Mike Moncrief hadn't been mayor of Fort Worth very long at the time, but he recalls that the city didn't hesitate to embrace it. "It was an exciting time for our city. Our western heritage was an attraction to Willie and his folks. [People here] anticipated this event, planned for it, put it on their calendars early on."

Indeed, from a marketing standpoint, Pam Minick saw a smooth road ahead. "It was so easy to get people interested because it was something new."

Fort Worth officials said they had no worries. "How could there be any concerns? We had the perfect place for it. We were happy to have him." The response from Jim Lane, a Fort Worth attorney who was a councilman in 2004, tells the story.

The Picnic had come a long way since 1976, when a Williamson County commissioner, still fuming over the '75 event, traveled one hundred miles to Gonzales to testify against it. Or when Gonzales citizens formed an organization to formally oppose it.

It seems reasonable that there would have been some people in Fort

Austin artist Jim Franklin designed the poster for the inaugural Picnic. Franklin said he didn't charge Willie for the artwork, and Willie returned the favor by performing for free when Franklin reopened the Ritz Theater the following year. Courtesy of Jim Franklin

▲ Willie Nelson performs alongside Kenneth Threadgill during the 1973 Picnic. Watt Casey.com

▶ Jim Franklin's poster for the 1975 Picnic in Liberty Hill. Courtesy of Jim Franklin

WILLIE NELSON'S
THIRD ANNUAL 4th OF JULY PICNIC

WILLIE, HIS FAMILY & FRIENDS:

Kris Kristofferson • Rita Coolidge • The Pointer Sisters
The Charlie Daniels Band • Doug Sahm Quintet • Billy Swan
Alex Harvey • Johnny Bush • Donnie Fritts • Billy "C"
Milton Carroll • Delbert McClinton

AT LIBERTY HILL from Austin take Hwy. 183 north then west on Hwy. 29. Tickets $5.50 advance $7.50 door. Mail Orders: Preston Ticket Agency, P. O. Box 12000, Dallas, Texas 75225.

▲ Jim Franklin's poster for the 1976 Picnic in Gonzales. Courtesy of Jim Franklin

▶ The poster Danny Garrett did for the 1978 mini-Picnic at the still-new Austin Opry House was the first iteration of the "Uncle Willie" design that would become well-known in the 1980s. Poster by Danny Garrett

Austin Opry House

Willie Nelson's 6th and 7th Annual 4th of July

July 3·4 PICNIC 1978

Willie Nelson performs at the 1979 Picnic alongside famed fiddler Johnny Gimble.
© *Bob Daemmrich photo*

When photographer Bob Daemmrich was brought into the 1979 Picnic, he was able to catch this shot of the crowd. © Bob Daemmrich photo

▲ Artist Steve Brooks had worked officially for Willie since the mid-1970s, but this is his only Picnic poster. Poster by Steve Brooks

▶ Austin artist Danny Garrett used this image on the poster for the trio of 1983 Picnics, and Willie liked it so much that it was used again in 1984, 1985, and 1987. Poster by Danny Garrett

I WANT YOU FOR WILLIE NELSON'S FOURTH OF JULY PICNIC

1984

THE SOUTH PARK MEADOWS — AUSTIN, TEXAS

Waylon Jennings　Jessi Colter　Jerry Jeff Walker　Billy Joe Shaver
Leon Russell　Joe Ely　Mo Bandy　Johnny Rodriguez
Kris Kristofferson　David Allen Coe　Carl Perkins　Farron Young
　　　　　　　　　　　　　　　　　　　　　　　　John Bush

Doors Open 8 a.m.　$18.00 Adults
10 to 10　$11.00 Children (Under 12)

Fireworks Display　**Concessions**

Chris Gates, a punk rocker in Austin in the 1980s, was making his living doing web development and commercial art in 2003. He was friends with Tim O'Connor and ended up designing the 2003 Picnic poster. Poster by Chris Gates

Gregory Ice designed the poster for the 2004 Picnic. After Poodie Locke struck Ice's signature from a proof of the poster, Ice hid the signature in the bottom left edge of the bandana. Poster by Gregory Ice, designer and creative director

▲ *Austin artist Billy Perkins created the poster for the 2010 Picnic. Poster design and illustration by Billy Perkins*

▶▲ *Roadies set up the stage during a break in the action at the 2017 Picnic. Photo by Dave Dalton Thomas*

▶▼ *Casey Kristofferson and bandmates watch Raelyn Nelson perform at the 2019 Picnic. Photo by Dave Dalton Thomas*

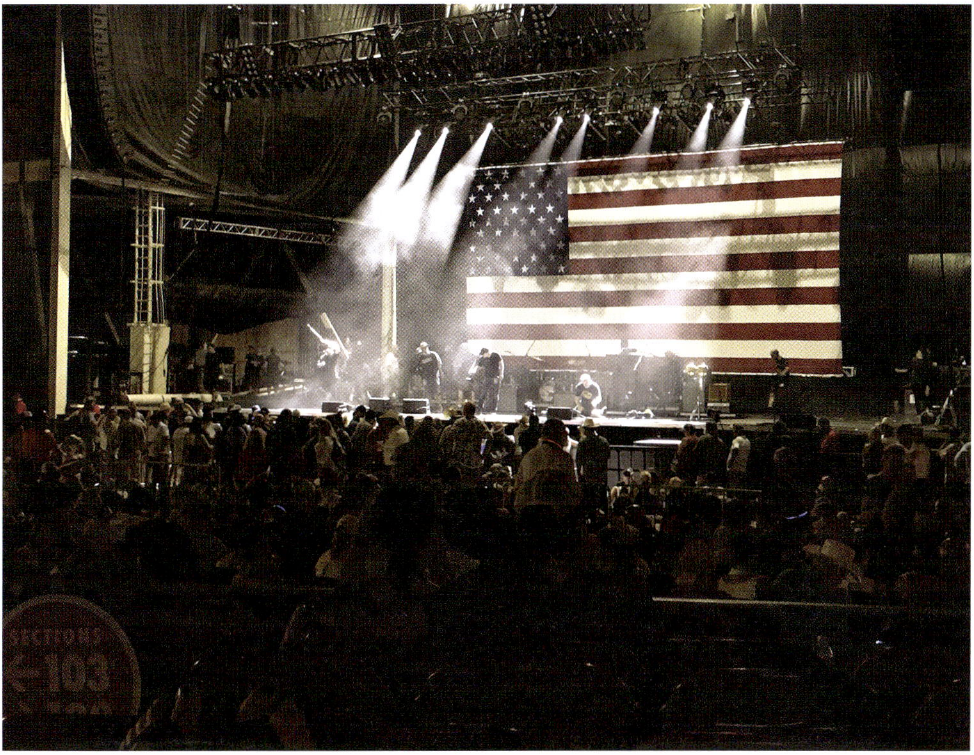
SECTIONS
←103

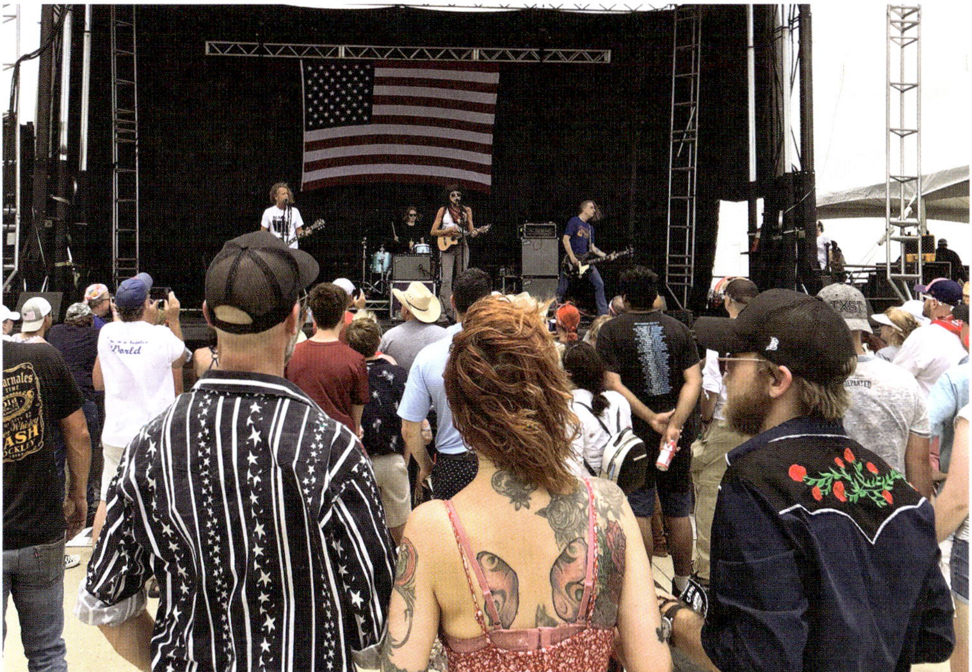

Willie Nelson performs at the 1997 Picnic in Luckenbach. The Picnic stayed in Luckenbach for five years (1995–1999) before promoters were caught off-guard by a revised state law in 2000. Photo by Rick Henson

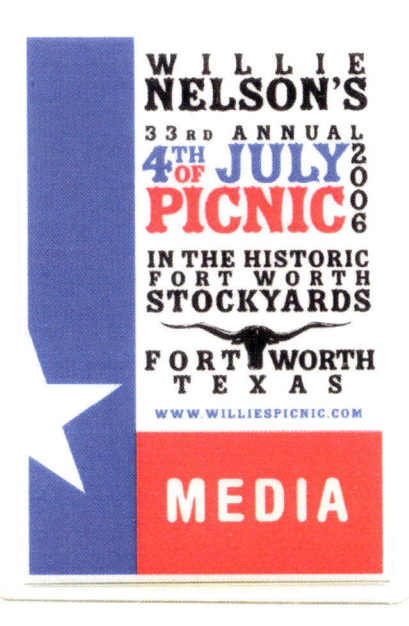

Backstage passes (clockwise from top left: 1987 in Carl's Corner, 1998 in Luckenbach, 2006 in Fort Worth, and 2016 at the Circuit of the Americas) were always highly sought-after. In the earlier years of the Picnics, Willie's team struggled to limit backstage access.

Willie Nelson performs at the 2022 Picnic at Q2 Stadium in Austin. At the age of 89, Willie now sat down throughout his shorter set, but the crowd's love for him was undiminished. Photo by Gary Miller

Worth who didn't want the Picnic, but questions about opposition came up empty. Tarradell said he could not recall any opposition, and Kennedy agreed: "I think that everything about the Picnic was an upside. I don't remember anybody complaining."

Moncrief said he had no concerns as long as public safety was assured. "Certainly, having a name and a quality product that Willie brought to our city was something we knew a lot of people would want to be a part of, even though at times he's been controversial."

The promise of a big payday bought the support of surrounding businesses. From the beginning, it was clear the Picnic was going to allow picnickers to come and go during the show. Of course, Billy Bob's was hoping to draw most of the picnickers to the club for a little air conditioning, cold beer, and clean restrooms, but surrounding bars and restaurants also would benefit greatly.

Marty Travis, general manager for Billy Bob's, said spreading the wealth throughout the Stockyards was key. "Everybody was going to get fat, from parking to restaurants to hotels and everything. So nobody really gave us too much static about it."

Billy Bob's Texas had impressive control over the vision and planning of the Picnic, and the club's years of experience engendered confidence. "I do not doubt for one moment that if the city officials in Fort Worth and the powers that be in Fort Worth needed convincing, I have absolutely zero doubt that [Billy Bob's leadership] convinced them," Tarradell said. "That is why Fort Worth the city embraced this Picnic."

Kennedy provided a deeper look at Fort Worth politics. "The rule in Fort Worth has always been that anything that's good for Billy Bob's is good for Fort Worth. When Billy Bob's wants to have something big, it's you know, 'Hey, everybody get on board.' Billy Bob's has had a tremendous say-so over politics in Fort Worth for many years."

No officials spoke on this topic, though it's worth noting that in his Picnic preview, Tarradell quoted Rick Smith as emphasizing the city's backing when he pitched the Picnic to Willie. "We've got the city of Fort Worth, from the mayor to the firemen giving us overwhelming support. . . . You couldn't buy that kind of support," Smith told Tarradell.

THE 1980 FILM *Urban Cowboy* stirred up a cultural craze in Texas that hadn't slowed down at all a year later. It was the perfect time for Billy Bob Barnett and Spencer Taylor to open their own cowboy nightclub—Billy Bob's Texas.

At 120,000 square feet, the "world's largest honky-tonk" is nearly as big as an average Target store. It can hold six thousand people and has its own bull-riding arena. On its busiest nights about forty bartenders work more than thirty bar stations. The massive building started as an open-air cattle barn in 1910, was enclosed during the Texas Centennial, housed an airplane factory during World War II, and was a department store in the 1950s.

Billy Bob's Texas opened on April 1, 1981. The avalanche of stars to perform in the first two years alone is incredible, including Ray Price, Merle Haggard, Bill Monroe, Jerry Lee Lewis, ZZ Top, Ray Charles, Bob Hope, Johnny Cash, Chuck Berry, Tina Turner, the Beach Boys, and Bo Diddley.

The high times didn't last, and Barnett's finances eventually faltered. When the club closed in 1988, four men teamed up to reopen it: Holt Hickman, Don Jury, Steve Murrin, and Billy Minick. Billy Bob's came back to life on March 31, 1989, with Willie on the main stage.

Starting in December 1998, the *Live at Billy Bob's Texas* recordings became an important part of the operation, particularly when it came to marketing. For as long as CDs and DVDs were vital, the Billy Bob's name would be in Walmarts and Buc-ee's locations all over Texas and beyond. The albums also helped strengthen ties with legendary artists and forge relationships with up-and-coming Texas and Red Dirt artists.

The key to those relationships was Rick Smith. More than just managing the logistics of the recordings, singer-songwriter Jason Boland recalls Smith as one of those people who "made you believe why we should be doing this and why you're the one chosen to do it. He was one of those people in your life who gave you supreme confidence."

Smith believed in the Stockyards and believed what he was doing was a key part of promoting country music and Texas culture. And he did it in an irrepressible way. "He was just a firecracker," Boland said. "He was one of those people that his spirit precedes him into the room a little bit—just a little bit larger than life, but still fun and accessible."

In a bit of marketing that couldn't have been planned better, Willie's *Live at Billy Bob's Texas* album was released two months before the Picnic, on May 4, 2004.

Marty Travis recalls the run-up to the first Picnic in Fort Worth as a stressful-yet-successful time. "Billy Minick came to me and he said, 'You got to run Willie's Picnic.' I said, 'Billy, twenty thousand people are gonna be in that field. I've never done anything that size!' He said, 'It's really easy son; don't run out of beer.'" He wouldn't run out of beer, but he would lose plenty of sleep.

The crowd came early for the 2004 Picnic and ultimately reached twenty thousand, making the North Forty pretty uncomfortable to navigate by late afternoon. Billy Bob's was a highly experienced venue, but they had never done anything like this before. Billy Bob's Texas

The Picnic was run by three partners. Billy Bob's Texas handled the operations, Willie and his people handled the musical acts, and Smith Music Group put together the sponsorships.

Having Smith Music handle the sponsorships allowed them to take money from Budweiser or Jack Daniels, because as a liquor permit holder, Billy Bob's was not permitted to do so. That was the reason the advertising and posters didn't say "at Billy Bob's" but rather "in the Fort Worth Stockyards."

Having Willie handle the talent was a given, Pam Minick said. "When you say, 'Willie's Picnic,' you've got pretty much no say-so in the artists. It's who he wants to play and how much he wants to pay them."

Billy Bob's handled the stages, the sound, lights, Porta Potties, marketing, ticket sales, counting money, and anything else that came up. "We learned from that first one," Pam said. "We learned so much we knew just what we didn't know about putting on an event like that."

One of the first things they learned is that Willie is partial to the Fourth of July. Billy Minick had asked Willie to move it to Saturday, July 3, and Willie's answer was clear. "He said 'Billy, I don't give a shit what you do on July 3, but if you don't mind, I'd like the Willie July Fourth Picnic to be on July Fourth,'" Marty Travis remembered.

Despite decades of running a club as large as Billy Bob's, Billy Minick said the Picnic was still daunting. "Operationally, it was a challenge because I didn't have that experience. I surrounded myself with people who did have that experience. Robert Gallagher was a big help."

Gallagher has spent more than three decades as entertainment director at Billy Bob's and has been with the club since it opened in 1981—there might not be anyone in Texas with more experience in preparing a venue for a big show. One of Gallagher's early decisions was to use two stages for the Picnic. The music would alternate between the main south stage (where Willie would close out the show) and the north stage. This would allow roadies to do setup on one stage while performances were being held on the other.

The music would flow nonstop, and any picnicker who has waited through thirty minutes of silence while Leon Russell and crew made adjustments could see the value in that. "The two-stage thing was the whole reason we could do twenty-seven acts," Gallagher said. "That's the absolute greatest thing, in my opinion, for that Picnic, because it allowed longer performances, on schedule."

Willie, however, was skeptical. "He didn't like it at first, because he didn't have access to everybody right there," Gallagher said. Willie wanted to visit with everyone, and having some buses parked on the north side might discourage that. Gallagher pointed out that the stages would be connected by a fenced-off service alley on the east side you could run golf carts through—anyone who wanted to come to Willie's bus would be accommodated.

This wasn't the first time Billy Bob's Texas had an event in the North Forty field with two stages. The year before they had held a smaller concert called the Dodge Stockyards Stampede with Hank Williams Jr. as the featured artist.

Marty Travis remembered that at this show, the north stage was small—a truck that transformed into a stage. It turns out they hadn't ironed out all the details. "Deryl Dodd was the last dude on that stage that particular night," Travis said. "And we had not factored in lights. So he was playing in the dark with ambient light from the Hank stage or light from the moon. He was like, 'Can y'all see me?'"

It was an important learning experience for everyone. "We had so many bugs that Hank show that we had to figure out, that I knew that we could fix any problems [with the Picnic]," Travis said.

For the first few months, the principals of the Picnic would meet once or twice a week and work out the details. "I worked with our bar managers on how many bars they thought were needed, worked out the entryways, exits, all that stuff," Gallagher said. Then, just over a week ahead of time, Gallagher went out with string, paint, and stakes and laid out the entire field, marking every vendor, tent, and bar.

Along the way, there were multiple meetings with the City of Fort Worth. "They would go over every detail," Robert said. "But the city was more than cooperative. As long as we had all the t's crossed, and the i's dotted, they were just wonderful about everything. They were confident that we knew what we were doing."

"WILLIE'S HIS OWN WORST ENEMY. His left hand has been bothering him for some time now, and we've tried to limit his sets to 90 minutes, but, you know, Willie just loves to play." Stage manager Poodie Locke was blunt about Willie's struggle with carpal tunnel syndrome in an interview with the *Austin American-Statesman* in early May as Willie considered surgery.

Willie ended up canceling all but one of his shows leading up to the Picnic, hoping that the rest would allow him to play. Billy Bob's officials say they were never worried that the Picnic would be called off. "It was a little bit concerning when the news first came out," Marty Travis said. "But as long as it wasn't his voice or his legs, I thought it would be okay."

Friend Ray Benson, who had also had problems with his hand, visited Willie before the Picnic to offer his advice. "I was over there to try to help him. I was trying to get him not to have the operation and do physical therapy. But I'm not a doctor, so what do I know? It was typical Willie . . . whatever it is, he'll deal with it."

Willie did have surgery on May 19, and by the beginning of July it was clear he wouldn't be able to play guitar at the Picnic. Fortunately, Willie had a plan. Joey Floyd had played Willie's son in the movie *Honeysuckle Rose*, sparking a lasting friendship. "Joey had been part of that Willie Nelson and Family, immersed in that for a long time," wife Laurin Floyd said. "And still kept up with Willie. They'd talk, tell jokes over the phone."

Fueling the friendship was the fact that Joey was one hell of a musician. As a child, he and his sister—Joey and Jill Floyd—had gone on the

Willie wasn't able to play guitar during the 2004 Picnic because he was recovering from surgery for carpal tunnel syndrome. Billy Bob's Texas

road with Willie for a time. He and Jill performed in the band Eldorado as adults, and by 1997, Joey was a multi-instrumentalist standout in Toby Keith's Easy Money Band.

As a child, Joey never took music lessons, Laurin said, because he grew up just knowing how to play. "He was one of those just great musicians. And he knew every single lick I think Willie ever did. He knew every song that Willie did. He never had to practice. He knew."

Given that Joey was from nearby Arlington, it was a natural fit for Willie to invite Joey to play his parts at the Fort Worth Picnic.

"IT'S ALWAYS SOMETHING. It's never what you think it's gonna be—it's always the little things." The gates had just opened on the Fourth of July when someone came to Marty Travis and said that the Porta Potties weren't working. "I said, 'What do you mean they aren't working? They're a hole, right?'"

He was busy and let it slide until another employee came and told him the same thing, and he decided he better check it out. "We didn't open the gates until eleven," Billy Minick said. "And I wasn't smart enough to put Porta Potties [outside the gate]. And as soon as they got in, and there was a thousand of 'em, they run for the Porta Potties."

However, when Porta Potties are transported, the doors are zip-tied shut. They had been unloaded and placed in the field, but nobody had thought to cut the zip ties "Oh shit," Travis said. "I ran over here real quick, grabbed two or three Leatherman tools or snips or whatever we had, passed them out . . . snap! snap! snap! snap! and people started cheering because they had to pee and couldn't get in there."

For subsequent Picnics, Billy Bob's made sure to have Porta Potties and concessions outside the gates. "We had no idea that people would line up at nine in the morning for a show that theoretically begins at noon, but really the headliners come on at eleven o'clock," Pam Minick said. "But they do. It's crazy."

Actually, the hard-core Willie fans are crazier than that. Linda Banks is one of those fans, known for her Willie blog, www.stillisstillmoving.com. The 2004 Picnic was her first, but she had already connected with

Cody Canada and Randy Ragsdale of Cross Canadian Ragweed perform at the 2004 Picnic. This Picnic was perhaps the last to be heavily focused on traditional country, but some up-and-coming bands made their way into the lineup. Billy Bob's Texas

other serious fans through Willie's website and knew the ropes. "We go to the Picnics or shows at the Backyard or something, and we'd get there at five in the morning and there's other people waiting to get in," Banks said. "There was just something about getting there and sitting there with everybody."

Those superfans were there to get prime spots on the front row, sure, but there was also a sense of community among them. "Willie has such a mix of fans who just love him from all walks of life," Banks said. "That's why his Picnics are so fun, because they really bring people from all over. And it's a fun crowd."

Craig Copeland, owner of Fort Worth's Longhorn Saloon, remembered the 2004 Picnic as hotter than hell, though everyone did their best to roll with it. "I haven't been to every one of them, but there's one thing that they all have in common: The closest cloud will be somewhere over Kansas. And the closest tree will be somewhere down south of Austin. There won't be a lick of shade.

"I've got a great picture of me and my son with Ray Price," Craig said. "Ray, I'm telling you, he had on a white shirt and blue jeans. And he had his shirt rolled up to his elbows, and the sweat was dripping off his cuffs. The old man was burning up."

The *Star-Telegram* reported that at least 125 people got medical treatment for heat problems, although only one was sent to the hospital. More than ever, the artists were glad to retreat to their air-conditioned buses. "It was too fucking hot," Ray Benson said. "And it was packed and kind of claustrophobic."

As more than twenty thousand people poured into the enclosed twenty-seven-acre site, tempers sometimes flared up. Early arrivals might stake out a spot and put down a blanket, only to find an hour later that they had been surrounded, with no way to the Porta Potty or beer tent except through someone else's space. Throw in ninety-three-degree heat and 55 percent humidity and people could get irritable.

"Of course, there's always a couple little fights because you stepped on my towel or you looked at my girlfriend wrong," Marty Travis said.

But the big picture was . . . this was a hit. "When we got there that morning and people were lined up, I felt from a marketing standpoint, 'Okay, my job is over now,'" Pam Minick said. "I didn't have to count the money. All I had to do was see the bodies."

For Mario Tarradell, covering the Picnic was a big moment in his career. "Here I am, country music critic for the *Dallas Morning News* in Texas, and I'm ten years in and I've been reading about the Picnics forever and a day and how legendary and infamous they are, and I've never seen one."

Tarradell spent the early part of the day walking the grounds, taking in the event from different vantage points. "It seemed like people were having a great time. I didn't see anybody that seemed otherwise. I can't remember anything that was not successful about it."

The two defining characteristics of the Fort Worth Picnics—the on-time schedule afforded by the two stages and the in-and-out policy—worked as well in practice as they did in theory. The predictable schedule and nonstop music weren't just a bonus for the fans; they also allowed Billy Bob's to coordinate with local radio stations.

Still, there were challenges.

"[The Picnics] had been run so loosely," Pam Minick said, "and the artists expected it to be run loosely. And so with it being more regimented, it wasn't always met with good grace from the artists."

Leon Russell backstage at the 2004 Picnic at the Stockyards. The two-stage approach to the 2004 Picnic meant that the music flowed nonstop. But a lot of Willie fanatics who camped out in front of the south stage missed old Willie friends performing at the north stage. Photo by Rick Henson

Jack Yoder, who had run the stage at the Luckenbach Picnics, said he was impressed with the two-stage operation. "The places we did it with Willie, we couldn't have really gotten two stages; it would have been a nightmare. But [Robert Gallagher's] logistics were a little bit better than ours. I thought they did a great job."

For the most hard-core Willie fans, however, having two stages meant not getting to see half the acts. "Willie fans just parked right in front of Willie's stage and just stayed there," Linda Banks said. "We would just sit in front of Willie all day and not worry about the other stages, but I didn't like it."

For the 2004 Picnic, ignoring the north stage meant missing Picnic regulars Johnny Bush, Leon Russell, and Ray Price. "I hated that," Banks said. "That was hard."

When Billy Minick was asked whether he considered not having an in-and-out policy at the Picnic, his answer was straightforward: "No. Because I own Billy Bob's. There was no discussion about it."

And the crowds definitely came. "Man, we got crushed," Marty Travis said. "In the first year, we were not as prepared inside as we should have been. And we got murdered. But it was good."

The big stars stayed backstage, but for those artists who could wander around mostly unrecognized, the urban room to roam was a nice departure. "Normally, if you wanted to get into some air conditioning, you had to go back to your bus because you're out in the middle of nowhere," Tyler Mahan Coe said. "There at Billy Bob's . . . they got plenty of air conditioning in there. It was almost like the Picnic moved uptown. It's like, 'Damn, we're doing all right this year.'"

Other Stockyards bars and restaurants also enjoyed the surge in business. "You gotta let people come and go so you support your neighbors, and our neighbors, they loved it," Robert Gallagher said. "They made big money on Willie days."

"ONE OF THE FUNNIEST THINGS that happened was someone called me and said the TABC has caught a guy in the parking lot selling beer." Billy Minick remembers this story pretty clearly.

"This college kid had the back of his pickup full of cases of beer, and he had a lawn chair and an umbrella; I mean he had it set up. Well, [the TABC] cleaned it all up, and this manager turned to me and said, 'Can you imagine a sumbitch being that dumb to do that?'"

Billy agreed it wasn't very bright, but it sure as hell was bold. "I said, 'Let me tell you something; when this is all cleared out, you go over there and see if you can hire that sumbitch, because I love him.'"

Just because the idea of Willie's Picnic was wildly popular in Fort Worth doesn't mean the authorities weren't keeping a close eye on things. "We would always have thirty or forty officers at those Picnics in addition to our thirty or forty security guys," Robert Gallagher said. "We'd have seventy-plus security people and hardly any trouble."

Over the years of handling big events at the Stockyards, the Fort Worth police were well practiced at handling people who had drunk more than they ought to and were wary of being heavy-handed in a tourist district. "If it was just somebody that was drunk, they'd give them a chance to call their parents or a friend," Gallagher said. "And if they weren't belligerent, they'd just hold them there. Somebody would come get them and [the police would let them go]."

By late in the evening, the *Dallas Morning News* reported, there had been just two arrests. One of the places security was crucial was around the RV where the gate and beer money was being brought and counted. In the days before debit cards could be used at beer stands, there was an enormous amount of cash. "We had a police officer in the RV with a weapon all the time," Marty Travis said. "And then anytime I went to go pick up money in a golf cart, I always had an officer right next to me. . . . We had a cop all the way until we brought the money into the mothership."

There was a lot of cash flowing and a lot of alcohol. The problem with the combination was that the money that came in was often wet. The bartenders (and Travis had hired some sixty of them to work the grounds) would reach into a tub of iced-down beers, take the money with wet hands, and hand the dripping beer can to the customer over the money tray.

In the office, one-dollar bills would stick to hundred-dollar bills, making counting the money frustrating as hell. For the following Picnics at the Stockyards, Billy Bob's made sure to rent an RV with a laundry setup, then run the money through the dryer.

That's right, they would literally launder the money before they counted it.

There were a few other problems. Travis had remembered all the permits . . . or at least he thought so until someone from the Health Department showed up and started giving him a hard time about the lack of hand-washing stations. "So we sent somebody up to Walgreens and

Henry and Jojo Garza of Los Lonely Boys perform at the 2004 Picnic. Los Lonely Boys was one of the hottest acts in Americana music at the time. Billy Bob's Texas

bought all their hand sanitizer and some water buckets, and we made do on the fly," Travis said. It cost me two hundred dollars of buying bullshit, but it kept me from having to shut down."

Parking was also a struggle. George Westby owned Quick Park, which handled the parking lots in the Stockyards, and he remembers there wasn't room to spare: "We parked everywhere. If it was bare, there was a car on it."

"WE WENT PRETTY HARD back in those days. We'd played the night before in Stillwater with Hank Jr. and had a big time up there, and then woke up in the Stockyards." That said, Jason Boland and his band were still up for a little bar hopping before their early-afternoon show. They felt welcome backstage at the Picnic, he said; however, they weren't in the circle of old Willie friends.

"At our age and who we were, there were a lot of conversations we weren't too involved in," he said. "Guys like us that were really pretty new to the scene still just couldn't believe we were playing Willie's Picnic. But the backstage was fun, though I never ended up hanging out with Willie."

Backstage, Robert Gallagher often had his hands full trying to keep the show on schedule. He remembered that Willie's young sons, Lukas and Micah, were playing in one of the early bands. "I was talking to 'em while they were getting ready and said, 'You got fifteen minutes.'"

Willie's wife, Annie, was standing nearby and stopped him. They're going to play forty-five minutes, she said. "I said, 'Annie, I got so many bands . . . ,' and she goes, 'Robert, my boys are going to play forty-five minutes.' I go, 'Yes ma'am, they sure are!'"

As the day progressed, the lineup turned legendary. Hot young acts Cross Canadian Ragweed and Los Lonely Boys played in the hottest part of the afternoon. Then came multigenre masters Gatemouth Brown and Leon Russell.

However, closing out the Picnic were Merle Haggard, Ray Price, Kris Kristofferson, and Willie Nelson. The Picnic would never be *this* country again.

"It was an insane lineup," Boland said. "I ended up riding around on a golf cart with Larry the Cable Guy. We tried to be unofficial mayors of Willie's Picnic and then just caught a bunch of shows. That's as heavy as country music gets. I think we were both pretty hard-core fans that day."

Marty Travis said he would occasionally stop his golf cart in the service alley and soak in a few moments of the lineup, but Pam Minick said that working with all of the top Picnic artists over the years left her and Billy at a disadvantage when it came to appreciating the moment. "Looking back now, I'm like, 'Wow,' but it didn't occur to me then that it was a Mount Rushmore of classic country music."

"Every time you see Willie in a concert photo, it's the tell-tale details of the picture: Trigger, red, white, and blue guitar strap. And you know, a lot of times, one hand will be raised and his finger will be pointing up to the heavens." Mario Tarradell had seen Willie perform a dozen times or more in his ten years at the *Dallas Morning News* and found it weird to see him come onstage without his famous guitar and start off with a handful of bluesy songs rather than "Whiskey River." "It was like, wow, okay, this is certainly a different Willie," he said. "It was kind of weird . . . but once again, in his own way, Willie is always the consummate pro."

Willie divided his set that night, playing with a bluesier band at first before taking a break and giving the stage to Kris Kristofferson.

Councilman Jim Lane had been a lifelong Willie fan and got to visit with him on the bus. "I told him, 'Willie, your music got a lot of us through the Vietnam situation—us Texas boys always wanted to come home when we heard your music.' He was kind of humble about it, but it's true."

Lane, who had worked hard to change the Fort Worth logo to the simple

Longhorn image with "Fort Worth" underneath it, had made new flags and presented one to Willie onstage at the Picnic. "He got the very first one," Lane said. "I know Pam and my wife came out onstage, and we presented it to him that night. He was very gracious."

Eventually, Willie returned to the stage with his Family Band, played "Whiskey River," and the Texas flag dropped down—the ritual that Willie fans had come to see.

"It was hard to see his hand in a brace and everything, because he's such a fantastic guitar player," Linda Banks said. "But people were just so happy to see him. It was just fantastic."

Joey Floyd was more than ready to play Willie's parts, but he was also more than aware of the scale of the moment. "It's the first time that I ever saw Joey even nervous about playing because he never was nervous," Laurin Floyd said. "But he knew every single lick; he knew every single song."

Laurin described the scene, Joey standing between Kris and Willie, who watched Joey play with a mixture of surprise and pride: "It was a very big deal for [Joey]. I just remember thinking how proud he was to be up there. And proud for me to see that happen."

ROBERT GALLAGHER SAID Willie ended up loving having two stages. "The morning after that first Picnic, he called me to the bus and said, 'Robert, let's celebrate.' He goes, 'That's the first time in thirty-one years that I've gotten to play a full set [at the Picnic].'" For years, chaos starting in the middle of the Picnic and a curfew at the end had shortened the host's set. Now, despite his initial misgivings, Willie was ready to celebrate at nine in the morning.

Marty Travis had arrived at 5 a.m. on July 4 and saw his second sunrise in the North Forty more than twenty-four hours later. He wasn't the only one putting in long hours—people stayed in the trailer counting money all night and all the next day.

The crowd of twenty thousand fell short of the thirty thousand that Rick Smith predicted, but the partnership between Willie, Smith Music Group, and Billy Bob's was successful—everyone made money. "We knew that fifteen thousand was gonna be profitable for everybody," Gallagher said. "I knew going in, presales were great enough; we knew it was gonna be good."

Bud Kennedy said he was among those who expected a bigger crowd. "We all really thought it would have a Woodstock kind of crowd because we'd heard the legend of Willie's Picnic. It had a big crowd. It didn't have a 'hanging from the rafters' kind of crowd."

Yet it's pretty clear that another ten thousand people would have put a serious strain on space and resources.

Water was key, Gallagher said. Almost every Picnic promoter has learned you've got to have more than you think. In the following years, Fort Worth Picnics would have big water stations and free water.

"There was nothing we could do about [the heat]," Pam Minick said. "But I don't know that anybody thought that people were going to come and stay all day long." They realized they would have to make it clearer where people could go to cool off. They realized that putting on their own fireworks show was too expensive. They realized that they needed to prepare for crowds outside the gate. "You learn a hell of a lot once you do one," Billy Minick said. "[However, 2004] probably went off better than most of 'em he ever did."

Jason Boland was among those who think that the Billy Bob's Picnics were remarkable, not just in production but also in establishing their own vibe. "I think they did a great job of picking the venue, a great job of lining it up. And then letting people have fun and not making everything so stuffy . . . they got the spirit of what we should be doing at music festivals." Things were organized but not regulated.

"I think they got it right," Mario Tarradell said. "From an almost philosophical standpoint, I think that the spirit of the Picnic was captured in Fort Worth. I don't remember anything worth mentioning even that went wrong that first year."

Pam Minick said the Picnic sold tickets in every state and several foreign countries and was a huge boost for everyone involved. "Not only did it make some money; we got a tremendous amount of publicity throughout the country—for Billy Bob's and the Stockyards and the city of Fort Worth."

Tarradell said the Picnic made Fort Worth more of a music festival town. Bud Kennedy took it a few steps further. "Fort Worth was a honky-tonk town. Willie started out here in the '60s, and then you had the Ernest Tubb history before that, but there wasn't as much interest in live music."

Billy Bob's always had live music, of course, but the smaller bars around the Stockyards, Bud said, were full of DJs playing current hits. The excitement spurred by the Picnic, paired with the rise of Texas and Americana music, started to change that.

"Now the bars that are full are the ones that have live music," Kennedy said. "It could be some guy from down the street who's a lawyer during the day and sings country at night, but still there's a bigger crowd for him than there is for the dance bars. There's so much music history

Merle Haggard performs at the 2004 Picnic at the Stockyards. The country music icon stood out among the legends at the 2004 Picnic. Photo by Rick Henson

here that had been lost, and Willie's Picnic helped Fort Worth get back in touch with all that."

Marty Travis said it's still a badge of honor that Billy Bob's ended up hosting seven Willie Nelson Picnics. The 2004 Picnic started a three-year run. "The next year we did it. I felt like it was cruise control. Anything after the first year was seemingly simple," he said. And after a four-year absence, the Picnic came back to the Stockyards for four more years.

"I'm more proud of that than so many other things," Robert Gallagher said. "They trusted us enough to host seven times. Just to have his trust, it says a lot about our organization, as well as Smith Music Group."

Mario Tarradell remembers Willie telling him that his intent for the Picnic was to move it around and not have it in the same place year after year. The Luckenbach Picnics showed he was willing to bend that rule for the right location. "Obviously Willie thought it was successful [in Fort Worth]," Tarradell said. "And really, that's the bottom line. Because if he didn't think it would be successful, he wouldn't come back."

By the time the 2012 Picnic rolled around, Craig Copeland had opened the Longhorn Saloon in the Stockyards, and he remembers reordering beer every two hours and writing the distributors what were essentially hot checks because he couldn't deposit the money in the bank fast enough. "It was a tremendous three days," Copeland said. "The Picnic was a very positive thing, and I'm not sure how Fort Worth let that get away."

Even as much as Fort Worth loved hosting the Picnic—former mayor Moncrief called it a "Fort Worth tradition"—the Picnic eventually moved on. The crowds for successive Picnics never matched the twenty thousand in 2004.

Billy Minick was blunt when explaining how the traditional Picnic lineup didn't hold up. "A bunch of his friends don't sell a hell of a lot of tickets. I admire his loyalty to all these people; he's always been that way, but it's hard to make it work."

The last two years that Billy Bob's hosted the Picnic, the Picnic started bringing in more contemporary artists to boost ticket sales, including Dierks Bentley in 2014. But it wasn't enough.

"What it actually costs to put on Willie's Picnic, the way we did it, is not a real good business model," Billy said. They made it work, but the risks of bad weather or performer cancellations couldn't be ignored.

Eventually, the partnership was history, but the memories remained.

Willie fan Linda Banks said the Fort Worth Picnics were her favorites. "I think they did such a great job. You hear music that you'll never hear anywhere else except in Texas. It was perfect."

"RICK OPERATED OUT OF PURE PASSION. And he was fearless." Pam Minick knew that as long as Rick Smith was involved, they could handle a Willie Picnic.

On July 8, the *Fort Worth Star-Telegram* reported that the Picnic would be back. "The day after the picnic, we hung out and [Willie] was just ecstatic," Smith told the paper. "He was really happy with the way everything turned out, so I asked him if he wanted to do it again. He said 'yeah.'"

A month later, the *Star-Telegram* printed Smith's obituary. He had suffered a heart attack in late July and died of complications a week later. He was forty-seven years old. Marty Travis said everyone was shocked by Rick's death, but Pam framed it differently. "He lived large. You're always shocked when somebody passes away, but he left nothing on the table, let's just put it that way."

After Smith's death, his brother Randy stepped up to take over Smith Music Group and continue the *Live at Billy Bob's* albums. Continuing the Picnic was another question. "We really didn't know if we had the guts to continue [with the Picnic]," Pam said. "Because the passion was his, and running Billy Bob's is a full-time job. But his brother really kind of stepped up [to help the Picnics continue]."

Fans went to the seven Fort Worth Picnics by the thousands, and they continue to go to Billy Bob's by the thousands. Very few of them have ever heard of Rick Smith. Behind the scenes, however, his presence still looms large. "That dude was crazy," Marty said. "But he helped us get the stars, the sun, and moon all lined up together. And it worked."

2005: Fort Worth Stockyards

SITE: *In the "North Forty" field adjacent to Billy Bob's Texas in the Fort Worth Stockyards*
ATTENDANCE: *Estimated at 18,000*
HEADLINERS: *Willie Nelson, Ray Price, Bob Dylan, Doobie Brothers, Los Lonely Boys*

When Bob Dylan finally took the stage at Willie Nelson's Fourth of July Picnic, thirty-two years after his rumored appearance at the inaugural Picnic, the crowd seemed divided. Half of the eighteen thousand were hanging on every word, and half were just trying to figure out what those words were. Then he hit the chorus of "Like a Rolling Stone," and the floodlights came on at just the right spot, illuminating the floating dust to give the whole crowd a ghostly appearance as they sang along together.

It was a moment.

For fans of songwriting, it was a hell of an hour, watching Billy Joe Shaver and Bob Dylan perform back to back—a fascinating pendulum swing between two masters of the craft.

Performers will tell you that backstage at the Picnic was a remarkably democratic place, where the up-and-comers got the chance to mingle with the legends. But in 2005, it was Dylan's kingdom, at least for a little bit. "I'm sitting on Willie's bus, and they shut down the entire stage and backstage," Ray Benson said. "Performers that were outside or on the [north] side, they couldn't get back there, even though they had the right pass." Suddenly, the stage, which usually had its own crowd of one hundred or so people on it, was empty. Willie told Benson, "Let's go see Bob."

It was Willie's Picnic, after all. But even that had its limits. "They did tell him where to stand onstage," Benson said. "Bob's thing was he didn't want to see anybody." Robert Gallagher, who was managing the south stage, was quick to defend Dylan, saying it wasn't all that drastic—just the area between Dylan's bus and the stage was barricaded off for a little bit.

Gallagher said it would have been a mess otherwise. "[Think about] the backstage at Luckenbach or somewhere like that. My God, can you imagine Bob trying to walk one hundred feet through that? He'd have never made it to the stage."

2006: Fort Worth Stockyards

SITE: *In the "North Forty" field adjacent to Billy Bob's Texas in the Fort Worth Stockyards*
ATTENDANCE: *Estimated at 12,000*
HEADLINERS: *Willie Nelson, Kris Kristofferson, Nitty Gritty Dirt Band, Randy Rogers, Stoney LaRue*

Starting the Friday before the Tuesday Picnic, Carl's Corner hosted a series of "warm-up" shows that culminated in a July 3 concert featuring Willie, Nitty Gritty Dirt Band, Billy Joe Shaver, and others. Was it a Picnic? Well, technically it was more of a pre-Picnic party. But Joe Nick Patoski said the "flashback" crowd, the presence of Carl Cornelius, and the involvement of Willie's promoter friends gave it somewhat of an old-school Picnic feel. "The one at Carl's Corner was kind of duct taped and chaotic, in the spirit of those Picnics of yesteryear," he said. "But the vibe wasn't quite the same."

The next day, at the Picnic proper in Fort Worth, David Allan Coe made the most of his biggest starring role at the Picnic since the 1970s. Though he had often performed early at the Picnic, in 2006 Coe was awarded the slot just before Willie, giving him a lot of time and visibility. Coe opened with a rap song and ran through such covers as "Midnight Rider," "Purple Rain," "We're an American Band," and "Whipping Post."

A year earlier, Coe had released *Rebel Meets Rebel*, a country metal album recorded with members of heavy metal band Pantera. At the Picnic, Coe and his band were in full hard-core mode, and Coe was absolutely magnetic. Whether you loved him or hated him, it was hard to take your eyes off him.

Tyler Mahan Coe, who was in his father's band at the time, laughed when asked about the inspiration behind the performance. "I actually don't remember the show. Because I got so fucked up beforehand. I wasn't doing any crazy drugs or anything.... Ben [Dorcy, Willie's right-hand roadie] just came over with some of Willie's weed."

2007: Washington State

SITE: *The Gorge Amphitheatre, west of George, Washington*
ATTENDANCE: *Unreleased*
HEADLINERS: *Willie Nelson, Son Volt, Drive-By Truckers, Old 97s*

An agreement to play David Letterman's Montana ranch on July 3 led to this pseudo-Picnic. If any fans made the trek from Texas hoping to escape the heat, it didn't work out. Temperatures brushed one hundred degrees for the half-day show, which featured no traditional Picnic performers.

Texas media breathlessly and erroneously reported that this was the first time the Picnic had ever left Texas. *Texas Monthly* tried correcting everyone, pointing out the show in New Jersey in 1983 (but forgetting that year's Picnics in Syracuse and Atlanta). Nobody mentioned the 1977 show in Tulsa or the 1978 show in Kansas City.

2008: San Antonio (July 4) and Houston (July 5)

SITE: *Verizon Wireless Amphitheater, San Antonio; Sam Houston Race Park, Houston*
ATTENDANCE: *Unreleased*
HEADLINERS: *Willie Nelson, Merle Haggard, Ray Price, Pat Green, Los Lonely Boys*

The dying Verizon Wireless Amphitheater in Selma held a depressing Picnic, where a small rain shower soaked a smaller afternoon crowd and David Allan Coe, dressed in black, performed against a backdrop of black. You couldn't swing an overpriced T-shirt without hitting a vendor hawking overpriced beers.

Johnny Bush appeared to hold a grudge against his hometown, defiantly telling the crowd that they play traditional country music and sarcastically showing them what a fiddle looked like. The day's real highlight was Ray Price, fronting a fourteen-piece band and sounding fantastic at eighty-two. "I'm going to do a song I did so many years ago I don't tell anyone when I did it," he said.

The next day, the new Sam Houston Race Park in Houston also had early-afternoon rains but a more spirited atmosphere. Merle Haggard, despite a good show in San Antonio the night before, canceled his Houston performance, so Willie just extended his closing set. A review in the *Houston Chronicle* noted that Shaver and Coe were particularly interesting but reserved the highest praise for Price and Willie.

2009: South Bend, Indiana

SITE: *Coveleski Stadium, South Bend, Indiana*
ATTENDANCE: *8,500*
HEADLINERS: *Willie Nelson, Bob Dylan, John Mellencamp*

Bob Dylan, Willie, and John Mellencamp went on a tour of minor league baseball parks in July and August 2009. With July 4 falling on a Saturday, a stop at Coveleski Stadium was promoted as a "Fourth of July Picnic," and Willie took Dylan's closing spot for the night.

Reviews were favorable, and a crowd of eighty-five hundred packed the park (even at ticket prices starting at $68.50), but it was a Picnic in promotion only.

The ballpark tour was the first Willie had done in decades without longtime stage manager Poodie Locke, who had died in May. Locke was celebrated at a memorial concert at Tim's Porch at the Backyard in Bee Cave on June 28—an event that felt much more like a Picnic than the Indiana show did.

CHAPTER NINE

2010: The (New) Backyard

SITE: *13801 Bee Cave Parkway, off Texas 71, in Bee Cave, west of Austin*
ATTENDANCE: *7,500*
HEADLINERS: *Willie Nelson, Kris Kristofferson, Ray Price, Leon Russell, Asleep at the Wheel, David Allan Coe*

Picnic VIP Update

Willie Nelson: The seventy-seven-year-old Willie was enjoying the success of his only 2010 album, *Country Music*, which was praised by critics. By the end of the year, his image as a marijuana spokesman would take a hit when he was arrested for possession in Sierra Blanca, Texas.

Kris Kristofferson: By 2010, the seventy-four-year-old music legend was in the legacy award stage of his career and was a year removed from one of his last albums, *Closer to the Bone*. As an actor, he remained busy, appearing in three films that year.

Leon Russell: Not quite sixty-eight in January 2010, Leon was working with Elton John on their collaboration album, *The Union*, when he had brain surgery for a brain fluid leak and treatment for heart failure and pneumonia. Leon recovered and the album was a hit.

Ray Wylie Hubbard: At sixty-three years old, Ray had reached full philosopher-poet status and was busy playing shows wherever he could. In January 2010, he released the critically acclaimed album *A. Enlightenment B. Endarkenment (Hint: There Is No C)*.

It was near midnight and the crowd was still waiting for Willie. The venue had long since run out of food and cold drinks. People who had been there ten, eleven, twelve hours were confused and upset. In hindsight, was there a kind of disregard for the audience?

Tim O'Connor considered the question. "I will agree with that. Was it a conscious 'fuck them, this is what we're gonna do?' No. But [we were following] the formula 'Let it ride.'"

After seven years of tightly produced Fourth of July Picnics, including a couple of pseudo-Picnics out of state, those within the Willie circle were excited that the Picnic was back in the hands of one of their own. O'Connor had recently reopened the Backyard, a little bit west of the original location in Bee Cave. Even though the venue held only seventy-five hundred at most, it quickly became the site of the 2010 Picnic.

The "let it ride" philosophy hearkened back to the older Picnics. What fun is a party on a timetable? Wasn't confusion part of the experience? "A little chaos makes it feel like a real Picnic," lighting director Budrock Prewitt said.

And, sure, there were Willie fanatics and Picnic veterans who shrugged off the inconveniences as the unfinished venue failed to keep up with the capacity crowd. But by now, many Texas music fans no longer were interested in chaotic adventures. They would pay high prices and wait in long lines, but they required a little comfort and predictability in return.

A lot of them left the 2010 Picnic very unhappy.

It was a lowlight for a venue with such a storied history. Tim O'Connor explained his vision for the original Backyard in a 1993 interview with the *Austin American-Statesman*'s Don McLeese: "I didn't see the beer garden of the Armadillo being duplicated. I didn't see anyone taking advantage of the Hill Country. I started seeing Austin not having as many good venues any more." McLeese explained to readers that, in industry parlance, the Backyard was a "shed"—an open-air amphitheater on the outskirts of a city.

O'Connor, along with restaurateur and celebrity chef Jeff Blank, extensively renovated the old Branding Iron restaurant and grounds into a multidecked, oak-shaded venue with a capacity that eventually reached five thousand. The partnership between O'Connor and Blank eventually dissolved, with O'Connor noting that the shows he was booking didn't jibe with Blank's vision of "six-course meals."

The Backyard, at Texas 71 and RM 620, west of Austin, opened on May 7, 1993, with Willie Nelson and Family. O'Connor was gambling that his "shed" was going to work.

It did.

Over the next fifteen years, the Backyard hosted hundreds of different acts, ranging from Morrissey to Merle Haggard and Leonard Cohen to Coldplay. "I always loved the Backyard because the name itself says it all," Paula Nelson said. "It was like being in a giant backyard with great sound and amazing artists. And you always had trouble finding your car at the end of the night."

The Backyard was an escape from the city, until the city came to it. By 2008, the Shops at the Galleria were bumping up against the Backyard, taking away some charm, as well as valuable parking space. The politics of development didn't jibe with impresario Tim O'Connor, and he closed the venue in October 2008.

The original site reopened briefly in 2009 as Tim's Porch at the Backyard for several shows, but by then, O'Connor was committed to a full-fledged comeback. In 2010, construction was under way on a new Backyard, west of the original site on Bee Cave Parkway. An *American-Statesman* update on the venue in January of that year made the first mention of that year's Picnic.

But the politics were still a problem, to hear O'Connor tell it. He had difficulties working with the city to get power to the land. He had difficulties working out the parking situation and the sewer line. On top of that, he was facing some financial difficulties getting everything set up in time for ZZ Top to open the venue in April. He hadn't even been able to purchase his own stage, so he had to rent one. "I was paying over twenty thousand dollars a month for the stage," O'Connor said. "Whether I had a show or not."

By July, when Budrock Prewitt arrived to set up for the Picnic, he was a little underwhelmed by the venue. "It was all done with portable buildings and generators. Nothing was permanent."

The 2010 Picnic was everything Pauline Reese wanted, including reconnecting with old friend Waylon Payne and talking to the legendary Kris Kristofferson. "I remember that was a really fun Picnic; it was a blast. I think that was the first time I had a bus; that was really exciting for me." She said she had a great time—even if she couldn't party in the traditional way. "I remember getting on [Willie's] bus and giving him a big hug," she said. "And he looked down at my stomach. I said, 'Oh yeah, I'm eight months pregnant right now.'"

If you've ever thought a Picnic was hot, keep in mind you haven't danced onstage while eight months pregnant. Reese wore a purple bandana, "not to imitate Willie," she said; "it was functional."

For those artists within the Willie circle, the Backyard was a homecoming. While Fort Worth had its moments, the cabins backstage and the green grass and trees in front of the stage at the Backyard felt more like a traditional Picnic. And almost every performer in 2010 was within the Willie circle. No artist seemed out of place, with the possible exception of Jamey Johnson, who would solve that problem by playing eight of the next nine Picnics.

CHAPTER NINE \ 199

Pauline Reese was pregnant during the 2010 Picnic and remembered the experience as a great time despite the heat. Photo by Scott Moore / The Backyard

David Allan Coe felt the spirit. He spent most of the day onstage, joining a few artists here and there and also pointing out—live on Sirius XM radio—that he doesn't get a lot of radio airplay "because I say *motherfucker* a whole lot!"

Even with the Backyard's troubles, production manager Jack Yoder said the Picnic got off to a good start. "There were a lot of things to fix and a lot of things to change on the day of the show. It's kind of that way with any new venue. But overall, the experience was good."

Budrock Prewitt wasn't quite as chipper. "They put the lighting board right behind this tree. I had to look through this tree all day long, and it kinda irritated me."

In the crowd, the first hours of the Picnic were fine. Those who arrived early didn't have to fight the chaos that parking would become, just navigate the slightly muddy lot. Food stands were plentiful, selling pizza and barbecue sandwiches, and, in true Austin style, hibiscus mint Popsicles. In an inspired move, there were extra-large blue coolers on stilts (they looked like miniature water towers) called "water monsters." Anybody could buy a bottle of water, then go to the water monster and refill it for free throughout the show. Though the water inside the monsters warmed up over the course of the day, tepid water was still better than passing out.

Austin photographer Gary Miller had to shoot the show from the front of the crowd, navigating the politics and personal space of the superfans. "It was my first interaction with what I call 'Willie's ladies'—the group of women that go to just about all his shows. They're always sitting in the front, and if you're smart, you made nice with those ladies because they'd give you hell if you didn't."

Freddy Powers, the elderly songwriter giving his last Picnic performance, flattered the front-row fans—mostly. "Looking at all these pretty girls in front of the stage is like looking at a rose garden," he said. Freddy paused for the crowd to say "awwww." Then he delivered the punchline: "Every now and then, there's a weed or two."

"ANY SINGLE OPPORTUNITY that I have had to watch Ray Wylie Hubbard play, I will sit there and watch his entire set. Lucas was playing with him, and I feel like Lucas was starting to figure out what he was doing on guitar and having more fun with that." As a second-generation Picnic musician himself, it made sense Tyler Mahan Coe would have noticed Lucas Hubbard playing alongside his father at the 2010 Picnic.

Lucas was seventeen years old at the time and had ventured out for a song or two at earlier Picnics, but this time was different. "That was a very special one," Ray Wylie Hubbard said. "That was one of the first ones where he came out and just played the whole set with me. He had no fear. He just stood up there flat-footed and played the lead. I was really proud of him."

Tyler Mahan Coe also performed at the Picnics alongside his father at an even younger age. "Before I could even read, he had me singing in the show with him. Before I even started going to elementary school. Bobby Bare and Bobby Bare Jr. had a hit with that song 'Daddy, What If?' We'd do that song. It was always a big crowd pleaser."

Tyler returned to his father's side when he dropped out of school at fifteen to play in his dad's band. Just like Willie intended, he found the Picnic to be a reunion of sorts. But where Willie was reuniting with his friends, Tyler was reuniting with their musically inclined children.

"Willie's Picnics were always truly a family reunion, running into [friends like] Shooter Jennings," he said. "You'd get to spend some time

Willie Nelson performs at the 2010 Picnic at the Backyard. By the time this Picnic rolled around, Willie took great comfort in sharing the stage with his children. Photo by Scott Moore / The Backyard

with them, then you go off and play your show, and then when you're done, you go back to hanging out. That was really fun." Part of the reason it was special, Tyler said, is the shared experience. "It's a real natural camaraderie. You know this person understands things about what your life has been like that no one else could possibly understand."

In addition to Lucas, Tyler, and Shooter, other second-generation Picnic artists have included Noel Haggard, Waylon Payne (son of Sammi Smith and Willie guitarist Jody Payne), and Eddy Shaver.

And then there are Willie's children.

Paula Nelson started performing at the Picnics in 1995. Folk Uke (Amy Nelson and Cathy Guthrie) joined in 2006. Sons Lukas and Micah played the Picnic as part of the band 40 Points in 2008, though they had been onstage a few years earlier in Fort Worth. "We always considered [the Picnic] a nepotism show, and we're really grateful to have it," Amy Nelson said. "We do it because we're invited, and we would never turn it down."

Paula, Amy, Lukas, and Micah didn't all perform at the same Picnic until 2011, but Amy said anytime they can get together it's a truly special event. "Sometimes we'll watch each other's shows on the side of the stage," she said. "But usually it's pretty hectic for everybody. Everyone's got a different show schedule, so we're just running around trying to find each other. We're not always successful—it's just kind of who you run into is who you hang out with backstage."

"POODIE WAS ENGAGED TO A WOMAN, and they were at Hank Cochran's beach house with Willie. I forget where it was, the Bahamas or Belize or somewhere."

Pauline Reese is telling a story about longtime Willie stage manager Poodie Locke. "They went down to this beach house on their time off, and then Willie had a couple of shows. So Poodie was going to be gone for a couple of weeks, and he told his fiancée just to stay at the beach and enjoy her time."

She apparently did. While Poodie was on tour with Willie, his fiancée ended up getting married to Hank Cochran, and they went on a honey-

The 2010 Picnic was dedicated to Poodie Locke, who had served as stage manager for Willie Nelson since 1974. Photo by Rick Henson

moon in Poodie's car. Understandably furious, Poodie went looking for Hank at a later show.

"Hank was hiding out, and he thought, 'I'll just hop onstage, and then he can't do anything,'" Reese said. "Poodie comes out onstage, and he walks out there and just cold-cocks him. And then he says, 'There, we're even.'"

But Poodie wasn't quite satisfied. On the way off the stage, he grabbed Hank's 1976 Martin guitar. The guitar stayed in Poodie's closet for twenty years. One day, when Reese told Poodie she had recently sold her guitar to pay the rent, Poodie took Hank's guitar and gave it to her.

The 2010 Picnic was the first true Picnic since 1974 without Randall "Poodie" Locke, who had died the year before. "Not having his presence [at the Picnic] running the show, that was definitely a hard thing," Paula Nelson said. "I've known Poodie since I can remember remembering, so that was definitely a tough one."

Willie was always the star, but somehow the man who controlled the stage had his own spotlight. "He was just so beloved," Amy Nelson said. "He had more friends than anybody I've ever met. I think he genuinely loved people, so he was a great person to pair up with Dad, because he was very similar to Dad in that way."

Jack Yoder, who worked alongside Poodie for many years, said that Poodie "went out of his way to be your friend, sometimes so much he ticked off the people he traveled with. I'd get twenty passes, but somehow Poodie got one hundred people backstage."

Connie Nelson remembered that the backstage experience was wide open, especially in Austin. "From the early Picnics on, it was just a circus. We'd joke, were there more people backstage or out front? How do we know?"

But the circus didn't extend to onstage. Poodie kept tight control over that. "He wanted everybody to be happy and have a good time, but when his job came into play, you knew when that happened," Yoder said. "If you crossed the line, he had no problem letting you know."

At the 2010 Picnic, a wooden statue of Poodie watched over the Picnic from the side of the stage—it was a little bit larger than life, just like the man.

"THERE HAD BEEN SOME TEST RUNS and that kind of thing, but nothing stresses a well-laid plan like a Willie Nelson Picnic." Musician and radio host Dallas Wayne served as the emcee, and he understood the "let it ride" nature of the Picnic.

A capacity crowd of seventy-five hundred at the 2010 Picnic ended up being more than the new Backyard could handle. Photo by Dave Dalton Thomas

But by 5 p.m. things had gotten out of hand. The capacity crowd of seventy-five hundred was many more than the venue could support. In the parking lot, there was chaos. There were long lines to get in, and because of safety issues, Bee Cave authorities wouldn't let people park elsewhere and walk along Texas 71 to the venue. "It was ridiculous," photographer Gary Miller said. "It was one lane in, one lane out. It took quite some time to get in."

Inside, the venue was crowded and uncomfortable. The bathrooms became a muddy mess. And then the vendors ran completely out of food. Then the cold beer was gone, and vendors had to scramble to get more.

Budrock Prewitt, who remembers he had to drink Dos Equis because they ran out of Budweiser, said the Backyard didn't yet have a liquor license. "That was all farmed out [to vendors], and they just underestimated what they were going to do, and they weren't able to get restocked. It's a shame."

On top of everything, whatever schedule there might have been was completely shot. Tim O'Connor told the *Austin American-Statesman* that "there is no schedule. There is an internal process that we go through, but it is helter-skelter, in a good way." This didn't appear to be the day for helter-skelter. Fans who had appreciated the two-stage process in Fort Worth now waited in the steamy heat, thirsty and hungry as set changes stretched on.

Dallas Wayne said the changeovers do take time, especially in a new venue when the procedures aren't practiced. "The problem with a lot of musicians is that everybody's used to doing their show on tour all year long. So they want things just the way they normally have them. Sometimes you can't quite do that at a Picnic."

But Scott Moore, the longtime house photographer for the Backyard said there wasn't a sense of urgency backstage. "The Willie shows, there's just as much of a party in the backstage areas as there is in the front of the house. I think there wasn't any big hurry to get out there."

Wayne said the artists were truly insulated from the discomfort of the crowd. "As far as the crew and the bands, it's a busy time back there; you're getting ready for a show or doing media obligations or those kinds of things. As long as it was not right in front of you, you're not quite aware of what's going on until after the fact."

Pauline Reese said she did hear "something" about the venue's problems. "I kind of thought to myself that you know, if Tim's in charge of this deal, it'll get handled. You know, he's not going to let this thing fail."

It didn't get handled. Reflecting on it a decade later, O'Connor didn't hesitate to take responsibility but was in no mood to elaborate. "It got bad," was all he said.

It was apparent that part of the problem was that this was not a crowd looking to re-create the legendary adventures of the 1970s. These were parents who paid full price to bring their children, expecting a fun time on a holiday. These were older country music fans who wanted to see Willie in a comfortable environment. These were recent arrivals to Texas who didn't know about the Picnic's history. These were professionals who had to be at work early the next morning.

By late afternoon, these were unhappy people.

Then, at sundown, there was a moment of Zen. Kris Kristofferson's performance was an acoustic wonder, a legend still at the peak of his powers. The Austin audience loved Kristofferson, and he loved them in return. For a little bit, everything was beautiful. "What a gentleman he was," O'Connor said. "And his music, the lyrics, and the way he put things together . . . stunning."

Kris Kristofferson was a highlight of the 2010 Picnic, delivering a stunning acoustic performance. Photo by Scott Moore / The Backyard

"WILLIE AND I WOULD SIT DOWN and talk about lineups. And when it came to family, there were parts that we didn't agree on, but I know who wrote the checks, you know?" Jack Yoder watched the trouble unfold from the side of the stage. It was very near to midnight, and the crowd was ready for Willie. After Leon Russell's set ended about 11:30, Dallas Wayne announced to the crowd that Willie was "coming up next."

Then the Reflectacles came out. A large portion of the crowd had zero idea that the drummer for this young band was Micah Nelson. To them, it was just a half-dozen whip-thin hipster kids who were all not Willie. They played a handful of songs, brought out a fire-breather, and then introduced the crowd to Gail Swanson, whose gentle music didn't jibe with many in the crowd. Some actually heckled her. Not to say that there weren't people who enjoyed everything, but large portions of the crowd were decidedly unhappy.

Finally, Willie appeared onstage, joining the Reflectacles for "This Land Is Your Land," along with Kris Kristofferson, Ray Benson, and others. Fortunately, Willie took that right into "Whiskey River."

By then, it was the Fifth of July.

A decade later, the Reflectacles' 2010 moment wasn't something people who worked with Willie or were part of the Family were interested in talking about. Asked if there was a reaction to or recognition of any hostility toward Micah's band, Tim O'Connor shouldered the responsibility again and just said, "Yep. And that's all I'm gonna say."

Photographers Scott Moore and Gary Miller both said they didn't remember any trouble. Asked about the upset fans, Budrock Prewitt said "I think a better word would be 'impatient.'"

Gail Swanson said her memories of the show were all positive. "I didn't hear, feel, or see anything negative. I was so happy to be there and part of the [Nelson] Family music. The day was magic to us, and we all remember a great vibe!"

Dallas Wayne said he didn't recall. "Willie runs things the way he wants to run it. Preconceived notions from audience members can be a challenge."

The Reflectacles took the stage just before Willie Nelson at the 2010 Picnic. Given the venue's struggles over the latter half of the event and the late hour, some in the crowd weren't excited to see them. Photo by Scott Moore / The Backyard

And Amy Nelson was quick to defend her brother. "I was watching the Reflectacles play with Kris Kristofferson standing next to me, and he was so excited. I just remember him running up to Micah afterward and telling him how talented he is and how impressed he was by his drumming and that he was just super impressed with him and his band."

However, Jack Yoder, long retired, was more open about it. "Micah's band was a very eclectic group to be put on the Picnic that late in the day. [They] might have made more sense in the middle of the afternoon." Asked if being put in that spot wasn't fair to the Reflectacles, Yoder agreed. "Considering what was going on, it wasn't fair to anybody up there."

Paula Nelson was among those in Willie's circle who saw the 2010 Picnic in a positive light. "I'm sure there were challenges for the crowd, but I definitely know the music was always amazing. If the show's amazing, then it's easy to look past any of the other stuff that might have fallen short." And it's true a lot of Willie's friends had gotten together and rolled out some great music. Budrock Prewitt called it "close to a real Picnic."

It turns out, many music fans weren't interested in a real Picnic. Online comments poured in on the *Statesman*'s Picnic stories, reflecting fans who were upset at the venue and upset at not seeing Willie all day.

David Allan Coe performs at the 2010 Picnic at the Backyard. Photo by John Carrico

"Shame on the Backyard charging $50 a ticket and running some sort of third-world venue," wrote one.

"Some of Willie's 'people' need to explain to him that as he's gotten older, so have we. . . . He has to understand we don't have air-conditioned tour buses to sit in 'til it's showtime," wrote another.

Many said they wouldn't attend another Picnic.

"We didn't do a good job," Tim O'Connor said a decade later. "Put that on me, one hundred percent. It was my event. It was my facility."

O'Connor blamed himself for "piss poor planning" but said he wasn't in the best financial situation at the time and had to contract out to vendors who weren't experienced or prepared for an all-day festival. And he acknowledged that the onstage delays only exacerbated the problems. "The thing that troubles me about that Picnic is we had a pretty darn good crowd. But it did get out of hand on the stage."

Budrock said the venue could have been better, but he defended Tim. "He was under the gun all the way, especially with money problems. It's really a miracle that he pulled it off with generators and portable buildings."

The Backyard limped along, holding its last shows in 2014. O'Connor tried to reinvent his prized idea a couple more times, even partnering with mogul John Paul DeJoria. They envisioned a fifty-acre entertainment venue and planned development district, including a hotel and a luxury residential community. There was a groundbreaking ceremony for the project in June 2017, but the plan eventually fell apart. O'Connor blamed the city politics.

"One of the funny things about the Picnic was always figuring out who was and wasn't going to get paid that year." Tyler Mahan Coe said his father would go play the Picnic knowing that he wouldn't get paid what he could make on his own and might not get paid at all.

Ray Wylie Hubbard agreed, saying that up until 2015, he never had a contract. "I never knew what I was gonna get paid. We used to always go on that old bus, and they just kinda started counting out twenties and hundreds."

Hubbard said he would get eleven hundred dollars one year, eighteen hundred dollars the next. "It didn't matter; we weren't doing it for the money. We're doing it because of the hang. Because it was such a very special, cool thing."

Budrock said that, whenever possible, Willie was generous with his friends, paying them first. "Willie paid everybody, but there was never enough for him. Willie said we'll let somebody else do it from now on because he'd like to get paid."

The 2010 Picnic started at noon on July 4, but Willie Nelson wasn't seen onstage until after midnight. Photo by John Carrico

And that was the end of the "let it ride" Picnics. From 2011 on, the Picnic would be a tightly run, highly organized event. "That was kind of the end of that era," Paula Nelson said. "It became more of a business rather than a show, I guess."

Paula grew up seeing the "balls-out crazy" Picnics of the 1970s and was sad to see it become more corporate, especially during its five-year run at the Austin360 Amphitheater, starting in 2015. But she understood that the crowd had moved on. "People expect, 'I paid a lot of money for these tickets, so I want a good parking spot' or whatever. I understand that, if you're paying to see a great show, you want the experience to be great." The important thing, she said, was that the music had to be good. "Times change and the size of the city changes and other things are going to change with it. But there's always been great music, and that definitely hasn't changed."

"THE LAST TIME I SAW POODIE was when Willie had the theater and the radio station up there at the truck stop at Carl's Corner. And a bunch of us are sitting around, Willie included." Dallas Wayne is describing the scene. Fellow radio DJ Bill Mack was there. As well as Ray Price and Poodie. It's early May 2009, and the older men were feeling their years.

"All of us are sitting there talking about how old we're getting and what medications we're taking and that kind of thing," Wayne said. "And it was time for Poodie to go to work, so he got up and said, 'Piss on you guys; I ain't been sick a day in my life.' Three days later, he was dead."

Poodie Locke was one of those guys who could embrace the chaos but still maintain control. He gave 100 percent, until it was suddenly over. He died May 6, 2009, of a suspected heart attack. He was fifty-six years old and had been working with Willie for thirty-four years. "He was one of these larger-than-life people that A, seem to come out of Texas, and B, seem to be drawn to the Willie Nelson camp," Wayne said. "These guys have given their childbearing years to support this idea and this dream that they all share."

2011–2012: Fort Worth Stockyards

SITE: *Inside Billy Bob's Texas and in the adjacent outdoor plaza in the Fort Worth Stockyards*
ATTENDANCE: *6,000 in 2011 and 4,000 in 2012*
HEADLINERS: *Willie Nelson, Jamey Johnson, Randy Rogers, Wade Bowen, Asleep at the Wheel, Ray Price (2011), Stoney LaRue (2012), Randy Houser (2011), Whispering Bill Anderson (2012)*

Willie had joined the Country Throwdown Tour in 2011 and brought it to Fort Worth on July 4, adding some traditional performers to make for a small Picnic. Billy Bob's set up a stage in the plaza outside, and the main stage was inside the air-conditioned honky-tonk.

After the drama of 2010, there were few problems of note. Micah Nelson's Reflectacles played at 4 p.m. to an appreciative crowd, Lukas Nelson jammed an hour later, and the whole event ran like clockwork.

With the indoor stage, the Picnic was not in the survival struggle it often was, and the music benefited from it, most notably Ray Price. This would be the legend's final Picnic, and his slow shuffle toward the microphone drew murmurs of concern. But he delivered the hits and the history, and the crowd loved him for it.

Jamey Johnson made the leap to Picnic headliner in his second year, and the advertised "surprise guest performance" in the spot just before Willie turned out to be an acoustic show from Randy Rogers and Wade

Bowen—cleverly keeping the audience entertained during the set change.

In 2012, the Picnic looked as if it were done. It had the same indoor-outdoor setup as 2011, and even during the heat of the afternoon, an actual seat in the shade was there for the taking in the plaza. There was no hiding that this was a small Picnic without a lot of star power.

That said, the event ran smoothly, and Willie sounded fantastic during his ninety-minute closing set. Earlier, during an interview on his bus, Willie said the days of the big outdoor Picnics might be over. "The thing about those is that they're expensive to put together. Especially when you have 'em out in somebody's pasture. It was a great idea forty years ago, but I think people now are accustomed to their comforts."

2013–2014: Fort Worth Stockyards

SITE: *In the "North Forty" field adjacent to Billy Bob's Texas in the Fort Worth Stockyards*
ATTENDANCE: *10,000 in 2013 and 12,000 in 2014*
HEADLINERS: *Willie Nelson, Ryan Bingham, Jamey Johnson, Gary Allan (2013), Kris Kristofferson (2013), Justin Moore (2013), Dierks Bentley (2014), Josh Abbott (2014), Charley Pride (2014)*

Billy Bob's tried to hit the sweet spot for the Picnic's fortieth anniversary, bringing the show back to the North Forty field, with north and south stages, but still hosting a few acts indoors. Picnickers faced a few interesting choices such as seeing David Allan Coe inside or Leon Russell outside.

The historical side of the Picnic was starting to see a little age and illness. Ray Price had to cancel his appearance, and Kris Kristofferson struggled to remember the words to his songs. But the Picnic's eighty-year-old host seemed to get stronger as his set progressed. For his part, Leon limped out to his keyboard in a white hat and white coat, and sparks flew during his powerful twenty-five-minute set.

By now, Billy Bob's required some more modern acts to sell tickets, and 2013 featured Gary Allan, Justin Moore, and Ryan Bingham. Of the three, Bingham definitely fit the traditional Picnic vibe, while Moore's theatrics and nonstop banter seemed comically out of place.

There was conjecture Willie was going to call it quits after forty years, and it felt like a positive end with many of the Picnic's traditional cadre doing their most traditional Picnic songs. But Willie wasn't interested in retirement or beholden to big round numbers. The Picnic returned to the Stockyards in 2014 to start its next decade.

The 2014 show leaned heavily on the star power of Dierks Bentley, who brought the fans in and whipped 'em into a frenzy during his action-packed seventy-five minutes. Analytically, he was just as out of place as Justin Moore, but his natural charisma and high energy made it hard not to like him.

Johnny Bush and Ray Wylie Hubbard did a lot of the heavy lifting during the afternoon, and Bingham was just as great during his second Picnic performance.

It's always special when the Picnic brings in a legendary artist for a first-time Picnic show, and Charley Pride made the most of his. He worked the stage, mike in one hand and white towel in the other, to mop the sweat from his head, never missing a note while he did so. The crowd loved hits like "Is Anybody Going to San Antone," "Kiss an Angel Good Mornin'," and "Kaw-Liga."

Willie was as cool as John Lee Hooker during his closing set, with seventy-five minutes of old hits and new songs. He brought everybody out to sing along in his finale, including his new "gospel" hit "Roll Me Up and Smoke Me When I Die."

During the course of seven Picnics in Fort Worth, Billy Bob's and Smith Music Group created something special—a fan-friendly Fourth of July Picnic. From 2015 on, there would be great music and lots of VIP options. But this would be the last truly comfortable Picnic for the average fan.

CHAPTER TEN

2015: Austin360 Amphitheater, Circuit of the Americas

SITE: *Within the F1 racetrack in Del Valle, east of Austin*
ATTENDANCE: *More than 14,000*
HEADLINERS: *Willie Nelson, Eric Church, Merle Haggard, Kacey Musgraves, Jamey Johnson, Jason Isbell, Sturgill Simpson, Chris Stapleton, Kris Kristofferson*

Picnic VIP Update
Willie Nelson: Now eighty-two years old, Willie had hardly slowed down. Following legalization of marijuana in several states, he established his own marijuana brand, "Willie's Reserve," and his collaboration with Merle Haggard, "Django & Jimmie," hit number one on the country charts.
Merle Haggard: "Django & Jimmie" was the last big splash for Merle, who also released his last solo album in June 2015 to lesser acclaim. At seventy-eight, he had faced several health scares but still performed as often as possible.
Jamey Johnson: When Jamey first played the Picnic in 2010, he was in the midst of much celebration for his songwriting. By 2015, the thirty-nine-year-old was struggling to write new music but was an important regular performer at the Picnic.
Billy Joe Shaver: The seventy-five-year-old was a year removed from the release of his last album, *Long in the Tooth*, but Billy Joe remained a vital performer and played dates from coast to coast. Shortly after the Picnic, he was slowed by hip-replacement surgery.

In 1973, the Picnic got off to a chaotic start on a rocky ranch west of Austin. Forty-two years later, it was still going, now in an amphitheater nestled within a four-hundred-million-dollar Formula One racetrack east of Austin. "That tells the story of Austin," author Joe Nick Patoski said, "and Austin's evolution during that period of time going from funky and cheap and earthy to sleek and shiny and international . . . everything got scaled up."

Patoski pointed out that when the Picnic started, the entertainment scene in Austin was a club scene, where a few hundred people could get together. Now, when people talk about Austin, he said, they're talking about South by Southwest or the ACL Festival, which attract people by the tens of thousands.

Fellow writer John T. Davis agreed that, for better or worse, the evolution of the Picnic mirrored the evolution of Austin. "In '73, this was a funky little college town. It had the university and the state legislature and an Air Force base, and that's about all it had going for it. Now you look at it and what it has transformed into, including Elon Musk and Google and everybody else."

Evolution. The first Picnic and the last Picnics were separated by more than forty-something years and forty-something miles. The whole mindset changed. Now you could just as soon find cheap rent in Austin as you could find the freewheeling feeling of the early 1970s.

"I think that those early Picnics basically planted a flag like no one else," Patoski said. "But the spirit of the early Picnics faded away by the

The Austin360 Amphitheater sits within the Circuit of the Americas F1 racetrack. The four-hundred-million-dollar facility was a far piece from the rocky field in Dripping Springs. Photo by Dave Dalton Thomas

early '80s. What's continued since is the franchise, the Picnic, the idea of Willie and his friends getting together for a big old show."

Musician and DJ Dallas Wayne said the evolution was necessary. "You gotta contain the comet to keep it burning. If it hadn't changed, I don't think it would have survived."

When the Picnic was announced on March 30, *Austin American-Statesman* music writer Peter Blackstock was taken aback by the lineup: "When I look back now at that one, that one was really impressive. They got just like a murderer's row of the best artists that they could get in that Americana realm." Of the twenty artists on the schedule, there were some traditional Picnic heavy hitters: Merle Haggard, Kris Kristofferson, and Jamey Johnson. And there was the now-expected nontraditional artist in the slot before Willie, Eric Church.

But the Picnic also featured Kacey Musgraves, Sturgill Simpson, Jason Isbell, and Chris Stapleton. "In future Picnics at the Circuit of the Americas, it would be like they would want one of those four," Blackstock said. "It's amazing they had all four." One of the reasons the lineup might have been so strong is that many of the artists were also part of a July 6 tribute to Waylon Jennings in Austin. The concert taping at ACL Live was later televised and released on DVD.

The Picnic would be split between the main stage in the amphitheater and a secondary "Grand Plaza" stage on a grassy lawn. Instead of the back-and-forth used so effectively in Fort Worth, the plaza stage would host the early acts, and the main stage would host the headliners—with a little bit of alternating in the late afternoon.

Tickets ranged from thirty-five to seventy-five dollars, with a range of VIP packages available for much more.

Dallas Wayne loved the lineup, noting that it takes a strong cast to get people to come out to the Picnic during the heat of the day instead of arriving late for the headliners.

Jack Yoder, a longtime production manager for Willie, said Willie still had relative autonomy on who showed up but understood the need to book and organize the Picnic in a way that would drive ticket sales. "At a four-hundred-million-dollar racetrack, he couldn't just have Billy Joe Shaver as a headliner. You had to go for some ticket buyers. I can only imagine what the overhead is before you even open the front gate."

"MY WILD GUESS IS WILLIE probably never made a dime on any Picnic until they moved to Circuit of Americas." Longtime Willie friend

Turk Pipkin knew that it was Willie's instinct to take however much the Picnic made and generously pay his friends . . . until there was little left for him.

Jack Yoder said it was about respect. "Willie had a lot of respect for the people he invited. Leon Russell is one of his idols. He paid him good money because he had respect for him."

But by 2015, Yoder said, Willie was clearly tired of writing the checks. This is where Live Nation/C3 Presents comes in.

National concert behemoth Live Nation had purchased a controlling interest in Austin's C3 Presents just the year before. It might have seemed odd to have this enormous corporation producing the 2015 Picnic, but there was actually a connection to the event on both sides.

Live Nation's roots go back to when New York entrepreneur Robert Sillerman created SFX Entertainment in 1997. He would quickly begin buying up independent promoters, including Fey Concerts (which produced the 1977 Tulsa Picnic and the 1978 Kansas City Picnic) and Pace Concerts (which produced the 1978 Texxas Jam and the 1984 and 1985 Picnics).

In 2000, Sillerman sold to Clear Channel Communications in a $4.4 billion deal, and five years later the radio giant would name its concert division Live Nation (which produced the 2007 and 2008 Picnics).

On the other side, C3 Presents was formed when Austinites Charlie Jones and Charles Attal joined their talents with Charlie Walker in 2007. Attal was a cofounder of the Stubb's music venue in downtown Austin and had produced Willie shows there. Walker began his career by working for Pace Concerts in 1994. When Pace Concerts and Direct Events started partnering on events, Walker began working out of an office at Tim O'Connor's Backyard.

Jones's connection to Tim, Willie, and the Picnic is much deeper. A student at Austin Community College, Jones had begun working for Direct Events as an intern for Tim's then-wife Allison Eklund at the Backyard in 1993. Jones did the ground-floor work of answering phones, serving as a runner, bartending, or whatever else was needed. Within a year, Tim offered Jones a full-time job. Jones quit school and entered what he called "the school of hard knocks in the music business working for Tim O'Connor."

Tim was a father figure of sorts and taught Jones a lot. However, getting involved in the resurgence of the Fourth of July Picnic in 1995 was particularly eye-opening and inspiring. "Tim took me up to Pedernales Studio and we sat on Willie's bus. And I watched him and Willie go through a long list of bands and decide offers and payments and who was going to play at what time, and I just took notes as fast as I could. I was very thankful for that moment in my life because it was the first festival that I was allowed to work on, which I didn't know at the time was going to steer my career."

Getting involved in the 1995 Picnic offered another opportunity to Jones. His father had attended the 1974 Picnic at the Texas World Speedway, and Jones had grown up hearing stories about how great it was. Willie was a hero to both men, and Jones saw a chance to repair a rift in their relationship.

"When I made the decision to go to work full time for Tim and not finish college, I think it upset my dad," Jones said. "When I invited my dad to [the 1995 Picnic] and had him watch it from behind the scenes and watch me work, he changed his look on my decisions and supported me from that point on."

Jones struck out on his own in 1998, though he remained close with Tim. In 2001, Jones joined forces with Attal to create Capital Sports and Entertainment, and the now-huge Austin City Limits festival would follow in 2002.

Walker had worked his way up through SFX and Live Nation after the acquisition of Pace. Leaving the corporate giant to come back to Austin in 2007 was considered a surprising move. But C3 Presents became a major industry player up through, and beyond, Live Nation acquiring a 51 percent interest for a reported $125 million in 2014.

Having Live Nation/C3 Presents promoting the Picnic would mean that the artists, including Willie, would get paid based on contracts and not Willie's people handing out cash on the bus. But it also meant a corporate clamp-down on the traditionally chaotic backstage scene. "Back in the day in the '70s, the stage had as many people on it as weight would allow," Ray Benson said. "Everybody was backstage who knew *somebody*."

Not everyone missed the chaos.

Dallas Wayne, who would broadcast live from the Picnic on Willie's Roadhouse on Sirius XM, stopped by the site a few days before July 4 and was impressed by the organization and efficiency. "From a broadcasting standpoint, you got a lot of issues that you need to get answered. Where are you getting your feeds from? Are we going to have monitors so we can actually see what's going on onstage without having to look through fifty people's butts? It was as civilized as you could make it."

"I REMEMBER BEING A KID, probably twelve years old, being there and being like 'I want to sing on stage at the Picnic.' So in 2015 when I finally got to do that, I was really nervous." Raelyn Nelson, Willie's granddaughter, said the Picnic had always been *the* big event and remembers

Raelyn Nelson, Willie's granddaughter, was excited to play her first Picnic after growing up watching them. She would continue to be a regular Picnic performer over the next four years. Photo by Gary Miller

watching her family members performing in Luckenbach and at later Picnics. When she was finally invited to perform in 2015, she was in her early thirties and more than ready to put a checkmark next to her long-time dream. "The Picnic was even more special to me just because I'd seen everyone do it my whole life," she said. "I was just on this super-elated high that day. I wanted to play insane onstage."

One of the things that was remarkable to Raelyn about the Picnic was the dedication of the fans. "There's always this massive crowd that comes even though it's so hot. They're just like uber-fans of my grandpa. It's a different experience than just any Papa Willie show."

Picnickers streamed into the Circuit of the Americas on July 4, 2015, riding in pedicabs from the free-but-remote parking lots and pausing to stand at attention during the national anthem. The Austin360 Amphitheater had been hosting shows for a couple years, but for many in the crowd—and onstage—it was the first time they had seen the site. "It seemed like an odd place for it," remembered Frank Mull, manager for Merle Haggard. "Seemed like we were kind of out there in the middle of nowhere getting to that place."

Cleve Hattersley and his band Greezy Wheels were returning to the Picnic for the first time in four decades after playing the first two. Hattersley was awed by how commercialization had "filled in the blanks" at the event: "The first few of those we did, you had trouble finding water. And now it's kind of like the Texas State Fair." That said, he detested the setting. "We hated the racetrack."

Other performers and guests kept the focus on the efficiency of the new site. "It was different than a lot of the Willie Picnics, you know, because a lot of 'em were, that old thing, 'the mud, the blood and the beer,'" Ray Wylie Hubbard said. "This was real efficient and real smooth."

Turk Pipkin said that once the racetrack started hosting the Picnic, he could no longer jokingly refer to it as "Willie's Fifth of July Picnic" because things stayed on schedule and Willie no longer hit the stage after midnight.

Yet the racetrack setting put a new spin on the Picnic's primary complaint. "It was, as it always is, hot as hell," Peter Blackstock said. "There was some physical discomfort involved."

The high temperature that day at the nearby Austin-Bergstrom airport was ninety-one degrees, but in the concrete bowl in front of the main stage, it was really cooking. "It was just damn hot," said photographer Gary Miller, who wondered why the amphitheater never built an awning over the seating area. In forty years of photographing shows, Miller said he's never fallen out but said that amphitheater staff helped keep everyone safe. "They watch out for people. If someone's looking a little woozy like they might fall out, the staff are keeping an eye on everybody."

With the exception of a grassy area in front of the secondary stage, everything was covered in concrete, something Amy Nelson couldn't quite accept. "I realized by the next day that it was not a smart idea to wear thin shoes, because the ground cooks [your feet]. It's kind of like a wok. I never got used to the fact that there was no way to be comfortable there. There was no nature; there was no shade. I just felt like those years were brutal."

Even though Folk Uke, the band Amy leads along with Cathy Guthrie, usually played early in the day, Amy said if she were going to a festival as a fan, she would probably show up late. "By the time [Willie's] bus would be pulling in, I would be limping. I don't know how people in the audience do it. How does anyone survive that day?"

Raelyn Nelson wasn't going to waste Grandpa's party. She took part in whatever fun she could find, even during the heat of the day. "They take the artists around in golf carts, so I talked one of the drivers into driving through the racetrack, but the golf cart made it maybe like fifty percent up

Ray Wylie Hubbard said the 2015 Picnic was the first one where he had a contract to play. Prior to that, he played for whatever money Willie's people handed him after the show. Photo by Gary Miller

the [first] hill and then it just started rolling back down. I had to change clothes five or six times that day because you just sweat through everything. The little trees they planted [at the racetrack] are so tiny, and there's no shade."

At just past 12:30, she took the stage, performing in between aunts Amy Nelson and Paula Nelson. Included in her set were Loretta Lynn and Joan Jett Covers. "[The fans] would embrace anything I did," she said. "I think if I came out there rapping, they would be okay with it."

Raelyn, raised on old country and gospel music, discovered Joan Jett, the Runaways, and Chrissie Hynde later in her twenties. "These powerful women paved the way in rock for us. And country elements have a rock to them; my grandpa's music has some rock elements to it. . . . Being able to combine those genres together, I feel like my band brings the rock for sure."

By the middle of the afternoon, there was little time to rest. There was a strong smell of marijuana around the front of the crowd during David Allan Coe's short set at 1:45. Greezy Wheels made their return to the Picnic after forty-one years at 2:45. And at 3:45, when Kris Kristofferson opened up the main stage, fans baked in the concrete heat to pay tribute to the icon.

One of the day's more compelling moments came when Sturgill Simpson played the main stage at 5:45. Simpson was still riding high on his compelling 2014 album *Metamodern Sounds in Country Music*, and when he performed at the Picnic, Kristofferson spent the entire show watching him from the side of the stage.

It wasn't a passing of the torch or anything like that, but it was surely a benediction of sorts.

"IT WAS JUST CRAZY. We would have parking lot parties and hang out in the parking lot. Because we can't get into the show." For all the talk about how the Willie Picnic experience changed, the most obvious

Ray Benson performs at the 2015 Picnic at Austin360 Amphitheater. Photo by Gary Miller

example was backstage. Amy Nelson explained that the artist credentials for the secondary stage did not apply to the main stage area.

If this seems particularly against the grain of the Picnic's spirit, it's because nearly everyone who played the secondary stage were old friends—Leon Russell, Johnny Bush, everyone who went by three names, and so on—or literal family.

Ray Benson, whose band Asleep at the Wheel played the secondary stage, says the setup would have limited him as well, except for the fact that he was pulling double duty and playing guitar with Willie at the end of the night. "It was all bifurcated. But playing for Willie, I could go anywhere."

For Raelyn, having to negotiate her way backstage at her grandfather's Picnic was upsetting. Recalling trying to get through the gate with her aunt Amy, she said the guard asked who they were. "[Amy] goes, 'I'm Willie's daughter.' And the guy goes, 'How many daughters does Willie have?' Amy's like, 'He's got a *lot* of daughters.' And it's true; all of us were there. It's kind of our family reunion. That was when we got to see each other and come together at the Papa Willie show portion. We're all gonna sing the gospel stuff together [at the end of Willie's show], and then we couldn't even get in?"

"MERLE WAS LATE, so we grabbed Jamey Johnson and Bobby Bare, who were two people I knew could sit down and at least fill twenty minutes or so with entertainment for people."

Dallas Wayne is telling a story about the 2015 Picnic's one big hiccup: Merle Haggard was late to the stage. Wayne, who had performed earlier in the day, was broadcasting live on Sirius XM and needed something to air. "We held them there, and we held them there, and we held them there, waiting for Merle. And finally, it looked like things were getting ready to go onstage."

Wayne thanked Johnson, who had finished his set not too long before, and Bare, who didn't perform that day but was good friends with Haggard. "Guys, we will let you go," Wayne told them. "You've been so gracious being with us for this amount of time. The last thing I hear Bobby Bare say as he's walking away with Jamey . . . he said, 'Let's go find Merle and kick his ass.'"

The delay lasted most of an hour. Wayne said he heard it was just because Haggard and Willie were on the bus visiting.

Being a legend has its benefits: Live Nation/C3 Presents can limit backstage access and run the show like clockwork, but who is going to

Merle Haggard performed at his last Picnic in 2015. Willie Nelson joined him onstage for a few songs, including "Pancho and Lefty" and "It's All Going to Pot." Photo by Gary Miller

be the one to tell Merle Haggard and Willie Nelson to break it up? "I don't know that it would do any good," Wayne said. "Because if they're having a great time . . . you know, they'll get there eventually."

Willie came out onstage to join Haggard during his set, a combined 160 years of country music history. Much to the crowd's delight, they kicked things off with "Pancho and Lefty," though it's notable that Willie sang the whole song instead of Haggard taking the last verse.

In what would be his last Picnic, Haggard appeared gaunt and a little stiff at first but loosened up a bit when he and Willie traded verses on "It's All Going to Pot."

Asked if Haggard enjoyed the Picnic, Manager Frank Mull said even if he didn't, Merle would have done it for Willie. "Merle rarely didn't give it all he had. But he would have tried harder on anything for Willie. They were extremely tight for an extreme amount of years. They had extreme loyalty to each other."

The audience wasn't alone in feeling that seeing the two together was a hell of a moment. Wayne compared it to Pete Seeger making a surprise appearance at Farm Aid in 2013, months before his death at the age of ninety-four. "Pete Seeger comes out onstage. And here's Willie, and here's Mellencamp, and here's Neil Young. Everybody wanted to see this because they knew it was going to be something special. And I think the same thing happened with [Merle at] the Picnic."

Willie *did* come out on the Fifth of July, thanks to the Merle Haggard delay, and took a relaxed, bluesy run through his decades of hits. The crowd thinned out a bit after his first few songs. Many of the all-day picnickers who impressed Amy Nelson so much—sunburned, glassy-eyed, and limping themselves—were clearly thinking, "Okay, we've seen Willie; let's go home."

Those who stayed until the 1:25 a.m. finale got to see the all-star gospel sing-along that ends these shows. All the performers who hadn't gone home themselves joined Willie onstage for "I'll Fly Away," "Roll Me Up and Smoke Me When I Die," and "I Saw the Light." Among those backup singers were Jamey Johnson, Eric Church, Pauline Reese, Kris Kristofferson, and Raelyn Nelson.

She made it.

"THAT'S WHY YOU WENT EARLY ON; you didn't know what the fuck was going to happen. And now it's climate-controlled. It's the difference between going to Woodstock and going to Coachella." Joe Nick Patoski

Willie Nelson and Family perform at the 2015 Picnic at Austin360 Amphitheater. Photo by Gary Miller

was there at the early Picnics and wasn't impressed by the final stage in its evolution. It wasn't just the relative placidity of the crowd but the predictability of the show. "No one's gonna improvise. They got every data point figured out. That's the modern world of the concert business."

Returning to the contrast between the first Picnic on the rocky ranch and its run at the racetrack, others long involved in the Picnics kind of shrugged and let it go.

Amy Nelson, who felt the Picnic lost something when the "human-to-tree ratio went all askew," thought about the evolution and said, "Well . . . if that's what success is."

Ray Wylie Hubbard took the same tack: "It's progress, I suppose."

But Peter Blackstock said the change was inevitable and that anything that was as long-lived and successful as the Picnic was bound to change over time. "I think they did about as good as they could and did it pretty well in the way they set things up. It's a credit to the Picnic's survival and continued relevancy that it was able to be that big of a deal in 2015."

As far back as 1995, journalists at the Picnics would climb into Willie's bus and ask, "How long are you going to keep doing this?" Willie's answer was usually some variation of "as long as it's still fun."

But the question missed the point. The end of the Picnic was not about Willie and his friends taking one last bow on stage together. Instead, it was a process. The Picnic's five-year run at the Circuit of the Americas' Austin360 Amphitheater served as that long good-bye to the old days.

Sure, Waylon, who had mostly stayed away from the Picnics since the early '80s before his 1996 appearance in Luckenbach, had died in 2002. And Ray Price died in 2013 during the Picnic's run in Fort Worth.

But the loss of Merle Haggard and Leon Russell—both died in 2016 and both played their last Picnic in 2015—really signified that the final years had come for the Picnic. "I knew that Merle was not gonna last forever, but I didn't know that it was gonna be that soon," Ray Benson said.

Kris Kristofferson performed his last Picnic in 2016 and retired from performing in 2020. Sammy Allred, the force behind the Geezinslaws, died in 2018, having last performed at the Picnic in 2010. Johnny Bush and Billy Joe Shaver performed at the last racetrack Picnic in 2019, and both died within a month of each other in 2020.

Given that Willie considered the Picnic to be a reunion for his friends and family, could it be that the loss of those friends diminished Willie's enthusiasm for the tradition? "Could be, could be," Dallas Wayne said. "Time will tell on that. I know the loss of people like Johnny Bush and Ray Price, that hit him very hard. Paul English passing hurt him a lot. . . . Leon Russell, losing him was a big blow."

Amy Nelson seemed surprised by the question. "Maybe so. When [Willie's] done with something, he's just done; he says, 'It's time.' But that might have had something to do with it."

Others aren't so sure. Turk Pipkin agrees that Willie, like everyone, is hit hard by losing friends, but "he's also really good at saying, 'Okay, now what's today going to bring?" "It's amazing how many friends the guy has. How many he's lost is incalculable, but nothing I think that Willie likes to talk about because he's living in the moment."

John T. Davis said Willie's love of showcasing younger talent—he mentions Margo Price, Kacey Musgraves, and Ryan Bingham—would keep him going. "Even though people like Ray Price and Ernest Tubb and those guys slipped away, I think he perpetuated a musical family with his own kids and with these other younger performers, who he sort of helped mentor and showcase on the Picnics."

"ONCE THE WILLIE PHENOMENA started, we were right there at the very D-Day. So we were always a part of it. And we always knew what was going to happen. It never surprised us." D-Day in Austin for Cleve Hattersley was that August 12, 1972, show at the Armadillo World Headquarters where Willie Nelson brought together the hippies and the rednecks.

The Armadillo was hedging its bets on Willie—Greezy Wheels were on the bill because they could bring in a sold-out crowd on their own. By the end of the night, nobody had any doubts about Willie. Hattersley said the convergence was real. He remembered being a long-haired hippie and fearing for his life when a truck full of rednecks pulled up next to him at a stoplight.

Willie's approach to music, combining the hip aspects of Nashville with the hippie scene in Austin created a whole new dialogue. "Rednecks talked to hippies and hippies talked to rednecks, beer drinkers smoked pot and pot smokers drank beer," he said. "And although the world still has all kinds of issues . . . that changed it."

The resulting dialogue changed more than interactions between young men on street corners, he said. Hattersley, who had just moved to Las Cruces, New Mexico, in 2022, said he was designing a college course for New Mexico State about the effect of music on politics and politics on music. He subtitled the course "Did Willie Change World Politics?" For him, the answer is clear: "Something about Willie being in Austin changed everything. And bless him for it."

2016–2017: Austin360 Amphitheater, Circuit of the Americas

SITE: *Within the F1 racetrack in Del Valle, east of Austin*
ATTENDANCE: *Unreleased*
HEADLINERS: *Willie Nelson, Jamey Johnson, Brantley Gilbert (2016), Alison Krauss (2016), Shakey Graves (2016), Kris Kristofferson (2016), Sheryl Crow (2017), Kacey Musgraves (2017), Turnpike Troubadours (2017), Steve Earle (2017)*

The Picnic settle in comfortably in its second year at the amphitheater, notable for the Picnic debut of Margo Price, the struggling-but-soulful Picnic finale of Kris Kristofferson, the realization that the combination of Jamey Johnson and Alison Krauss was fantastic, and the comically out-of-place preening and flexing by Brantley Gilbert.

Kristofferson, one of the Picnic's three octogenarians (along with Willie and Johnny Bush), played solo acoustic in the heat of the day. He fought with his harmonica and his memory but was embraced by the Austin fans, who gave him a standing ovation.

Gilbert took the stage to smoke machines and helicopter sound effects. He grabbed the brass knuckles on his microphone and tried to let everyone within earshot know just how tough he was, as if everyone there hadn't seen Billy Joe Shaver just a few hours ago.

The following year was the biggest year for women at the Picnic since 2000, with Margo Price and Kacey Musgraves as headliners and Sheryl Crow taking the ringer spot ahead of Willie. Crow definitely took to the Picnic quickly, welcoming a rare Willie appearance onstage for a cover of "Midnight Rider." At the end of the night, she could be seen with a beer bottle in hand, singing with Steve Earle and Margo Price during the Willie gospel finale.

It was Steve Earle's first Picnic, and the day took a talk-show turn when Hayes Carll—who was with Earle's ex-wife Allison Moorer—debuted a song with the lyrics "I think she left you because you wouldn't shut your mouth." There was some speculation that Earle might retaliate onstage. Instead, he did one better by completely blowing away Carll's set, and pretty much everyone else's.

Both years Willie was absolutely timeless—as worn as his guitar Trigger, yet as eternal as the songs he played. Each year, he seemed a little reluctant to leave the stage. In 2016 he decided to play a few more songs after the gospel finale; the next year he turned around while walking off and came back to wave to the crowd.

2018: Austin360 Amphitheater, Circuit of the Americas

SITE: *Within the F1 racetrack in Del Valle, east of Austin*
ATTENDANCE: *Unreleased*
HEADLINERS: *Willie Nelson, Sturgill Simpson, the Head and the Heart, Ryan Bingham, Edie Brickell & New Bohemians, Margo Price, Lukas Nelson & Promise of the Real*

The 2018 Picnic was only four sets under way when an approaching thunderstorm brought the show to a halt. Fans were evacuated for three hours, either waiting in their cars or huddled in buildings while the rain poured down. "We stayed on the air," said Dallas Wayne, broadcasting with Willie's Roadhouse on Sirius XM. "We're in this pelting rainstorm and the wind's blowing and the speaker stacks are swaying. I felt like I was on the Weather Channel."

When the rain finally ended, people outside the track could see that the secondary stage was already being dismantled. It was clear the Picnic wasn't going to squeeze any missed sets in but would skip ahead to the main-stage portion of the show.

Among those whose sets were canceled were regulars Billy Joe Shaver and Ray Wylie Hubbard. *Austin American-Statesman* music writer Peter Blackstock joked on Twitter that it was the first-ever Picnic without a three-named performer.

The Picnic resumed about 5:30, and the remainder of the show was cool and soggy. The night took a weird turn when Democratic US Senate candidate Beto O'Rourke came out for a short speech, to the delight of some fans and the dismay of others. Willie didn't care if anyone didn't like it. He brought O'Rourke back onstage at the end of the night to play guitar with him and the Family.

2019: Austin 360 Amphitheater, Circuit of the Americas

SITE: *Within the F1 racetrack in Del Valle, east of Austin*
ATTENDANCE: *Unreleased*
HEADLINERS: *Willie Nelson, Luke Combs, Nathaniel Rateliff & the Night Sweats, Alison Krauss, Jamey Johnson, Steve Earle*

Alison Krauss brought her soaring soprano and Luke Combs brought the beer ballads; however, the final Picnic at the Austin360 Amphitheater was business as usual for the most part. Willie at eighty-six walked stiffly to the microphone, just as his mentor Ray Price did in 2011, and his set was shortened to an hour, but he was great nonetheless and he worked in a few songs from his latest release, *Ride Me Back Home*.

If age and good-byes were the subplot to this Picnic, the contrast between David Allan Coe's and Johnny Bush's sets showed the right and the wrong way to do it. Both started out a little rough, but Coe's band tip-toed around the aging outlaw's ragged vocals, clearly not wanting to be accused of upstaging him. Bush's band, however, was having a helluva time and brought the San Antonio legend along with them. Bush, long the traditional country heart of the Picnic, ended strong. Coe just ended.

The Picnic also saw its last performance from Billy Joe Shaver, who looked shaky and had his four-song set list scrawled on his arm yet remained as irrepressible as ever.

Steve Earle was the man of the day, introducing Bush, hugging Shaver, and just singing the hell out of his own songs and a fine collection from his Guy Clark tribute album. Earle was among the many who came out onstage at the end of the night for the all-too-brief Willie finale—a single gospel song and it was over.

2020: The Virtual Picnic

SITE: *Portions of the show were streamed live from Luck; others were prerecorded*
HEADLINERS: *Willie Nelson, Sheryl Crow, Lyle Lovett, Steve Earle, Robert Earl Keen, Charley Crockett (live), Asleep at the Wheel (live)*

The temperature hit one hundred degrees in Austin on July Fourth. This time, fans at Willie Nelson's Fourth of July Picnic did not care. The virtual Picnic, thanks to Covid, was something new entirely. The show featured a half-dozen performances streamed live from Willie's ranch, Luck, plus more than twenty prerecorded performances and a handful of interviews with people such as Dahr Jamail, Mickey Raphael, and Freddy Fletcher.

The disparity between the live and prerecorded sets felt a little misleading. There were forty minutes of Charley Crockett in the afternoon and about three minutes of Steve Earle in the post-sundown finale. However, the two-hour finale was interesting and fast-paced.

The interviews desperately needed more context—they were a combination of surprising new information and old myths and exaggerations. Some of the interviewees were good at telling stories, and some were definitely not.

The virtual Picnic featured more diversity than ever in regard to black performers—Ziggy Marley's reggae-ish cover of "On the Road Again" was awesome—but the Picnic still remained pretty much a boys' club. It didn't help that Margo Price's prerecorded performance was left off the July Fourth broadcast (though it was added when the show was rebroadcast).

The Willie finale was quite good, or at least it was reassuring to see him healthy and rested during the pandemic. Willie talked about how he would like to return to Dripping Springs and get all the bands and fans together.

Those early Picnics were discussed with no small amount of reverence, even as the interviewees emphasized the chaos and heat and dust. Ray Wylie Hubbard explained it best. "You wanted to be a part of it. Each one was like a magical thing that wasn't happening anywhere else in the world. You would show up there early. You'd stay as long as you could.

It was such an incredible world that you didn't want to leave that Willie world and go back to the rest of it."

2022: Q2 Stadium, Austin

SITE: *In the soccer stadium for Austin FC in North Austin*
ATTENDANCE: *Unreleased*
HEADLINERS: *Willie Nelson, Jason Isbell and the 400 Unit, Allison Russell, Tyler Childers*

With the deaths of Johnny Bush and Billy Joe Shaver in late 2020, the Picnic wasn't going to be the same, and, in the end, Willie didn't try. Putting everything in the hands of Live Nation/C3 Presents, the Picnic featured ten acts at Austin's new twenty-thousand-seat soccer stadium.

Only opening act Asleep at the Wheel had any ties to the Picnic's history, and only Micah Nelson's Particle Kid was there to represent the extended Nelson family.

Promoters put ten thousand extra seats on the field, which at first looked like a bad move. Much of the crowd didn't arrive early, and those who did were spread out around the stadium in search of shade and refreshments. The crowd grew through the afternoon as the headliners' set times approached.

Peter Blackstock, covering the event for the *Austin American-Statesman*, wrote that the Picnic was "perhaps the most impressively booked and presented Picnic since Willie moved them back to Austin in 2015." Blackstock said the crowd responded strongly to Tyler Childers's set, who got the coveted sunset slot.

As he did in 2018, Beto O'Rourke, now running for governor, joined Willie onstage. O'Rourke and his son played guitar along with "On the Road Again." Willie got in the soccer spirit, wearing a jersey with the number 420. Willie's now-shortened performance featured a few surprises, including closing the show with the Mac Davis cover "It's Hard to Be Humble."

2023: Q2 Stadium, Austin

SITE: *In the soccer stadium for Austin FC in North Austin*
ATTENDANCE: *Unreleased*
HEADLINERS: *Willie Nelson, Tyler Childers, Dwight Yoakam, Shakey Graves*

The fiftieth-anniversary Picnic deserved to be epic, but the epic-ness was all spent on Willie's ninetieth-birthday concerts a few months prior. The Picnic had only eight artists and little buzz.

Tyler Childers was in the ringer spot ahead of Willie, playing for a crowd who had responded loudly when the emcee asked if this was their first Picnic. Fans across the stadium were wearing his name, and the end of his set was met with a sustained roar of appreciation.

For the few Picnic veterans, Dwight Yoakam was likely their pre-Willie highlight. Dwight pulled out a surprise cover of Ray Wylie Hubbard's "Redneck Mother" and played his own hits with an obvious sense of joy. Dwight took the Picnic back to the old days for just an hour in the evening. The people in the floor seats were dancing in the aisles.

During his set, Willie's right-hand man was Micah Nelson, and they made a strong pair. At ninety years old, Willie, who now sits down for his hour-long set, can no longer carry a whole show without a moment of rest now and then.

Micah was there to lean on, contributing three songs over the course of the Willie show. "Die When I'm High" was the first, answering the question of why Micah didn't play his most Picnic-friendly song during his opening set as Particle Kid.

For a minute there, all of us were old outlaws, still on the run.

> *I was born in a barn and the door was wide open*
> *I ran out before I learned to crawl*
> *and if die when I'm high, I'll be halfway to heaven*
> *or I might have a long way to fall*

CONCLUSION

In December 1975, Willie did an interview with Norma Sosa of the *Corpus Christi Caller-Times*. He talked about the Picnics and the difficulty of putting them on. He said he was looking for a place for the '76 Picnic. But he definitely wasn't thinking long term: "The only thing I say is that I don't ever want to get to the point that I'm saying, 'Welcome to the 38th Annual Willie Nelson's Fourth of July Picnic.' No sir."

It didn't happen every year, but the Picnic kept going, surviving several "last Picnics"—both announced and assumed. It hit the thirty-eighth not-quite-annual mark in Fort Worth in 2011 and continued years beyond that.

So why did it last?

John T. Davis was there from the beginning and said he assumed the event would just peter out after a few years. But when it became a multigenerational event, for Willie's family and for the fans, he thinks Willie's outlook changed. "I think that gave him real pleasure," Davis said. "[Willie's] north star has always been family. And I think when he saw whole families coming out and building their holiday weekend around this, I suspect that meant a lot to him."

Turk Pipkin, who said the Picnic survived because it changed with the times and took on different forms, underscored the family aspect. "I think Willie likes to go out on the Fourth of July and celebrate this great American holiday with friends who are old and new. And that includes people in the audience. That Willie and Family Band thing, people who are longtime fans, they feel like they're part of that family."

That family all starts with Willie Nelson.

Dallas Wayne described how he's seen today's popular country artists quickly acquiesce to what Willie wants at the Picnics. And Tyler Mahan Coe said Willie also has the respect of his fellow legendary country artists. "He's truly a patriarch of this scene; no one would dispute it. It was Willie who brought this family together through everything he did."

Raelyn Nelson said that's her grandfather's gift: bringing people together.

It's obvious onstage. The Picnic, long presumed to be a space for country and Americana music, always has featured a little diversity, from the Pointer Sisters in 1975 to the Bells of Joy during the Luckenbach years to Del Castillo in the 2000s. The Picnic was a place to be introduced to an artist or a band fans wouldn't have otherwise seen or appreciated.

But Willie also brought different people together. Not just the hippies and the rednecks, but the working class and the executives, the rural and the urban.

"He's the coolest; he's for everyone," Raelyn said. "I feel like he stands for freedom. I think that's why he wants to celebrate [the Picnic] on Independence Day. Let's celebrate our freedom to be who we are, to be who you are, to be unique. Let's celebrate that."

She laughed. "I just got goosebumps," she said.

The Picnic was pioneering. Joe Nick Patoski pointed out that Willie was the first personality to have a mass gathering tied to his name and that gathering was a sort of magnet for the musical hybrid that was emerging in Austin.

What was key, Dahr Jamail said, was that in addition to showcasing Willie's own exceptional talent, the Picnic was about Willie's generosity in promoting other music. "In a way, I would say the Picnic was a real

Derek Trucks, Derek O'Brien, and Susan Tedeschi were all part of the blues-flavored 2000 Picnic. Willie joined them onstage among many, many others. Photo by John Carrico

expression of Willie's love of music and playing with his friends. He gave them a stage to show people what he loved."

When questioned about the legacy of the Picnic, Jack Yoder said the Picnic showed both Willie's loyalty to friends and fans and his devotion to Texas music. "I don't think people will forget that for generations."

Dallas Wayne said anything could happen at the Picnics, especially considering the heat, but that he never considered any of them to be an artistic failure. "It may not have been the crowd they wanted at the time, or the weather might have not cooperated, or all these other variables like that, but the artist lineups are always impeccable. And it's everybody who wants to be there because of Willie, which in and of itself was magical to me."

As for the Picnic's longevity, you could view it two ways.

One way is to consider how it has changed over the years. It evolved—sometimes grudgingly—to be relevant to successive generations.

The other is to realize the Picnic remained long enough to become its own monument. "In a world where the Austin music scene has changed so much in the last fifty years, this is a bit of continuity," said historian Travis D. Stimeling. "To me it's one of those major touchstones. It's a pillar of Texas music history."

Even hard times can make a treasured memory, given enough distance and a comfortable place from which to consider them. The heat and the chaos of the Picnic are no different for those involved. "It was extremely cool to be a part of it," John T. Davis said. "Even when I was roasting in the middle of a cotton field somewhere and the whole thing was just going to hell in a handbasket in front of your eyes . . . looking back on it, I've had a wonderful time. I wouldn't trade for it."

Photographer Scott Newton agreed. "It all runs together. And when you try to think about it, it's the trying to drink out of a firehose thing, you know; it just comes back at you. So my thoughts are scattered, but I was there and I enjoyed the hell out of myself."

Ray Wylie Hubbard performed at more Picnics than anyone other than Willie, edging out Asleep at the Wheel. Along the way Hubbard sobered up and became a renowned songwriter and then a beloved elder statesman of the scene. Throughout that journey, Hubbard's commitment to the Picnic remained steady. "It's been something that I always looked forward to. It was a reunion and it was . . . it's a cliché, but they were magical in a way. It's been a thrill and an honor to be a part of it."

Connie Nelson was deeply involved in all of the early Picnics and said it was always a whirlwind, before and during the event. What carried her

Willie Nelson at the 1979 Picnic on the golf course at his Pedernales Country Club. The Picnics were often difficult but always—well, almost always—looked back upon fondly. Photo by Rick Henson.

through—and Wille as well—was the music. "The best way that I've always been able to describe it is one foot on a merry-go-round, if you can imagine. It's like, 'Oh, God, the Picnic is coming up. Oh, God, it's tomorrow.' And then the next thing you know, it's over. Like, wow, I don't even know how we did all that. Even during the heat of the day, which was always brutal. You just kind of put that aside, and the music and everything just engulfed you, and before you know it, it's just done."

Appendix A

Artists Who Played the Fourth of July Picnics

1973: Dripping Springs
Confirmed: Willie Nelson, Leon Russell, Kris Kristofferson, Waylon Jennings, Rita Coolidge, John Prine, Sammi Smith, Tom T. Hall, Charlie Rich, Billy Joe Shaver, Lee Clayton, Kenneth Threadgill, Greezy Wheels, Marc Benno and the Nightcrawlers, Steve Fromholz
Program and later written accounts: Johnny Darrell, Bobby Smith & the Country Blues, George Chambers and the Country Gentlemen, the Storytellers, the Threadgills, Troy Seals, the Geezinslaws, Buster Brown, Jerry Lane, Jimmy Velvet, Garland Brady
Didn't show/didn't play: Doug Sahm, Freda and the Fire Dogs

1974: College Station
Note: This chaotic Picnic doesn't readily allow for individual performances to be confirmed on each day. The reviews aren't comprehensive, many acts were bumped at the last second, and others were added at the last moment. Listed below is the "Tentative Schedule" as printed in the official program. Performers who have been confirmed as performing at some point during the festival are italicized.

July 4: *Willie Nelson, Asleep at the Wheel, Bobby Bare, Jimmy Buffett, Guy Clark*, Milton Carroll Band, Lefty Frizzell, *Freda and the Firedogs, Lost Gonzo Band, John Hartford, Waylon Jennings*, Darrell McCall, *Michael Murphey, Sammi Smith, B. W. Stevenson*, Red Steagall, *Jerry Jeff Walker*

July 5: *Willie Nelson*, Hank Cochran, Billy Jim Baker, Moe Bandy, Alvin Crow, Dick Crouse, Johnny Dallas, Kinky Friedman, Steve Fromholz, Larry Gatlin, Tompall Glaser, the Geezinslaws, Linda Hargrove, *Doug Kershaw, Augie Meyers*, Buzz Rabin, *Leon Russell*, Kenneth Threadgill, Billy Walker, Rusty Wier

July 6: *Willie Nelson, David Carradine*, George Chambers, *Lee Clayton*, David Allan Coe, Ewing St. Times, Alex Harvey, *Ray Wylie Hubbard*, Barefoot Jerry, Jerry Lane, Dee Moeller, Tracy Nelson, *Rick Nelson, Doug Sahm, Billy Joe Shaver*, Spanky & Our Gang, *Willis Alan Ramsey, Greezy Wheels*

Unscheduled: Johnny Bush, Johnny Duncan, Billy Gray, Red Lane, Plum Nelly, Kenny O'Dell, Magic Cowboy Band, Silver City Saddle Tramps, Don Williams, *Nitty Gritty Dirt Band, Floyd Tillman, John Sebastian*

1975: Liberty Hill
Confirmed: Willie Nelson, Kris Kristofferson, Johnny Bush, Rita Coolidge, the Pointer Sisters, Doug Sahm, John Sebastian, Charlie Daniels, Billy Swan, Alex Harvey, Donnie Fritts, Billy C, Milton Carroll, Delbert McClinton, Floyd Tillman, David Allan Coe

1976: Gonzales
Confirmed: Leon and Mary Russell, Kris Kristofferson, Rita Coolidge, David Allan Coe, Jerry Jeff Walker, Doug Sahm, George Jones, Ray Wylie Hubbard, Asleep at the Wheel, B. W. Stevenson, Rusty Wier, Floyd Tillman, Steve Fromholz, the Point, Billy C, Linda Hargrove, Milton Carroll

Rained out: Willie Nelson (he did sit in with Sahm and Russell), Waylon Jennings

Program and later written accounts: Billy Joe Shaver, Hoyt Axton, Alvin Crow, Roger Miller, Jody Payne, Jessi Colter, Bobby Bare, Tompall Glaser

1977: Tulsa
Confirmed: Willie Nelson, Waylon Jennings, Jessi Colter, Lynyrd Skynyrd, Jerry Jeff Walker, Asleep at the Wheel

1978: Kansas City
Confirmed: Willie Nelson, Waylon Jennings, Jessi Colter, the Grateful Dead, Jerry Jeff Walker, Missouri

1978: Dallas
Confirmed: Willie Nelson, Waylon Jennings, Jessi Colter, Ray Wylie Hubbard, Charlie Daniels Band, Kris Kristofferson, Rita Coolidge, Emmylou Harris, Billy Swan

1978: Austin
Confirmed: Willie Nelson, Steve Fromholz
Advertised: Larry Hudson

APPENDIX A \ 241

1979: Pedernales
Confirmed: Willie Nelson, Leon Russell, Ernest Tubb, Bobby Bare, Ray Wylie Hubbard, Johnny Paycheck, Steve Fromholz, Johnny Gimble, the Geezinslaws, Cooder Browne Band
Advertised: Don Bowman, Johnny Rodriguez, Larry Hudson

1980: Pedernales
Confirmed: Willie Nelson, Dyan Cannon, Slim Pickens, Asleep at the Wheel, Johnny Paycheck, Fiddlin' Frenchie Burke, the Geezinslaws, Ray Price, Ernest Tubb, Merle Haggard, Delbert McClinton, Leon Russell, Hank Cochran, Faron Young, Don Bowman
Didn't show or canceled: Jerry Jeff Walker, Charlie Daniels

1983: Syracuse
Confirmed: Willie Nelson, Merle Haggard, Linda Ronstadt, Emmylou Harris, Stray Cats

1983: New Jersey
Confirmed: Willie Nelson, Merle Haggard, Waylon Jennings, Jessi Colter, Linda Ronstadt, Emmylou Harris, Stray Cats

1983: Atlanta
Confirmed: Willie Nelson, Merle Haggard, Waylon Jennings, Hank Williams Jr., Linda Ronstadt, David Allan Coe, Stray Cats

1984: South Park Meadows
Confirmed: Willie Nelson, Waylon Jennings, Jessi Colter, Kris Kristofferson, Leon Russell, Joe Ely, Jerry Jeff Walker, Billy Joe Shaver, David Allan Coe, Delbert McClinton, Johnny Rodriguez, Johnny Bush, Steve Fromholz, Moe Bandy, Floyd Tillman, the Geezinslaws, Faron Young, Jackie King, Townes Van Zandt (played between sets)
Canceled: Carl Perkins
Advertised: Gary Busey

1985: South Park Meadows
Confirmed: Willie Nelson, Johnny Cash, Kris Kristofferson, Waylon Jennings, the Highwaymen, Neil Young, June Carter Cash, Jessi Colter, Jerry Jeff Walker, David Allan Coe, Asleep at the Wheel, Rockin' Sidney, Johnny

Bush, Jubal Clark, Rattlesnake Annie, Jerry Max Lane, the Unforgiven, Ray Wylie Hubbard, the Geezinslaws, Steve Fromholz, Floyd Tillman, Freddy Powers, Faron Young

Advertised: Bonnie Bramlett, Hank Snow

1986: Farm Aid II at Manor Downs

Note: With too many acts to individually confirm, this is the lineup as it was promoted in the *Austin American-Statesman*. Reviews said the event "ran like clockwork."

From 7 a.m. until 10 a.m.: Cherokee Rose (with Willie Nelson), Jerry Max Lane, Jubal Clark, Danny Cooksey, Lee Clayton, Boxcar Willie, Johnny Bush, Gary P. Nunn, Rusty Wier, the Geezinslaws, Bill and Bonnie Hearne, Ray Wylie Hubbard, Steven Fromholz, Willie Nelson, Julio Iglesias, Willie and Waylon Jennings, Alex Harvey, Willie and David Lynn Jones, the Beach Boys, Johnny Paycheck, J. D. Souther with the Nelsons, B. W. Stevenson, David Allan Coe, Dusty Rhodes, War, Roy Head, Minnie Mouse and the Disney characters

From 10 a.m. until 1 p.m.: Judy Collins, Patty Loveless, Vern Gosdin, Charlie Haid, Little Joe y la Familia, Exile, the Blasters, Judy Rodman, Don Johnson, Jerry Jeff Walker, Rob Lowe, David Lindley and El Rayo-X, Sawyer Brown, the Rock and Roll All-Stars (Willie Nelson, Jon Bon Jovi, Vince Neil, Dickey Betts, Joe Walsh)

From 1 p.m. until 4 p.m.: George Jones, Gary Morris, Robert Guillaume, Nils Lofgren, Billy Joe Shaver, Playboy Girls of Rock n Roll, David Soul, Dave Mason, Dwight Yoakam, John Anderson, Bonnie Raitt, Roger McGuinn, Taj Mahal

From 4 until 7 p.m.: William Lee Golden, the Fabulous Thunderbirds, John Prine, Roger Miller, the Nelsons, X, John Schneider, Asleep at the Wheel, Doug Kershaw, the Unforgiven, Joe Ely

From 7 p.m. until 10 p.m.: the Bellamy Brothers, Alabama, Green on Red, Christopher Hewitt, Los Lobos, Jack Wagner, John Cougar Mellencamp with Maria McKee, Arlo Guthrie, Kris Kristofferson, Jason and the Scorchers

From 10 p.m. until 1 a.m.: Rick James, Neil Young, Rita Coolidge, Steppenwolf, John Conlee, Delbert McClinton, Stevie Ray Vaughan and Double Trouble, Kip Addotta, Leslie Phillips, Felix Cavaliere, Willie Nelson and Family, All-Star Finale

Also: Bob Dylan and Tom Petty (via satellite), Rosanne Cash, Emmylou Harris

1987: Carl's Corner
Confirmed: Willie Nelson, Bruce Hornsby and the Range, Kris Kristofferson, Roger Miller, Joe Walsh, the Fabulous Thunderbirds, Eric Johnson, Joe Ely, Asleep at the Wheel, Billy Joe Shaver, Rattlesnake Annie, Jackie King, Darden Smith, the O'Kanes, Don Cherry, Floyd Tillman, Roy Garrett and Linda Elaine, Darrell John, Jimmie Dale Court, Benny Kirby and the Country Dummies, David Lynn Jones, the Unforgiven, Celinda Pink and the Cellar Dwellers

Advertised: Steve Pryor and the Mighty Kingsnakes, the Geezinslaws, Mack Abernathy, T. Gosney Thornton, Billy Roy, Alex Harvey, the Nelsons, Cherokee Rose, Jubal Clark, Gary McClung and the Drifters

Canceled: Merle Haggard, Emmylou Harris, Jerry Jeff Walker, David Allan Coe, Dwight Yoakam

1990: Zilker Park, Austin
Confirmed: Willie Nelson, Johnny Cash, Waylon Jennings, Kris Kristofferson, the Highwaymen, David Allan Coe, Kimmie Rhodes, Little Joe y la Familia, Billy Joe Shaver, Shelby Lynne

Advertised: Kinky Friedman, Asleep at the Wheel, Original Riders of the Purple Sage, Steve Fromholz, Darden Smith, the Geezinslaws, Johnny Gimble, Little Whisper & the Rumors

1993: Backyard
Confirmed: Willie Nelson, the Geezinslaws, Kimmie Rhodes
Advertised: Bells of Joy, the Kyle Sisters, Asleep at the Wheel

1995: Luckenbach
Confirmed: Willie Nelson, Kris Kristofferson, Leon Russell, Ray Price, Robert Earl Keen, Little Joe y la Familia, David Allan Coe, the Geezinslaws, Jesse Dayton, Ray Wylie Hubbard, Gary P. Nunn, Steve Fromholz, Kimmie Rhodes, Aaron Allen, Paula Nelson, Craig Dillingham, Titty Bingo, Johnny Rodriguez, Monte Montgomery, Doc and Ava Mason, Jimmy Lee Jones, Maggie Montgomery

Advertised: Shelby Lynne, Tab Benoit, Karen Brooks, P. C. Nelson, the Offenders (with Johnny Bush), Freddy Powers, Uranium Savages, Hays County Gals

1996: Luckenbach
Confirmed: Willie Nelson, Waylon Jennings, Leon Russell, Ray Price, Little Joe y la Familia, Robert Earl Keen, Billy Joe Shaver, Asleep at the Wheel,

Ray Wylie Hubbard, Gary P. Nunn, Paula Nelson, Jesse Dayton, Kinky Friedman, Antone's Blues Band, Kimmie Rhodes, Supersuckers, Tenderloin, Monte Montgomery, Aaron Allan, Titty Bingo, Jimmy Lee Jones, Doc and Ava Mason, Maggie Montgomery

Advertised: PC Cowboys, Geronimo Trevino, Craig Dillingham, Jubal Clark, 8 1/2 Souvenirs, Steve Fromholz, Lee Rocker, Freddy Powers, Doug Supernaw, the Geezinslaws

1997: Luckenbach

Confirmed: Willie Nelson, Ray Price, David Allan Coe, Joe Ely (with Dwight Yoakam), Jimmie Dale Gilmore, Little Joe y la Familia, Ray Wylie Hubbard, Mary Cutrufello, Steve Fromholz, 8 1/2 Souvenirs, the Geezinslaws, Rogers & Hammerhead, Joey and Jill Floyd, Doc Mason, Ava Mason, Jimmy Lee Jones

Advertised: Leon Russell, Titty Bingo, Jesse Dayton, Loose Diamonds, Paula and Amy Nelson, Bells of Joy, Kimmie Rhodes

Canceled: Merle Haggard

1998: Luckenbach

Confirmed: Willie Nelson, Leon Russell, Ray Price, Emmylou Harris, Robert Earl Keen, Billy Joe Shaver, Asleep at the Wheel, Ray Wylie Hubbard, Paula Nelson, Ronnie Dawson, Larry Butler, Steve Fromholz, Freddy Powers, Derek O'Brien Blues Band, Kimmie Rhodes, Billy Walker, Gary P. Nunn, 8 1/2 Souvenirs, the Geezinslaws, Jesse Dayton, Fryed Brothers, Jack Ingram, Alvin Crow, Craig Dillingham, Bad Rodeo, Bells of Joy, Jimmy Lee Jones, Doc Mason

Advertised: Toni Price, Peter Rowan, Titty Bingo

1999: Luckenbach

Confirmed: Willie Nelson, Leon Russell, Ray Price, Billy Joe Shaver, Paula Nelson, Ray Wylie Hubbard, Johnny Bush, Little Joe y la Familia, Tab Benoit, Pat Green, Steve Fromholz, Kimmie Rhodes, Derek O'Brien Blues Band, Rogers & Hammerhead, Sisters Morales, Pumpskully, Monte Montgomery, Bells of Joy, Doc Mason, Ava Mason, Cowjazz, Mark David Manders, Jimmy Lee Jones

Advertised: Larry Gatlin, Asleep at the Wheel, Paula Nelson, the Geezinslaws, Jackie King, Supersuckers, Claude Grey, Patsy Thompson, Razzy Bailey, Titty Bingo, Lee Rocker, Janis Ian, Fryed Brothers Band, Bobby Boyd, Bastard Sons of Johnny Cash

2000: Southpark Meadows
Confirmed: Willie Nelson, Leon Russell, Ray Price, Pat Green, Joe Ely, David Allan Coe, the Geezinslaws, Toni Price, Shelby Lynne, Susan Tedeschi and Francine Reed, Kimmie Rhodes, Jimmie Dale Gilmore, Ray Wylie Hubbard, Billy Joe Shaver, Titty Bingo, Johnny Bush, Rusty Wier, Johnny Gimble, Mark David Manders, Willie K, Cory Morrow

Advertised: Steve Fromholz, Asleep at the Wheel, Little Joe y la Familia, Larry Butler, Derek O'Brien, Freddy Powers, Bill McDavid, Lost Trailers, Doc Mason, Bobby Boyd, Doug Supernaw, Patsy Thompson, Bells of Joy, Craig Dillingham, Fryed Brothers, Jimmy Lee Jones, Rodney Hayden, Mustang Sally & the Blame

2003: Two River Canyon
July 4 Confirmed: Willie Nelson, the Dead with Joan Osborne, Ray Price, Toby Keith, Pat Green, Merle Haggard, Leon Russell, Johnny Bush, Kimmie Rhodes, Stephanie Urbina Jones, Bells of Joy, South Austin Jug Band, James Hand

July 4 Advertised: the Geezinslaws

July 5 Confirmed: Willie Nelson, Neil Young, Billy Bob Thornton, Billy Joe Shaver, Patty Griffin, Ray Wylie Hubbard, Shawn Colvin, Los Lonely Boys, Cross Canadian Ragweed, Del Castillo, Cory Morrow, Titty Bingo, Paula Nelson, Jeff Haney Band, Stephanie Urbina Jones, Bells of Joy

July 5 Advertised: Pauline Reese, Waylon Payne, Matt Powell, Jack Ingram

2004: Fort Worth Stockyards
Confirmed: Willie Nelson, Kris Kristofferson, Calhoun Brothers, Ray Price, Merle Haggard, Ron White, Leon Russell, Clarence "Gatemouth" Brown, Los Lonely Boys, Cross Canadian Ragweed, Larry the Cable Guy, Asleep at the Wheel, Johnny Bush, Django Walker, Vince Esquire, David Allan Coe, Del Castillo, Ray Wylie Hubbard, the Geezinslaws, Cowboy Johnson, Jason Boland, Jack Ingram

2005: Fort Worth Stockyards
Confirmed: Willie Nelson, Bob Dylan, Los Lonely Boys, Doobie Brothers, Ray Price, David Allan Coe, Billy Joe Shaver, Jessi Colter, James Hand, Paula Nelson, Pauline Reese, the Geezinslaws, Marty Dread, Los Maui Boys, Django Walker, Johnny Bush, Heather Myles, Janie Fricke, Freddy Powers and Bill McDavid, Lost Trailers, Texas Playboys, Troubadillos, Ray Wylie Hubbard

2006: Fort Worth Stockyards
Confirmed: Willie Nelson, Kris Kristofferson, David Allan Coe, Ray Price, Billy Joe Shaver, Nitty Gritty Dirt Band, Ray Wylie Hubbard, Leon Russell, Randy Rogers, Harmonic Tribe, Shooter Jennings, Paula Nelson, Noel Haggard, Folk Uke, Stoney LaRue, Titty Bingo, Johnny Bush, Del Castillo, Bonnie Bishop, Pauline Reese, the Mothertruckers, the Geezinslaws, James Hand, Freddy Powers and Bill McDavid, No Justice, Jimmy Lee Jones, Mike Graham, Heather Myles

2007: Washington State
Confirmed: Willie Nelson, Son Volt, Old 97s, Drive-By Truckers, Amos Lee, 40 Points

2008: San Antonio
Confirmed: Willie Nelson, Merle Haggard, Ray Price, Los Lonely Boys, Del Castillo, Asleep at the Wheel, Pat Green, Johnny Bush, Ray Wylie Hubbard, Billy Joe Shaver, David Allan Coe, 40 Points

2008: Houston
Confirmed: Willie Nelson, Ray Price, Los Lonely Boys, Asleep at the Wheel, Ray Wylie Hubbard, Billy Joe Shaver, David Allan Coe, 40 Points
Advertised: Johnny Bush, Del Castillo
Canceled: Merle Haggard

2009: South Bend, Indiana
Confirmed: Willie Nelson, Bob Dylan, John Mellencamp, the Wiyos

2010: The (New) Backyard
Confirmed: Willie Nelson, Kris Kristofferson, Ray Price, Leon Russell, Asleep at the Wheel, David Allan Coe, Jack Ingram, Jamey Johnson, Paula Nelson, Randy Rogers, Ray Wylie Hubbard, the Reflectacles, Del Castillo, the Geezinslaws, Kevin Fowler, Freddy Powers, Folk Uke, Johnny Bush, Pauline Reese, Jody Nix and the Texas Cowboys, Blackwood Quartet, Waylon Payne
Canceled: Billy Joe Shaver

2011: Fort Worth Stockyards
Confirmed: Willie Nelson, Ray Price, Jamey Johnson, Randy Houser, David Allan Coe, Ray Wylie Hubbard, Wade Bowen, Randy Rogers, Asleep

at the Wheel, Billy Joe Shaver, Lukas Nelson, Micah Nelson and the Reflectacles, Lee Brice, Brantley Gilbert, Paula Nelson, Craig Campell, Folk Uke, Drake White, Johnny Bush, Bleu Edmondson, Austin Lucas, Brent Cobb, Caitlyn Smith, Adam Hood, Dani Flowers, Erin Enderin, Ashley Ray

2012: Fort Worth Stockyards
Confirmed: Willie Nelson, Jamey Johnson, Stoney LaRue, Randy Rogers Band, Wade Bowen, Asleep at the Wheel, Ray Wylie Hubbard, Billy Joe Shaver, Whispering Bill Anderson, Shy Blakeman, Dirty River Boys, Folk Uke, Paula Nelson, Deadman, Johnny Bush, Whiskey Myers, Lukas Nelson, Corey Smith

2013: Fort Worth Stockyards
Confirmed: Willie Nelson, Gary Allan, Kris Kristofferson, Ryan Bingham, Leon Russell, Jamey Johnson, Asleep at the Wheel, Randy Rogers, Justin Moore, Dallas Wayne, Billy Joe Shaver, David Allan Coe, Dale Watson, Ray Wylie Hubbard, Folk Uke, Insects vs. Robots, Jody Nix, Sonny Throckmorton, Paula Nelson, Johnny Bush, Dirty River Boys, Quebe Sisters, Amber Digby
Canceled: Ray Price, Lukas Nelson

2014: Fort Worth Stockyards
Confirmed: Willie Nelson, Dierks Bentley, Josh Abbott, Ryan Bingham, Lukas Nelson, Ray Wylie Hubbard, Jamey Johnson, David Allan Coe, Charley Pride, Johnny Bush, Folk Uke, Insects vs. Robots, Amber Digby

2015: Austin360 Amphitheater, Circuit of the Americas
Confirmed: Willie Nelson, Eric Church, Merle Haggard, Kacey Musgraves, Jamey Johnson, Jason Isbell, Asleep at the Wheel, Sturgill Simpson, Leon Russell, Chris Stapleton, Billy Joe Shaver, Kris Kristofferson, Johnny Bush, Greezy Wheels, Ray Wylie Hubbard, David Allan Coe, Dallas Wayne, Paula Nelson, Raelyn Nelson, Folk Uke, Hudson Moore, Amber Digby, Pauline Reese

2016: Austin360 Amphitheater, Circuit of the Americas
Confirmed: Willie Nelson, Brantley Gilbert, Jamey Johnson, Alison Krauss, Shakey Graves, Jamestown Revival, Kris Kristofferson, Cody Johnson, Lee Ann Womack, Billy Joe Shaver, Margo Price, Johnny Bush, Ray Wylie

Hubbard, Asleep at the Wheel, Raelyn Nelson, Folk Uke, Dallas Wayne, Amber Digby

Canceled: Leon Russell, David Allan Coe, Paula Nelson

2017: Austin360 Amphitheater, Circuit of the Americas
Confirmed: Willie Nelson, Sheryl Crow, Kacey Musgraves, Jamey Johnson, Turnpike Troubadours, Steve Earle, Margo Price, Asleep at the Wheel, Hayes Carll, Lukas Nelson & Promise of the Real, Ray Wylie Hubbard, Johnny Bush, Insects vs. Robots, Billy Joe Shaver, Folk Uke, Raelyn Nelson, David Allan Coe

2018: Austin360 Amphitheater, Circuit of the Americas
Confirmed: Willie Nelson, Sturgill Simpson, the Head and the Heart, Ryan Bingham, Edie Brickell & New Bohemians, Margo Price, Lukas Nelson & Promise of the Real, Folk Uke, Particle Kid, Raelyn Nelson, Yellow Feather

Rained out: Jamestown Revival, the Wild Feathers, Asleep at the Wheel, Johnny Bush, Billy Joe Shaver, Ray Wylie Hubbard, Gene Watson

Canceled: David Allan Coe

2019: Austin360 Amphitheater, Circuit of the Americas
Confirmed: Willie Nelson, Luke Combs, Nathaniel Rateliff & the Night Sweats, Alison Krauss, Jamey Johnson, Steve Earle, Colter Wall, Hayes Carll, Ray Wylie Hubbard, Gene Watson, Billy Joe Shaver, David Allan Coe, Folk Uke, Johnny Bush, Casey Kristofferson Band, Raelyn Nelson

2020: The Virtual Picnic
Streamed live from Luck: Charley Crockett, the Peterson Brothers, Particle Kid, Shakey Graves, Vincent Neil Emerson, Asleep at the Wheel

(Mostly) prerecorded finale: Willie Nelson, Sheryl Crow, Lyle Lovett, Steve Earle, Robert Earl Keen, Ray Wylie Hubbard, Ziggy Marley, the McCrary Sisters, Edie Brickell, Jamey Johnson, Lukas Nelson & Promise of the Real, Randy Rogers and Wade Bowen, Matthew Houck (of Phosphorescent), Kurt Vile, Kinky Friedman, John Doe, Devon Gilfillian

Also prerecorded: Gina Chavez, Monte Warden, Trey Privott, the War and Treaty, Kalu James, Parker McCollum

Missed live stream but added for rebroadcast: Margo Price

2022: Q2 Stadium, Austin
Confirmed: Willie Nelson, Jason Isbell and the 400 Unit, Tyler Childers, Allison Russell, Osborne Brothers, Midland, Charley Crockett, Particle Kid, Steve Earle & the Dukes, Asleep at the Wheel

2023: Q2 Stadium, Austin
Confirmed: Asleep at the Wheel, Tyler Childers, Sierra Ferrell, Shakey Graves, Particle Kid, Shane Smith and the Saints, Willie Nelson, Dwight Yoakam

Appendix B

Events Often Confused with Fourth of July Picnics

Dripping Springs Reunion: This event was held March 17–19, 1972, at the same site outside Dripping Springs that would host the inaugural Picnic the following year. It is often confused with the Picnic, though it was not a Willie-organized event. It is most well-known for being where Waylon Jennings first ran into Billy Joe Shaver. Waylon promised to record some of Billy Joe's songs, a promise he quickly forgot about. Billy Joe didn't forget and later confronted Waylon in Nashville. The result was Waylon's 1973 *Honky Tonk Heroes* album.

Labor Day Picnic: This event was set for September 2, 1973, in Lewisville, near Dallas, but it was canceled the week before when negotiations over the site broke down.

Abbot Homecoming: This event was held November 4, 1973, in Willie's hometown of Abbott. It attracted a crowd of more than ten thousand and stretched over twelve hours, including performances from Willie, Michael Murphy, Jerry Jeff Walker, Billy Joe Shaver, Sammi Smith, and Johnny Bush. Profits were promised to the local PTA, but any money taken in vanished along the way.

48 Hours at Atoka: This event was held Labor Day weekend in 1975 near McAlester, Oklahoma. Willie, Waylon Jennings, Jerry Jeff Walker, David Allan Coe, Jerry Lee Lewis, Don Williams, and Freddy Fender were among the headliners. Some people consider this concert the beginning of the "outlaw country" era. The concert was originally billed as a "country-rock" fest, but when locals balked, the "rock" was removed from the advertising.

California Picnic: For two years, Willie hosted these summer events in Sacramento. The August 2, 1980, event included Merle Haggard, Emmylou Harris, and Lacy J. Dalton. The June 28, 1981, event included the Oak Ridge Boys, Rosanne Cash, and Delbert McClinton. There also was an event advertised as "Willie Nelson's California Picnic" in 1977. The Santa Clara event was to feature Freddy Fender and Donna Fargo.

Aloha Picnic: This event was held March 25, 1978, in what was then called Rainbow Bay Music Park, near Hawaii's Aloha Stadium. The concert included the Charlie Daniels Band, Bonnie Raitt, and Pure Prairie League.

Bull Creek Party Barn: The barn was a historic music venue outside Austin in the 1970s. A well-known photo by Scott Newton of Willie and Waylon performing there in 1975 has a Picnic vibe, but it was an April concert that also featured Jerry Jeff Walker and the Lost Gonzo Band.

The Woodlands Picnics: Starting in 1999 and ending in 2002, the Cynthia Woods Mitchell Pavilion in The Woodlands, near Houston, did host four events billed as a Willie Picnic. With the exception of the 2000 show in October, the shows were held in early August.

San Antonio Picnic: This event was held August 11, 2001, at the Verizon Wireless Amphitheater. The lineup included Dwight Yoakam, Robert Earl Keen, Dennis Quaid, Rodney Crowell, Pat Green, and Gary Allen.

Country Throwdown Tour: In the middle of its three-year life span, Willie Nelson joined this touring fest in 2011. The tour actually did intersect with the Fourth of July Picnic on July 4, 2011, in Fort Worth, bringing artists such as Drake White, Randy Houser, and Brantley Gilbert to the Picnic alongside traditional acts such as Ray Price, Johnny Bush, and Ray Wylie Hubbard. Other dates were decidedly not Picnics.

Outlaw Music Festival: Willie Nelson headlined this Americana touring fest, which got its start in 2016. The event was not held in 2020 due to the Covid pandemic. The August 22, 2021, show at Austin's Germania Insurance Amphitheater sort of stood in for the Picnic that year, with sets from Chris Stapleton, Ryan Bingham, and Yola.

Appendix C

Suggested Reading

Clark, Rob. *Live from Aggieland: Legendary Performances in the Brazos Valley.* College Station: Texas A&M University Press, 2017.
One of the chapters is a detailed and excellent account of the 1974 Fourth of July Picnic.

Garrett, Danny. *Weird Yet Strange.* Fort Worth: TCU Press, 2015.
Artist Danny Garrett devotes considerable space to talking about his Willie Nelson Picnic posters, the Picnic itself, and working with Willie Nelson.

Nelson, Susie. *Heartworn Memories.* Austin: Eakin Press, 1987.
Susie shares good information and observations about the 1973 and 1980 Picnics.

Nelson, Willie, and Bud Shrake. *Willie: An Autobiography.* New York: Simon and Schuster, 1988.
Willie tells the story of the 1987 Picnic in the book's first chapter.

Patoski, Joe Nick. *Willie Nelson: An Epic Life.* New York: Little, Brown, 2008.
This is the definitive biography of Willie Nelson.

Querry, Ronald B., ed. *Growing Old at Willie's Nelson's Picnic and Other Sketches of Life in the Southwest.* College Station: Texas A&M University Press, 1983.
William C. Martin's essay on the 1974 Fourth of July Picnic is one of the best things ever written about the Picnic.

Reid, Jan. *The Improbable Rise of Redneck Rock.* Austin: Heidelberg Publishers, 1974.
This is the guidebook for progressive country music fans, and the chapter on the 1973 Fourth of July Picnic captures the chaos and culture.

Roberts, Woody. *Horse Racing & Rock 'n' Roll.* Austin: Press 709, 2019.
Woody's story is not widely known, but he played a crucial part in the 1973 Picnic and also details some of his involvement in the 1986 Farm Aid II/Picnic.

Wilson, Eddie, with Jesse Sublett. *Armadillo World Headquarters.* Austin: TSSI Publishing, 2017.
This is one of the great books about the Austin music scene with a detailed chapter on the 1973 Picnic.

Yorks, Terrence. *Silver Eagles Taking Flight: A Trip Back in Musical Time with Willie Nelson and Friends.* Smithfield, UT: High Level Press, 2016.
Essentially a photo essay, this book provides an incredible look at the 1974 Picnic from setup to finale.

Sources

Introduction
ARTICLES
Lewis, Grover. "Hillbilly Heaven: Take the Money and Go Limp." *Rolling Stone*, April 27, 1972, 42–46.
INTERVIEWS
Terry Allen, Bill Bentley, Johnny Bush, Dahr Jamail, Steve Kirk, Delbert McClinton, Tim O'Connor, Janis Tillerson

Chapter One
1973: Dripping Springs
BOOKS
Nelson, Susie. *Heartworn Memories*. Austin: Eakin Press, 1987.
Nelson, Willie, with David Ritz. *It's a Long Story*. New York: Little, Brown, 2015.
Patoski, Joe Nick. *Willie Nelson: An Epic Life*. New York: Little, Brown, 2008.
Reid, Jan. *The Improbable Rise of Redneck Rock*. Austin: Heidelberg Publishers, 1974.
Roberts, Woody. *Horse Racing & Rock 'n' Roll*. Austin: Press 709, 2019.
Wilson, Eddie, with Jesse Sublett. *Armadillo World Headquarters*. Austin: TSSI Publishing, 2017.
ARTICLES
Doerschuk, Bob. "Long-Hairs, Middle America Drawn Together by Picnic." *Austin American-Statesman*, July 5, 1973, 1.
Gracey, Joe. "Willie & Mike Get Together." *Austin American-Statesman*, August 19, 1972, 40.
Hyun, Paula. "What Happened at Willie's Picnic?" *Los Angeles Free Press*, July 13, 1973, 27.
Miller, Townsend. "Austin's Music Scene Overflowing." *Austin American-Statesman*, June 23, 1973, 26.
———. "Kris and Rita: 'Beautiful People.'" *Austin American-Statesman*, July 14, 1973, B24.
———. "Willie Nelson Bringing 'Em All Together (and Ain't It Wonderful!)." *Austin American-Statesman*, August 12, 1972, 37.

———. "Willie's Fest Smash Success." *Austin American-Statesman*, July 7, 1973, A27.
Milner, Jay. "This Has Got to Be the Biggest Gathering of Hippies and Rednecks Ever." *Iconoclast*, July 13, 1973, 4–5.
Thomas, Dave. "Dawn of the Picnic." *Austin American-Statesman*, June 30, 2013, D1.
———. "Reunion Planted Austin's Country Roots." *Austin American-Statesman*, March 17, 2012, E1.
Thompson, Greg. "Willie Nelson's Country Picnic Draws 50,000." *Denton Record-Chronicle*, July 5, 1973, 2A.

INTERVIEWS

Tony Airoldi, Marcia Ball, Steve Brooks, Thomas Chapman, Lee Clayton, Sandy Gravenor, Johnny Gross, Lissa Hattersley, Brad Hurlbut, Dahr Jamail, Louis Karp, Tim O'Connor, Joe Nick Patoski, Alan Pogue, Woody Roberts, Thomas Sheldon, Bobby Earl Smith, Mike Tolleson, Melinda Wickman, Eddie Wilson

1974: College Station

BOOKS

Clark, Rob. *Live from Aggieland: Legendary Performances in the Brazos Valley*. College Station: Texas A&M University Press, 2017.

ARTICLES

Martin, William C. "Growing Old at Willie Nelson's Picnic." *Texas Monthly*, October 1974, 94–98, 116–24.

INTERVIEWS

Marcia Ball, Judy Hubbard, Bobby Earl Smith

1975: Liberty Hill

ARTICLES

Harvey, Lynn. "Willie's Third Fourth." *The Tennessean*, July 13, 1975, 103.
Mintz, Sandie. "Letter Alleges July 4 Picnic Health Dangers." *Austin American-Statesman*, July 31, 1975, 3.
———. "Picnic Fare Upsets Commissioner." *Austin American-Statesman*, July 6, 1975, 1.
Nolan, Joe. "Willie's Bash Crowd Pleaser." *Fort Worth Star-Telegram*, July 13, 1975, 81.
Powers, Kay. "Liberty Hill 'Hosts' Divided after Picnic." *Austin American-Statesman*, July 18, 1975, 13.

INTERVIEWS

Joe Nick Patoski

Chapter Two
1976: Gonzales
ARTICLES

Alexander, Wiley. "Willie Wouldn't Change a Thing." *San Antonio Express*, September 16, 1976, Pae 6A.

Besaw, Larry. "Willie's Fest Ties Up Roads." *Austin American-Statesman*, July 4, 1976.

———. "Willie's Fourth of July Picnic Ends on Soggy Note." *Austin American-Statesman*, July 6, 1976, 13.

———. "Willie's Picnic Getting Longer before a Note Is Even Heard." *Austin American-Statesman*, June 29, 1976, B1.

Bode, Winston. "Willie Nelson Aftermath." *Victoria Advocate*, July 22, 1978, 8A.

"Burn Victim Sues Nelson over Picnic." *Austin American-Statesman*, December 29, 1976.

Copeland, Becky. "Violence Also Played at Music Fest." *Austin American-Statesman*, July 5, 1976.

Copeland, Becky, and Larry Besaw. "Gonzales Besieged by Campers Headed for Picnic." *Austin American-Statesman*, July 3, 1976, 9.

Deal, Jerry. "Suit Looms on Nelson Festival." *San Antonio Express-News*, May 20, 1976, 1.

"George Jones Finds Youth Like Him Too." *Valley News* (Van Nuys, CA), August 27, 1976, 66.

Harvey, Lynn. "Willie Nelson Says Annual Picnic Off." *The Tennessean*, May 21, 1976. Page 57

"Henry, Genevieve Vollentine: Pillars of the Community." *Gonzales Inquirer*, March 31, 2017.

House, Bob. "Willie Can Have His Picnic." *Austin American-Statesman*, June 15, 1976, B1.

———. "Willie Nelson July 4th Concert Hits Sour Note." *Austin American-Statesman*, May 20, 1976, B1.

———. "Willie's Concert Draws Static." *Austin American-Statesman*, May 19, 1976, 1.

"Houston Cotton Munson Jr." *Victoria Advocate*, June 18, 2017, B6.

Kelley, Mike. "The Things They Say about Willie in Gonzales." *Austin American-Statesman*, May 30, 1976, B1.

Mayes, Dave. "DA Reaps Nelson Picnic Profits." *Austin American-Statesman*, July 18, 1976, 1.

———. "Willie Charge May Only Make a Point." *Austin American-Statesman*, July 31, 1976, B1.

Miller, Townsend. "Willie Chooses Gonzales as Site for His Annual 'Pick-Nick.'" *Austin American-Statesman*, April 29, 1976, C5.

"One-Day Gonzales Stand May Be Enough." *Austin American-Statesman*, June 6, 1976, B2.

"147 Arrested during Picnic." *Austin American-Statesman*, July 6, 1976, B1.

"Petitions Circulate Supporting Willie's Picnic in Gonzales." *Austin American-Statesman*, May 26, 1976, B3.

"Picnic Backers Want Willie to Play Anyway." *Austin American-Statesman*, May 23, 1976, B3.

Powers, Kay. "Rancher Wiser after Nelson Fest." *Austin American-Statesman*, July 22, 1976.

———. "Singer Nelson Hit with Another Lawsuit." *Austin American-Statesman*, March 24, 1977, B7.

———. "Willie Nelson's July 4th Bash Stirs Discord." *Austin American-Statesman*, May 19, 1976, 1.

———. "Willie Reduces Picnic to 1 Day." *Austin American-Statesman*, June 9, 1976, B1.

Prince, Jeff. "Phases and Stages." *Fort Worth Weekly*, January 7, 2009.

"Rain Sogs Willie's Fourth." *The Tennessean*, July 8, 1976, 40.

"Seguin Lawyer Is Appointed to District Attorney Vacancy." *Austin American-Statesman*, June 1, 1984, B4.

Taggart, Patrick. "Willie's 4th Party's Over." *Austin American-Statesman*, July 6, 1976.

"Toilet Trouble Plagues Picnic." *Austin American-Statesman*, July 1, 1976, 1.

"Weekend Orgy of Music Prepared." *Austin American-Statesman*, July 2, 1976.

"Willie Faces Yet Another Picnic Suit." *Austin American-Statesman*, August 26, 1976, B8.

"Willie Keeps Saying, 'No Picnic,' but Is Anybody Listening?" *Austin American-Statesman*, June 2, 1976, 1.

"Willie Nelson May Cancel Picnic Tonight." *Austin American-Statesman*, June 4, 1976.

"Willie Suddenly Says Picnic's On." *Austin American-Statesman*, June 5, 1976.

"Willie Worries Bell Sheriff." *Austin American-Statesman*, May 25, 1976, B3.

INTERVIEWS

Rodeo Barton, Mike Benestante, Debbie Munson Bumpass, Tyler Mahan Coe, Debbie Culak, Freddy Fletcher, Ray Wylie Hubbard, Dahr Jamail,

Mark Kelley, Susie McCoslin, Scott Newton, Joe Nick Patoski, Laurie Kelley Taylor, Steve Taylor, Perry Tong, Melinda Wickman

DOCUMENTS

Application to Gonzales County for music festival, filed by Houston Munson on April 30, 1976.

Application (amended) to Gonzales County for music festival, filed by Houston Munson on May 28, 1976.

Texas Department of Health Resources report, *Mass Gathering–Gonzales County, Willie Nelson's Fourth of July Picnic (1976)*, filed July 9, 1976.

1977: Tulsa

ARTICLES

Bledsoe, Bob. "There's Hot Time for All at Tulsa Picnic Concert." *The Oklahoman*, July 4, 1977, 1.

Woolley, John. "Willie's Back: Country Outlaws Team Up Once Again." *Tulsa World*, February 27, 2007.

1978: Kansas City, Dallas, and Austin

ARTICLES

Besaw, Larry. "Two Pounds Bite the Dust Thanks to Willie Nelson." *Austin American-Statesman*, July 8, 1978, D1.

Curry, Bill. "Tame Picnic; Country Tunes at the Cotton Bowl; Willie Nelson on Artificial Turf." *Washington Post*, July 4, 1978, B1.

Davis, John T. "10 Years of Fun and Games, Wet Stages, Dry Humor, Good Times, Bad Times at the Opera House." *Austin American-Statesman*, June 5, 1987, B9.

Frolik, Joe. "Concerts Set for Next Year." *Austin American-Statesman*, July 7, 1978, D1.

1979: Pedernales

ARTICLES

Burger, Frederick. "Yahoo! What a Party: Willie's Annual 4th-of-July Picnic." *Miami Herald*, July 8, 1979, 3L.

Frolik, Joe. "Ticket Sales Languid." *Austin American-Statesman*, June 27, 1979, B1.

———. "Willie Draws Big Crowd, but Few Problems." *Austin American-Statesman*, July 5, 1979.

Garcia, Guillermo. '79 Picnic Fun, Not Profitable." *Austin American-Statesman*, July 5, 1979, B1.

Lomax, Lucius. "High Times: Medical Staff Has Busy Day Keeping Picnickers on Ground." *Austin American-Statesman*, July 5, 1979, B6.

———. "Suit to Stop Willie's Picnic Filed." *Austin American-Statesman*, June 26, 1979, B3.

Chapter Three
1980: Pedernales
BOOKS

Nelson, Susie. *Heartworn Memories.* Austin: Eakin Press, 1987.

Patoski, Joe Nick. *Willie Nelson: An Epic Life*. New York: Little, Brown, 2008.

ARTICLES

Applebome, Peter. "Dallas Story: Fortune Made in a Hurry, Lost in a Hurry, Then Death at 39." *New York Times*, May 29, 1979.

Associated Press. "50,000 Beer-Guzzling Country Music Lovers Flock to Willie's Last Picnic." *Longview Journal*, July 6, 1980, 2-A.

Coggins, Cheryl. "'Last Props Set for Willie's Fete." *Austin American-Statesman*, July 4, 1980, B1.

———. "Willie Takes Home $62,000 from Final Picnic." *Austin American-Statesman*, July 16, 1980, B1.

Crewdson, John M. "The Last of the Best Little Picnics in Texas." *New York Times*, July 6, 1980.

Curry, Bill. "Woodstock for Rednecks: Beer, Willie Nelson." *Los Angeles Times*, July 6, 1980, 1.

Douthat, Bill. "If Suit Filed, Frank Says He'll Stop Willie's Picnic." *Austin American-Statesman*, April 29, 1980.

———. "Medics Treat 300 at Picnic." *Austin American-Statesman*, July 5, 1980, 1.

Eipper, Laura. "Willie's Picnic Becomes Lone Star Woodstock." *The Tennessean*, July 8, 1980, 13.

Garcia, Guillermo. "'Willie Packing Up for His Last July 4th Picnic." *Austin American-Statesman*, May 14, 1980.

Hoffard, Vince. "40 Years after Willie Nelson said His 4th of July Picnic Was Over, It Lives On—This Year, Online." *Southern Illinoisan*, July 1, 2020.

Kelly, Lee, and Patrick Taggart. "'Honeysuckle' Premiere Star-Studded." *Austin American-Statesman*, July 4, 1980, G1.

Kirkland, Bruce. "Forget the Heat, It's Showtime at Willie Nelson's." *Ottawa Journal*, July 7, 1980, 1.

Lomax, Lucius. "Justice Will Prevail at Willie's Bash." *Austin American-Statesman*, April 16, 1980.

Messina, Lynne. "'Blue Jeans Fadin' in the Rain." *Austin American-Statesman*, July 9, 1980, C1.

Patterson, Rob. "The Last Holler for Willie Nelson's Picnic." *The (Streator) Times*, July 22, 1980, 11.

Smith, Rick. "Judge's Day at Picnic Duller than Average." *Austin American-Statesman*, July 5, 1980, A6.

———. "Nelson's Notes Die Out amid Litter." *Austin American-Statesman*, July 6, 1980, B1.

———. "Willie's Picnic Proves Too Much for Manager." *Austin American-Statesman*, July 6, 1980, B1.

Taggart, Patrick. "'Willie Undaunted by Role in 2nd Time before Cameras." *Austin American-Statesman*, July 5, 1980, 31.

Trachtenberg, Jay. "Willie's Last Picnic: His Best." *Daily Texan*, July 7, 1980.

Ward, Ed. "Missing Helicopter Kept Charlie Daniels Band from Nelson Picnic." *Austin American-Statesman*, July 9, 1980, D6.

Ward, Ed, John T. Davis, and Adam Block. "Chaos, Country Rule at Willie's Last Picnic." *Austin American-Statesman*, July 5, 1980, A7.

Wilson, Janet. "'Picnic Bench Overturned." *Austin American-Statesman*, July 3, 1980, B2.

INTERVIEWS

Ray Benson, Tommy Blackwell, Steve Brooks, Roger Collins, Freddy Fletcher, Delbert McClinton, Connie Nelson, Scott Newton, Tim O'Connor, Fran Szal, Jay Trachtenberg

1981 and 1982

ARTICLES

Associated Press. "Gilley's 4th Bash a Bust." *Longview News-Journal*, July 7, 1981, 4-B.

Beck, Marilyn. "Willie's Annual Picnic Held Las Vegas-Style." *Chicago Tribune Service*, July 10, 1981, E5.

Connelly, Christopher. "Willie Nelson Woos Caesar's Palace Leisure Suit Crowd." *Fort Lauderdale News*, July 31, 1981, 29S.

Szilagyi, Pete. "When He's Not on the Road Again, Willie Prefers Austin." *Austin American-Statesman*, July 26, 1981, A7.

1983: Syracuse, New Jersey, and Atlanta

ARTICLES

Croyle, Jonathan. "Willie Nelson's 'Texas Woodstock' Becomes Syracuse Sauna in 1983." Syracuse.com, June 30, 2016.

DeVault, Russ. "Hank Got Them Cooking, but Willie Fixed the Boiling Point." *Atlanta Journal-Constitution*, July 5, 1983, 4B.

———. "It Was No Picnic for Willie, Press." *Atlanta Journal-Constitution*, June 21, 1983, 3B.

Martz, Ron. "Fans Party and Sweat for Nelson." *Atlanta Journal-Constitution*, July 5, 1983, 1B.

Martz, Ron, and Russ DeVault. "The Sounds Were Hot While the Fans Tried to Stay Wet and Cool." *Atlanta Journal-Constitution*, July 5, 1983, 4B.

Chapter Four
1984: South Park Meadows
ARTICLES

Associated Press. "Willie's Neighbors Not Happy with Latest Concert." *Paris News*, July 2, 1984, 3A.

Booth, William, and Jerry White. "Willie's Back Home: 18,000 Music Fans Revel at July Fourth Picnic." *Austin American-Statesman*, July 5, 1984, 1.

Corcoran, Michael. "Little Lambs to Slaughter Lane: A History of Southpark Meadows." *MichaelCorcoran.net*, August 8, 1995.

Davis, John T. "Legendary Picnic Rewards Fans on the Fourth." *Austin American-Statesman*, July 6, 1984, C1.

———. "Nelson Glad to Take Picnics Back Home." *Austin American-Statesman*, June 14, 1984, C10.

———. "Outdoor Concert Center to Be Built for 30,000 in South Travis." *Austin American-Statesman*, June 14, 1984, 1.

———. "Picnic Hotter than Fourth of July." *Austin American-Statesman*, July 5, 1984, A7.

Gibson, Elise. "Willie Fans Run Gamut from Bikers to Feisty Grandmas." *Austin American-Statesman*, July 5, 1984, A6.

Goodrich, Terry. "Security Net Spread across Meadows." *Austin American-Statesman*, July 4, 1984, H4.

Millard, Bob. "Willie Warms Austin with Tradition." *Fort Worth Star-Telegram*, July 5, 1984, 2A.

Phillips, Jim. "Details Submitted for Willie's Concert." *Austin American-Statesman*, June 22, 1984, B1.

INTERVIEWS

Michael Ballew, Tyler Mahan Coe, Roger Collins, John T. Davis, Joe Ely, Sharon Ely, Freddy Fletcher, Danny Garrett, Sandra Madrid, Scott Newton, Tim O'Connor, Joe Nick Patoski, Travis D. Stimeling, Jerry White

1985: South Park Meadows
ARTICLES

Davis, John T. "Rain Adds Muddy Splash to Willie's Picnic." *Austin American-Statesman*, July 5, 1985, F1.

Knapp, Becky. "Willie's Fans Remain Loyal at Wet Picnic." *Austin American-Statesman*, July 5, 1985, A14.
White, Jerry. "Festive Crowds Revel in July Fourth Rain." *Austin American-Statesman*, July 5, 1985, 1.

INTERVIEWS

Roger Collins, Tim O'Connor

1986: Farm Aid II at Manor Downs

BOOKS

Roberts, Woody. *Horse Racing & Rock 'n' Roll*. Austin: Press 709, 2019.

ARTICLES

Bryant, John. "The Benefit Beat: Farm Aid II Ends Minutes Late and Dollars Short, but Thumbs Up.'" *Austin American-Statesman*, July 6, 1986.
———. "Willie Nelson Keeps Concert 'Rolling Right Along.'" *Austin American-Statesman*, July 5, 1986, A8.
Davis, John T. "Performers Weather Acoustics, Odd Duets for Rousing Spectacle." *Austin American-Statesman*, July 5, 1985, A8.
Phillips, Jim, and John Bryant. "40,000 Crowd Manor Downs for Farm Aid." *Austin American-Statesman*, July 5, 1986, 1.

Chapter Five

1987: Carl's Corner

BOOKS

Nelson, Willie, and Bud Shrake. *Willie: An Autobiography*. New York: Simon and Schuster, 1988.

ARTICLES

Associated Press. "Carl's Corner Ready for Willie's Picnic." *Paris News*, May 14, 1987, 1.
———. "Nelson Plans Big July Picnic." *Sheboygan Press*, May 12, 1987, 20.
Canning, Whit. "Best Little Truckstop in Texas." *Fort Worth Star-Telegram*, June 28, 1987, sec. 6, 6.
Davis, John T. "Faces & Stages: Annual Picnic Reunites Old Friends, New Talent." *Austin American-Statesman*, July 3, 1987, E1.
———. "Problem-Free Picnic Reminiscent of Willie Past." *Austin American-Statesman*, July 5, 1987, A8.
Guinn, Jeff. "What's-His-Name's Picnic Lacks Friends." *Fort Worth Star-Telegram*, July 5, 1987, 1.
Hull, C. Bryson. "Carl's Corner a Roadside Oz for Travelers." *Galveston Daily-News*, August 15, 1999, B2.

Jinkins, Shirley. "Picnic with Willie." *Fort Worth Star-Telegram*, July 3, 1987, 20.

———. "Willie Saves the Day by Filling the Gap for Missing Stars." *Fort Worth Star-Telegram*, July 5, 1987, sec. 1, 10.

Matustik, David. "A Truckstop Operator with Vision." *Austin American-Statesman*, June 15, 1987, 1.

Shropshire, Mike. "How Willie Nelson Saved Carl's Corner—Again." *D Magazine*, November 2006.

Staff and Wire. "Gettin' Down to Willie's Jam." *Fort Worth Star-Telegram*, July 4, 1987, sec. 1, pt. 2, 1.

Trott, Bob. "Thousands Attend Annual Willie Nelson Picnic." *Kilgore News-Herald*, July 5, 1987, 1.

UPI. "Willie's Picnic May Attract 90,000 Fans." *Tyler Courier-News*, July 2, 1987, sec. 2, 7.

Weingarten, Paul. "Carl Is the Ultimate Big Wheel in a Strange Land of 18-Wheelers." *Chicago Tribune*, February 5, 1989, sec. 1, 5.

"Willie's Picnic Smooth, Concert-Goers Pleased." *Hillsboro Reporter*, July 9, 1987.

INTERVIEWS

John T. Davis, Jeff Guinn, Bruce Hornsby, Tim O'Connor, Budrock Prewitt, Rattlesnake Annie, Janis Tillerson, Jimmie Vaughan, Bob Wishoff

1988 and 1989

ARTICLES

MacCambridge, Michael. "Music in the Parks to Light Up Fourth Celebration." *Austin American-Statesman*, July 4, 1988, B8.

INTERVIEWS

Tim O'Connor

1990: Zilker Park, Austin

ARTICLES

MacCambridge, Michael. "Highwaymen Top Picnic with a Musical Dessert." *Austin American-Statesman*, July 5, 1990, A9.

Szilagyi, Pete. "'Small Loss' Predicted for Picnic.'" *Austin American-Statesman*, July 7, 1990, Time Out, 3.

Szilagyi, Pete, and Julie Bonnin. "Singing the Spirit of the 4th: Heat Greets Austin Revelers, Willie Declares Zilker Picnic 'Smoothest Ever.'" *Austin American-Statesman*, July 5, 1990, 1.

INTERVIEWS

Turk Pipkin

Chapter Six
1995: Luckenbach
ARTICLES
Thomas, Dave. "Willie's Fans Have a Picnic." *San Angelo Standard-Times*, July 5, 1995, 1.
INTERVIEWS
David Anderson, Monica Andrews, Matthew Carinhas, VelAnne Clifton, John T. Davis, Jesse Dayton, Cris Graham, John Graham, Little Joe Hernandez, Ray Wylie Hubbard, Dahr Jamail, Jimmy Lee Jones, Milton Jung, Robert Earl Keen, Doc Mason, Paula Nelson, Tim O'Connor, Joe Nick Patoski, Budrock Prewitt, Kimmie Rhodes, Richard Skanse, Bob Wishoff, Jack Yoder, Zip Zimmerman

1996–2002
ARTICLES
Martin, Margaret. "Kenny Wayne Shepherd, Willie Nelson Jam." *Shreveport Times*, July 10, 2001, D1.
Riemenschneider, Chris, and Kim Sue Lia Perkes. "Willie Sings One for Austin." *Austin American-Statesman*, July 5, 2000, B1.
Scheibal, Stephen. "Austin to Welcome Willie after He's Forced to Pack Up His Picnic." *Austin American-Statesman*, June 1, 2000, 1.
INTERVIEWS
Grant Alden, Matthew Carinhas, VelAnne Clifton, Nancy Coplin, Cris Graham, Tim O'Connor, Budrock Prewitt
DOCUMENTS
Personal notes, 1996–99 Picnics.

Chapter Seven
2003: Two River Canyon
ARTICLES
Corcoran, Michael. "Breakin' in the Canyon Willie Style." *Austin American-Statesman*, April 10, 2003, XLENT, 22.
———. "Willie's Picnic, Back with the Dead." *Austin American-Statesman*, June 29, 2003, 1.
Corcoran, Michael, Melissa Ludwig, and Jeremy Schwartz. "Country Fans, Deadheads Dance Together at 4th of July Picnic." *Austin American-Statesman*, July 5, 2003, A10.
Gray, Christopher. "Willie's July 4th Party Showers Spicewood with More than Just Fireworks." *Austin Chronicle*, July 11, 2003.
Gross, Joe, Melissa Ludwig, and Jeremy Schwartz. "A New Day at Willie's Picnic." *Austin American-Statesman*, July 6, 2003, B1.

Langer, Andy. "Ruling the Roost: The Live Music Capital's Notorious Captain of Industry, Tim O'Connor." *Austin Chronicle*, June 1, 2001.

Plohetski, Tony, Melissa Ludwig, and Jeremy Schwartz. "Traffic Was No Picnic." *Austin American-Statesman*, July 5, 2003, 1.

INTERVIEWS

Roger Collins, Michael Corcoran, Ed Crowell, John T. Davis, Mark del Castillo, Rick del Castillo, Alfredo Tomas Garcia, Deana Hebert Gideon, Patty Griffin, James Hyland, Dahr Jamail, Charlie Jones, Stephanie Urbina Jones, Darren Morrison, Paula Nelson, James Oakley, Tim O'Connor, Budrock Prewitt, Alex Ruiz, Josh Spurgers, Jack Yoder, Bob Wishoff

BLOGS

"The Grateful Dead in Texas 1968–88 (Miles and Miles of Texas)." lostlivdead.blogspot.com, April 6, 2017.

Chapter Eight

2004: Fort Worth Stockyards

BOOKS

Billy Bob's Texas: 40 Years at the World's Largest Honky-Tonk. Fort Worth: Billy Bob's Texas, 2021.

ARTICLES

Corcoran, Michael. "Injury Has Willie's Fans Singing the Blues." *Austin American-Statesman*, May 12, 2004, B1.

Curry, Matt. "Willie Nelson Suffers Reaction after Surgery, Not Playing Guitar." Associated Press, July 2, 2004, 6A.

Jinkins, Shirley. "Nelson Bringing Lots of Friends to Stockyards Picnic." *Fort Worth Star-Telegram*, April 17, 2004, 9B.

Kennedy, Bud. "Willie's Fourth of July Picnic Here to Be a Hot One." *Fort Worth Star-Telegram*, March 2, 2004, 4B.

Mayhew, Malcolm. "Concert Producer Pitched Big Ideas." *Fort Worth Star-Telegram*, August 8, 2004, 5B.

———. "It's Almost Official: Willie's Picnic Is Coming Back." *Fort Worth Star-Telegram*, July 8, 2004, 11A.

"Nelson in Cowtown July 4th." *Fort Worth Star-Telegram*, February 23, 2004, 12A.

Penland, Caren, and Stefan Stevenson. "Willie's Picnic as American as July Fourth." *Fort Worth Star-Telegram*, July 5, 2004, 11A.

Tarradell, Mario. "Willie's Eager to Celebrate in Fort Worth." *Dallas Morning News*, July 4, 2004, 1G.

INTERVIEWS

Linda Banks, Ray Benson, Jason Boland, Tyler Mahan Coe, Craig Copeland, Laurin Floyd, Robert Gallagher, Bud Kennedy, Jim Lane, Billy Minick, Pam Minick, Mike Moncrief, Mario Tarradell, Marty Travis, George Westby, Jack Yoder

2005–2009
ARTICLES

Asher, Tizzy. "The Heat Was No Picnic, but Willie Nelson's Party Was Cool." *Seattle Post-Intelligencer*, July 5, 2007.

Corcoran, Michael. "Poodie-ful Music: Despite Heat, 2,000 Gather for Outpouring of Love." *Austin American-Statesman*, June 29, 2009, 1.

Guerra, Joey. "Willie's Family Tradition Continues." *Houston Chronicle*, July 7, 2008.

Hughes, Andrew S. "Despite Rain, Concert a Good Time." *South Bend Tribune*, July 6, 2009, A2.

INTERVIEWS

Ray Benson, Tyler Mahan Coe, Robert Gallagher, Joe Nick Patoski

DOCUMENTS

Personal notes, 2005, 2006, 2008 Picnics.

Chapter Nine
2010: The (New) Backyard
ARTICLES

Allen, Ed. "Backyard's Green Redevelopment Launched with High Hopes, Praise." *Austin American-Statesman*, July 1, 2017, B2.

Caldwell, Patrick. "Shortages and Delays in the Evening at Nelson's Picnic." Austin360.com, July 5, 2010.

———. "Willie, Fans Give a Downhome Welcome to the New Backyard." *Austin American-Statesman*, July 5, 2010, 1.

Gross, Joe. "Musicians Serenade Backyard like There's No Tomorrow." *Austin American-Statesman*, October 27, 2008, 1.

McLeese, Don. "Backyard Plugs Austin into 'Shed Circuit.'" *Austin American-Statesman*, May 4, 1993, F5.

———. "Sexton Gets Offer He Can't Refuse." *Austin American-Statesman*, May 24, 1994, E5.

INTERVIEWS

Tyler Mahan Coe, Ray Wylie Hubbard, Gary Miller, Scott Moore, Amy Nelson, Connie Nelson, Paula Nelson, Tim O'Connor, Budrock Prewitt, Pauline Reese, Gail Swanson, Dallas Wayne, Jack Yoder

DOCUMENTS
Personal notes, 2010 Picnic.

2011–2014
DOCUMENTS
Personal notes, 2011–14 Picnics.

Chapter Ten

2015: Austin360 Amphitheater, Circuit of the Americas
INTERVIEWS
Ray Benson, Peter Blackstock, John T. Davis, Cleve Hattersley, Ray Wylie Hubbard, Charlie Jones, Gary Miller, Frank Mull, Amy Nelson, Raelyn Nelson, Joe Nick Patoski, Turk Pipkin, Dallas Wayne, Jack Yoder
DOCUMENTS
Personal notes, 2015 Picnic.

2016–2023
INTERVIEWS
Dallas Wayne
DOCUMENTS
Personal notes, 2016–23 Picnics.

Conclusion
ARTICLES
Sosa, Norma. "Willie Nelson." *Corpus Christi Caller-Times*, December 12, 1975, 20C.
INTERVIEWS
Tyler Mahan Coe, John T. Davis, Ray Wylie Hubbard, Dahr Jamail, Connie Nelson, Raelyn Nelson, Scott Newton, Joe Nick Patoski, Turk Pipkin, Travis D. Stimeling, Dallas Wayne, Jack Yoder

Index

Abernathy, Mack, 109
advertising/promotion, 12–13, 15–16, *45*, 46, 49, 52, 93–94, *color photo section*
Airoldi, Tony, 19, 26
Alabama, 89
Alden, Grant, 148
Allan, Gary, 212
Allen, Nelson, 48
Allen, Terry, 1
Allred, Sammy, 88, 135, *141*, 227
"Amazing Grace" (at Farm Aid II), 104
Anderson, David (Luckenbach bar supervisor), 131, 134, 145
Anderson, David (Pedernales coordinator), 64–65, 69
Anderson, John, 105
Andrews, Monica, 140, 144
Angel (assistant), 46
"Angel from Montgomery" (at Farm Aid II), 104
Armadillo Farm, 127
Armadillo World Headquarters, 10–12, 14, 15, 30–31, 32, 228. *See also* Wilson, Eddy
arrests: Carl's Corner, 112; Fort Worth Stockyards, 185; Gonzales, 58; Luckenbach, 132, 134, 145; Pedernales, 76; South Park Meadows, 96, 102; Two River Canyon, 166; Zilker Park, 120
Arrowhead Stadium, Kansas City, 63–64, 217, 240
Asleep at the Wheel, 7, 66, 76, 105, 121, 172, 223, 232. *See also* Benson, Ray
Atlanta Journal-Constitution, 87
Atlanta Picnic, 87
Atlanta Picnic (1983), 241
Attal, Charles, 217, 218
attendance, during the 1970s: Austin, 63; College Station, 34; Dallas, 63, 64; Dripping Springs, 9, *20c*; Gonzales, 37, 38, 49–50, 51–52; Kansas City, 63; Liberty Hill, 35, 36; Moulton benefit, 44; Pedernales, 64, 65, 69; Tulsa, 63
attendance, during the 1980s: Atlanta, 87; Carl's Corner, 105, 106, 115; Farm Aid II, 103; Gilley's picnic, 86; New Jersey, 87; Pedernales, 66, *71c*, 83; South Park Meadows, 88, 102; Syracuse, 87
attendance, during the 1990s: Backyard, 121; Luckenbach, 122, *129c*, 147, 149; Zilker Park, 120
attendance, during the 2000s: Austin360 Amphitheater, 214; Backyard, 196, *204c*; Fort Worth Stockyards, 172, *177c*, 182, 188, 192, 193, 211, 212; South Bend, *195*; South Park Meadows, 149; Two River Canyon, 152, *155c*, 166
Austin American-Statesman (article topics): Armadillo venue, 10; Nelson's film, 67; Nelson's hand problem, 179; no-Picnic years, 86, 119; Stone Mountain venue, 150
Austin American-Statesman (Gonzales Picnic coverage): aftermath, 58, 59; announcement of, 40, 44, 46; attendance, 52; opposition, 49; permit problem, 43, 49; rape reports, 56; site preparations, 50, 51
Austin American-Statesman (Picnic coverage): Austin360 Amphitheater, 216, 230; Backyard, 198, 204–5, 208–9; Carl's Corner, 109; Dripping Springs, 19; Kansas City, 64; Pedernales, 65, 70–71, 76, 83, 84–85; Q2 Stadium, 232; South Park Meadows, 90, 91, 94, 96, 99, 101, 102; Two River Canyon, 152, 153, 156, 159, 160, 166; Zilker Park, 120
Austin360 Amphitheater Picnics: artists listed, 247–48; atmosphere, 210, 214–16, 222–23, 225–26; backstage passes,

270 / INDEX

color photo section; management of, 216–18, 219–20, *color photo section*; performances, 218–19, 221–23, *224*, *225*, 228–29, 230–31, *color photo section*; photos, *215*, *219*, *221*, *222*
Austin Chronicle, 160
Austin City Limits, 218
Austin Music Hall, 157
Austin Opera/Opry House, 63–64, 80, 90, 157, 240, *color photo section*

backstage atmosphere: after corporate management, 218; Austin360 Amphitheater, 222–23, 230; Backyard, 205; Dripping Springs, 26–28; Fort Worth, 186, 193; Gonzales, 56; Pedernales, 79–80; Poodie's role, 203; South Park Meadows, 98–99
backstage passes, *color photo section*
Backyard, O'Connor's ownership, 157, 217
Backyard mini-Picnics, 6, 121
Backyard Picnics: aftermath, 208–10; artists listed, 243, 246; atmosphere, 196–97, 198–201, 204–5; as end of "let it ride" era, 210; performances, 205–8, *210*; photos, *199*, *201*, *204*, *207*, *208*, *210*; Poodie's absence, 202–3; poster, *color photo section*; preparation challenges, 198, 199, 204
Baez, Joan, 44, 48
Ball, Marcia, 24, 26, 34
Ballew, Michael, 95–96, 99
ballpark tour, 195
Bandy, Moe, 97
Banks, Linda, 181–82, 184, 191
Barbarosa (film), 96
Bare, Bobby, 200, 223
Bare, Bobby Jr, 200
Barnett, Billy Bob, 175–76
Barton, Rodeo, 54
Bassler, Jerry, 83
Beach Boys, 118, 176
Bee Cave. *See* Backyard Picnics
beer rules: Luckenbach, 131, 132, 146; South Park Meadows, 88–89
beer sales-parking lot story, 184–85

Bells of Joy, 236
Benestante, Mike: after Gonzales Picnic, 62; background, 41–42
Benestante, Mike (Gonzales Picnic): aftermath, 61; on Geno's behavior, 48; kidnapping story, 38, 57–58; during performances, 56–57; permit application, 43, 46, 49; preparations, 50
Benno, Marco, 29
Benson, Ray: and Del Castillo Band, 154; recording with Hornsby, 114; and Willie's hand problem, 179
Benson, Ray (at Picnics): Austin, *222*, *223*; Backyard, 207; Fort Worth Stockyards, 182, 193; as frequent performer, 7; Pedernales, 76, 78, 84. *See also* Asleep at the Wheel
Benson, Ray (commenting on): backstage atmosphere, 80, 218; golf course condition, 71; Haggard's death, 227; his band's success, 172; longevity of Picnics, 84; reunion aspect, 81; Trader, 74
Bentley, Bill, 5, 20, 21, 22, 26, 29, 32
Bentley, Dierks, 191, 213
Berry, Chuck, 176
Besaw, Larry, 64
Biel, Walter, 150
Billboard Magazine, 63
Billy Bob's, 175–77, 184, 185, 188, 189–90, 211–12. *See also* Fort Worth Stockyards Picnics
Bingham, Ryan, 212, 213, 227
Blackstock, Peter, 5, 216, 220, 226, 230, 232
Blackwell, Tommy, 74–75, 76, 82
Blank, Jeff, 197
Blundell, Jerry, 75
Boatright, Paul Lenden, 54
Boland, Jason, 176, 186, 187, 189
Bolt, Tommy, 73
Bon Jovi, Jon, 104
Bowen, Wade, 211–12
Bowie, David, 101
"A Boy Named Sue" (at Zilker Park), 120
bribes, 12, 46

Brooks, Steve, 22, 68, *69*, 80, 94, *color photo section*
Brotherton, Rich, 140
Brown, Clarence "Gatemouth," 138, 187
Bumpass, Beth Munson, 40, 43, 46, 62
Burchard, Bob, 60
Burke, Delta, 119
Busey, Gary, 96
Bush, Johnny: career highlights, 88, 152; death of, 4, 227, 232; on Picnic idea, 3; in Price's band, 66
Bush, Johnny (at Picnics): Austin, 223; Austin360 Amphitheater, 228, 230; Fort Worth Stockyards, 184, 213; as frequent performer, 7; San Antonio, 195; South Park Meadows, 96
Byrds, 32
304 pages
Caeser's Palace party, 86
Canada, Cody, *181*
Cannon, Dyan, 66, 78, *79*
Capital Ambulance Services, 60
Capital Plaza Cinema, 66
Capital Sports and Entertainment, 218
car fires, 35
Carinhas, Matthew, 130, 151
Carlan, Willobee, 155, 156, 170
Carll, Hayes, 229
Carl's Corner Picnic: artists listed, 243; attendance, 105, 106, 109, 115; backstage passes, *color photo section*; failure factors, 117–19; performances, 112–15; photos, *107*, *111*, *113*, *116*, *117*; publicity for, 108; site location, 105, 108, 117–18
Carradine, David, 35
Carter, Jimmy, 66
Cash, Johnny, 44, 102, 120, 176
Cash, June Carter, 102
Castle Creek Club, 156
Cat (assistant), 46
Chapman, Thomas, 22, 24
Charles, Ray, 176
Charlie Daniels Band, 49
Cherokee Rose, 104
Childers, Tyler, 232, 233

"China Cat Sunflower" (at Two River Canyon), 164
Church, Eric, 216, 225
Circuit of the Americas. *See* Austin360 Amphitheater Picnics
Citizens for Law, Order, and Decency (CLOD), 42–43, 49, 61
City of New Orleans (Nelson), 88
Clark, Dick, 55
Clark, Guy, 18, 148, 231
Clark, Roy, 44
Clayton, Lee, 1, 18, 26
Clear Channel Communications, 217
Clifton, VelAnne, 123, *125*, 126–27, 135, 137, 139, 147, 148
CLOD (Citizens for Law, Order, and Decency), 42–43, 49, 61
cocaine, 3, 11, 54, 72, 80
Cochran, Hank, 202–3
Coe, David Allan (at Picnics): Atlanta, 87; Austin360 Amphitheater, 221, 230; Backyard, *208*; Carl's Corner, 109; Fort Worth Stockyards, 193–94; as frequent performer, 7; Gilley's, 86; Gonzales, 49, 53–54; Houston, 195; Liberty Hill, 36; Luckenbach, 143; San Antonio, 195; South Park Meadows, 97–98
Coe, David Allan (career highlights), 37, 122, 172
Coe, Tyler Mahan, 53, 97–98, 184, 194, 200–201, 209, 235
Cohen, Leonard, 197
Cohn, Nudie, 98
Coldplay, 197
College Station Picnic, 34–35, 239–40
Collins, Roger: on fan base, 82; Pedernales, 79–80, 84; South Park Meadows, 89, 98–99, 102; on Trader, 73, 74; Two River Canyon, 156, 159, 160
Colter, Jessi, 7, 99
Columbia/Sony, 124
Colvin, Shawn, 168
Combs, Luke, 230
concessionaires: Backyard, 199, 204; Carl's Corner, 108, 110; Gonzales, 51, 52, 58–59; Liberty Hill, 36; Luckenbach,

140, 146; South Park Meadows, 89, 96; Syracuse, 87
Cook, Mark, 96
Coolidge, Rita, 12, 28, 49
Cooper, Billy Ray "B. C.," 12
Cooper, George W., 28
Copeland, Craig, 182, 191
Coplin, Nancy, 148
Corcoran, Michael, 152, 159
Cornelius, Carl (Carl's Corner Picnic): as failure factor, 118–19; money dispute, 105–6; negotiations for, 107–8; promotional activity, 108, 109–10, 118
Cornelius, Carl (property development), 106–7
Corpus Christi Caller-Times, 235
Cotton Bowl, Dallas Picnic, 63–64, 240
Country Dummies, 109
Country Throwdown Tour, 211
"Courtesy of the Red, White and Blue" (Keith song), 161
Coveleski Stadium, 195
Covers, Joan Jett, 221
"Crazy" (at Two River Canyon), 162
Crockett, Charley, 231
Cross Canadian Ragweed, *181*, 187
Crouch, Becky, 126
Crouch, Cris, 126
Crouch, Hondo, 126
Crow, Sheryl, 229
Crowell, Ed, 156
Crowell, Rodney, 90
Crumley Grocery, 102
C3 Presents, 158, 217, 218
Culak, Debbie, 59–60
"Cumberland Blues" (at Two River Canyon), 154, 161–62
Cusic, Don, 58

D. E. Crumley Grocery, 102
"Daddy, What If?" (Coe performances), 200
Daily Texan, 77
Dallas Morning News, 118, 173, 182, 185
Dallas Picnic, 63–64, 240
Daltrey, Roger, 78

D'Angelo, Annie, 105, 124
Daniels, Charlie, 78
Darnell, Jimmy, 42
Davis, John T. (comments about): Austin's music evolution, 215; Carl's Corner, 106, 110, 113–14, 117, 118; concert line ups, 91, 96–97; Luckenbach, 137, 140, 144, 146; music variety, 138; Nelson's celebrity status, 89, 90; O'Connor, 106; Pace Concerts management, 91; Picnic longevity, 235; Picnic magic, 237; Picnic motivations, 101; South Park Meadows, 95, 98, 99, 102; Willie's music mentoring, 227; Willie's music transition, 124
Davis, Mac, 232
Day, Jimmy, 142
Dayton, Jesse, 125, 135
Dead, 152, 154, 155, 159, 164–65, 170
dehydration. *See* heat problems
DeJoria, John Paul, 209
Del Castillo, Mark, 154, 166
Del Castillo, Rick, 154, 166–67, 171
Del Castillo band, 153–54, 166–67
de Menil, Francois, 12, 16
Denton Record-Chronicle, 32
Dependable Dodge, 30
"Desperados Waiting for a Train" (Walker performance), 18
Diddley, Bo, 176
"Did Willie Change World Politics?" (course title), 228
"Die When I'm High" (at Q2 Stadium), 233
Direct Events, 157, 217
diversity factor, Picnic longevity, 235–36
"Django & Jimmie" (Nelson and Haggard song), 214
documentaries, Picnic, 12, 16, 34, 44, 53, 54–55, 120
Dodd, Deryl, 178
Dodge Stockyards Stampede, 178
Dorcy, Ben, 194
Doug Sahm and Friends (Sahm album), 13
"Down by the River" (at Two River Canyon), 168
Dripping Springs Picnic (1973): aftermath,

29–33; artists listed, 239; atmosphere, 21–24, 26–27; fan arrival problems, 18–21; film plan, 16; performances, *17*, 18–19, 24, 26, 28–29; photos, *17*, *20*, *25*, *27*; planning/promotion, 9–16; poster, *color photo section*; power outage, 28–29; preparations for, 15, 16–17
Dripping Springs plan (2000), 149–50
Dripping Springs Reunion (1972), 1, 14–15, 29, 32
drowning, Gonzales Picnic, 55
drug consumption: College Station Picnic, 34; Dripping Springs, 5, 21, 22, 23, 26; Gonzales, 37–38, 39, 48, 54, 56; Pedernales, 65
drug dogs, 134, 146
drunkenness, 36, 37–38, 111–12, 137, 145. *See also* arrests
Duke, Red, 109, 112
The Dukes of Hazzard (film), 172
dusty conditions, 21, 26, 95, 114
DWI cases, Carl's Corner, 112. *See also* arrests
Dylan, Bob, 13, 16, 24, 32, 44, 48, 52, 172, 192–93, 195

Earle, Steve, 90, 229, 230–31
Eastwood, Clint, 66
Easy Money Band, 180
Eipper, Laura, 78
Eklund, Allison, 217
"El Paso" (at Two River Canyon), 164
Ely, Joe: Carl's Corner, 114; Luckenbach, 149; Mickey Mantle story, 92–93; in 1990s Texas music scene, 124; South Park Meadows, 97, 98; on Southpark shopping center, 102
Ely, Sharon, 93
Emmons, Bobby, 148
Engel, Benno, 129
Engel, Elizabeth, 129–30
Engel, John, 129
English, Paul, 28, 36, 227
<LS>
Fabulous Thunderbirds, 114, 115
family/friendship factor, 80–81, 142–43, 169, 200–201, 223, 225, 235
fan base, aging impact, 91, 118
"Fantasy Island," 80
Farm Aid, 147, 225
Farm Aid II, 84, 103–4, 242
Feelin' Good (Geezinslaws album), 122
fencing: Dripping Springs, 15, 19, 20–21, 23; Gonzales, 50, 52–53; Luckenbach, 128; Pedernales, 70, 83
Fey, Barry, 63
Fey Concerts, 217
field courthouse, 70
films, Picnic, 12, 16, 34, 44, 53, 54–55, 120
films, Willie's, 66–67, 96, 105, 119, 172, 179
fireworks, 52, 56, 99
Fletcher, Freddy: Gonzales, 46, 48, 54, 60, 61; Pedernales, 67; South Park Meadows, 89; Trader story, 72–73; Virtual Picnic, 231
Floyd, Jill, 179–80
Floyd, Joey, 66, 179–80, 188
Floyd, Laurin, 179–80, 188
Folk Uke, 7, 201, 220
"Folsom Prison Blues" (at Zilker Park), 120
Fonda, Jane, 86
Fortenberry, Lloyd, 17
Fort Worth Star-Telegram, on Rick Smith's death, 192
Fort Worth Star-Telegram (Picnic coverage): Carl's Corner, 109, 110, 111, 112; Fort Worth Stockyards, 173, 182, 191–92; South Park Meadows, 88, 98
Fort Worth Stockyards Picnics: artists listed, 245–47; atmosphere, 181–86, 189; backstage passes, *color photo section*; performances, *181*, 186–87, 192–94, 211–12, 213; photos, *177*, *180*, *181*, *190*; poster, *color photo section*; preparations for, 176–81; success factors, 188–91; support for, 173–75
Fort Worth Weekly, 47
40 Points band, 201
Fourth of July Picnic, overviews: artists listed, 7, 239–49; country-rock merge, 32, 228; evolution summarized, 84, 215–16, 237; interview challenges, 3–4;

longevity factors, 235–37; origins, 1, 3, 6; performer payments, 209, 216. *See also specific topics*, e.g., Carl's Corner Picnic; family/friendship factor; Nelson entries; O'Connor, Tim
Foust, Wesley, 43
Fox, C. L., 90
Frank, Raymond, 69
Franklin, Jim, 12, 13, 94, *color photo section*
Freda and the Firedogs, 24, 26, 34
Friedman, Kinky, 148
friendship/family factor, 80–81, 142–43, 169, 200–201, 223, 225
"Friends of Willie" (in Gonzales), 43
frog sculptures, Carl's Corner, 106, 107, 115
Fromholz, Steve, 7, 53, 96

Gallagher, Robert, 178, 179, 184, 185, 186–87, 188, 190, 193
Garcia, Alfredo Tomas, 161, 164, 166, 167, 168
Garcia, Jerry, 152
Garrett, Danny, 12, 93–94, *color photo section*
Garza, Henry, *186*
Garza, Jojo, *186*
gate receipts. *See* ticket prices/sales
Gates, Chris (poster by), *color photo section*
Geezinslaws, 7, 88, 96, 122, *133*
Gideon, Deana (earlier Hebert), 153, 155, 160, 165, 166, 169–71
Gilbert, Brantley, 228, 229
Gilley, Mickey, 86
Gimble, Jimmy, 142, *color photo section*
Gittin' Up (Geezinslaws album), 122
golf, 62, 72–73
Gonzales community, characterized, 39–40
Gonzales Picnic: aftermath, 58–61; artists listed, 240; atmosphere, 3, 37–39, 51–53, 54–56; opposition to, 41, 42–43, 44, 48–49, 58, 61, 174; performances, 53–54, *57*; permit process, 42–45, 46–47, 48–49; photos, *39, 50, 52, 55, 57, 59, 61*; poster, *color photo section*; preparations for, 40–42, 46–47, 49–51
Gracey, Joe, 10
Graham, Cris, 127, 128, 131, 134, 135, 142, 144, 151
Graham, John, 126, 127, 128, 131, 133–34, 141, 145, 146
Grateful Dead, 152, 159, 164–66
Gravenor, Sandy, 14–15, 19, 21, 22
Green, Pat, 125, 150, 164, 173
Greezy Wheels, 19, 26, 220, 221, 228
Greshman, Tom, 12
Griffin, Patty, 165, 166, 167–69
Guinn, Jeff, 111–12, 114
guns: Carl's Corner, 118; and concert promoting, 73; Dripping Springs, 1, 23, 27, 30; Gonzales, 3, 39, 48, 55, 57–58; Liberty Hill, 36; Luckenbach, 125; and Willie-Armadillo partnership, 30–31
Guthrie, Cathy, 220

Haden, Charlie, 114
Haggard, Merle: album with Nelson, 89; at Billy Bob's, 176; career highlights, 66, 214; death of, 227
Haggard, Merle (at Picnics): Atlanta, 87; Austin360 Amphitheater, 223–25; Backyard, 197; Carl's Corner, 109; Fort Worth Stockyards, 187, *190*; as frequent performer, 7; Houston, 195; Pedernales, 77, 81; Two River Canyon, 163
Haggard, Noel, 201
Hall, Tom T., 12, 29
Hall of Fame, 122
Ham, Bill, 154
Hard Rock Cafe, 109
Harris, Emmylou, 109, 149
Hattersley, Cleve, 220, 228
Hattersley, Lissa, 26
Hayden, Tom, 86
Head, Roy, 104
headliners listed, at the 1970s Picnics: Austin, 63; College Station, 34; Dallas, 63; Dripping Springs, 9; Gonzales, 37; Kansas City, 63; Liberty Hill, 35; Pedernales, 64; Tulsa, 63

headliners listed, at the 1980s Picnics: Atlanta, 87; Carl's Corner, 105; Farm Aid II, 103; New Jersey, 87; Pedernales, 66; South Park Meadows, 88, 102; Syracuse, 87

headliners listed, at the 1990s Picnics: Luckenbach, 122, 147, 149; Zilker Park, 120

headliners listed, at the 2000s Picnics: Austin360 Amphitheater, 214, 228, 229; Backyard, 196; Fort Worth Stockyards, 192, 193, 211, 212; Houston, 194; Q2 Stadium, 232, 233; San Antonio, 194; South Bend, 195; South Park Meadows, 149; Two River Canyon, 152; Viritual Picnic, 231; Washington State, 194

Healing Hands of Time (Willie album), 124

Health Department permit, Fort Worth Stockyards, 185

Heartworn Memories (Susie Nelson), 21, 75

heat problems: Austin360 Amphitheater, 220–21; Carl's Corner, 112; Dripping Springs, 21–22, 26; East coast Picnics, 87; Farm Aid II, 104; Fort Worth Stockyards, 182, 189; Gonzales, 54; Luckenbach, 137, 140, 147; Pedernales, 76; South Park Meadows, 89, 96; Tulsa, 63; Two River Canyon, 161; Washington State, 194; Zilker Park, 120

Heaven's Gate (film), 105

Hebert, Deana (later Gideon), 153, 155, 160, 165, 166, 169–71

Hebert, James, 153, 155, 170

Hedderman, Bobby, 12, 27, 30–31

helicopter story, Gonzales, 48

helicopter travel, Pedernales, 74–75, 78, 79, 86

"Help, I'm White and I Can't Get Down" (Geezinslaws song), 122

Hernandez, Little Joe, 137–38

Hickman, Holt, 176

Highwaymen, 101, 102, 120–21

Hillsboro Reporter, 112

Hoffard, Vince, 77, 78

Honeysuckle Rose (film), 66–67, 179

Honky Tonk Heroes (Jennings album), 37

Hope, Bob, 176

Hornsby, Bruce, 113, 114–15

"House of Blue Lights" (Asleep at the Wheel song), 105

House of Blues Concerts, 150

Houston Chronicle, 195

Houston Picnic, 194, 246

Hubbard, Judy, 34

Hubbard, Lucas, 200

Hubbard, Ray Wylie: career highlights, 37, 152, 196; conversation about Nashville, 90; on evolution of Picnics, 226; at Luckenbach honkytonk, 126; on magic of Picnics, 231–32, 237; on payment uncertainties, 209; in 1990s Texas music scene, 124–25

Hubbard, Ray Wylie (at Picnics): Austin360 Amphitheater, 220, *221*, 230; Backyard, 200; College Station, 34; Fort Worth, 213; as frequent performer, 7; Gonzales, 52, 53; Luckenbach, 143; Two River Canyon, 167

Huddleston, Dianne, 28

Hurlbut, Brad, 29, 32–33

Hurlbut Ranch, 32–33. *See also* Dripping Springs *entries*

Hurlbut, Burt, 12, 15, 23, 30

Hurlbut, James, 15, 29

Hyland, James, 154, 161, 163, 165, 171

Hynde, Chrissie, 221

Ice, Gregory (poster by), *color photo section*

Iconoclast newspaper, 45

Iglesias, Julio, 89

"I'll Fly Away" (at Austin360 Amphitheater), 225

The Improbable Rise of Redneck Rock (Reid), 16, 24

"I'm Ragged, but I'm Right" (at Gonzales), 54

Ingram, Jack, 125, 166

Iraq War, 161

IRS, 121

Irving, Amy, 67

"Is Anybody Going to San Antone" (at Fort Worth Picnic), 213

"I Saw the Light " (at Austin360 Amphitheater), 225
Isbell, Jason, 216
"It's All Going to Pot" (at Austin360 Amphitheater), 224, 225
It's a Long Story (Nelson biography), 18, 24, 60
"it's Hard to Be Humble" (at Q2 Stadium), 232
"I Wanna Be a Cowboy's Sweetheart" (at College Station), 34

"Jack Straw" (at Two River Canyon), 164
"Jacob's Ladder" (Hornsby song), 114
Jamail, Dahr: Dripping Springs, 10, 12, 31; Gonzales, 5, 38, 41–43, 46, 48, 49, 50, 53, 54, 60; interview openness, 5; Luckenbach, 142, 145; on Picnic legacy, 236–37; Two River Canyon, 154–55, 159, 164–65, 168–69; Virtual Picnic, 231
Jamail, Joe, 9, 10, 12
Jennings, Shooter, 200
Jennings, Waylon: career highlights, 9, 88; death, 227; Dripping Springs Reunion, 26; recordings with Nelson, 89–90
Jennings, Waylon (at Picnics): Atlanta, 87; College Station, 35; Dripping Springs, 12, 18, 28; as frequent performer, 7; Gonzales, 3, 38, 49, 52; Luckenbach, 133, 147–49; South Park Meadows, 99; Tulsa, 63
Johnson, Eric, 113–14
Johnson, Jamey, 7, 198, 211, 214, 216, 223, 225, 228
Johnson, Lyndon Baines, 79–80
Johnson, Wayne, 112
Jones, Charlie, 158, 217–18
Jones, George, 49, 53–54
Jones, Jimmy Lee, 127, 135, 145
Jones, Stephanie Urbina, 154, 161–62, 171
Juice Newton, 89
"Jumpin' Jack Flash" (at Gonzales), 57
Jung, Milton, 123, 130–31, 132, 134, 135, 137, 139, 145
Jury, Don, 176
"Just One Love" (at Luckenbach), 142

Just One Love (Nelson album), 122

Kansas City Picnic, 63–64, 217, 240
Karp, Louis, 22, 24, 29
"KawLiga" (at Fort Worth Picnic), 213
Keen, Robert Earl, 35, 122, 124, 126, 140, 148
Keith, Toby, 161, 163–64, 180
Kelley, Mark, 41, 59
Kelley, Sterling, 39, 41, 58, 60. *See also* Gonzales Picnic
Kennedy, Bud, 173, 175, 188, 189
kidnapping story, 38, 57–58, 62
Kimmel, Jim, 111
King, Jackie, 97
Kirby, Bennie, 109
Kirk, Steve, 3
Kirkland, Bruce, 76
"Kiss an Angel Good Morning" (at Fort Worth Picnic), 213
Kolsburn, John, 94
Koock, Guich, 126
Krauss, Alison, 228, 230
Kristofferson, Casey, *color photo section*
Kristofferson, Kris: career highlights, 37, 105, 196; retirement, 227
Kristofferson, Kris (at Picnics): Austin360 Amphitheater, 216, 221–22, 225, 228–29; Backyard, 198, 205, *206*, 207, 208; Dripping Springs, 12, 18, 26; Fort Worth Stockyards, 187, 188, 212; as frequent performer, 7; Gonzales, 49; South Park Meadows, 98, 99, *100*
KRMH radio, 30
Kucinich, Dennis, 161

Lam, Mike, 50, 57
Lane, Jim, 174, 187–88
law enforcement: Carl's Corner, 112, *117*; Dripping Springs, 1, 22; Fort Worth Stockyards, 185; Luckenbach, 130, 136–37; Two River Canyon, 166. *See also* security services
lawsuits, 16, 60, 61, 64
La Zona Rosa, 157
Lennon, John, 5

INDEX \ 277

Letterman, David, 194
Lewis, Grover, 1
Lewis, Jalapeno Sam, 127
Lewis, Jerry Lee, 86, 143, 176
Liberty Hill Picnic, *2*, 35–36, 41, 43, 240, *color photo section*
"Like a Rolling Stone" (Dylan's performance), 192
Live at Billy Bob's Texas recordings, 172, 173, 176, 192
Live Nation, 217, 218
Live Nation/C3, 217, 223, 232. *See also* Austin360 Amphitheater Picnics
Locke, Poodie: conflict with Cochran, 202–3; death of, 195, 211; at 2009 gathering, 210–11; on golf, 72; Gonzales, 57–58; Luckenbach, 127; Pedernales, 80; poster design, *color photo section*; Two River Canyon, 154, 161, 163; on Willie's hand problem, 179
"Long Black Limousine" (at Carl's Corner), 113
Longhaired Redneck (Coe album), 37
Longhorn Saloon, 182, 191
Long in the Tooth (Shaver album), 214
Los Angeles Free Press, 28
Los Angeles Times, 77
Los Lonely Boys, 166, *186*, 187
"Luckenbach, Texas" (at Tulsa Picnic), 63
"Luckenbach, Texas" (at Zilker Park), 121
Luckenbach Inn, 130
Luckenbach Picnics: agreement for, 126–27, 131; artists listed, 243–44; atmosphere, 122–23, 135–36, 142–47; backstage passes, *color photo section*; community resistance, 128–30, 139; lineup for, 132–33; loss of, 151; music scene context, 124–25; performances, 122–23, 135, 137–38, 140–42, 147–49, *color photo section*; photos, *123*, *129*, *138*, *139*, *141*, *143*, *144*, *146*; preparations for, 131–32, 133–34
Lynn, Loretta, 221

Mack, Bill, 16, 211
Madrid, Sandra, 93, 95, 96, 99

Manor Downs, 103–4
Mantle, Mickey, 92–93
marijuana. *See all Picnics*, e.g., Dripping Springs
Marley, Ziggy, 231
Marshall Tucker Band, 44
Mason, Ava (Ava Pine), 131, 145
Mason, Doc, 122, 131, 140, 145
McCall, Diane, 15
McCall, Randy, 15, 30
McCartney, Paul, 5, 52
McClinton, Delbert, 77–78, 81–82, 84
McConaughey, Matthew, 166
McCoslin, Geno: Dripping Springs, 12, 15, 27; Liberty Hill, 36; reputation, 47–48; Trader relationship, 73; Wilson's comment about, 9
McCoslin, Geno (Gonzales Picnic): afterwards, 60, 62; cocaine story, 3; drug consumption, 37, 48; kidnapping story, 38, 57–58, 62; promotion tactics, 5, 52; Sheridan conflict, 48
McCoslin, Susie, 47–48, 62
McKeown, Ron, 18
McLeese, Don, 197
medical services: Carl's Corner, 109; Dripping Springs, 15, 22–23; Fort Worth Stockyards, 182; Gonzales, 42, 56; Luckenbach, 125, 131, 139–40; Pedernales, 65, 76; Two River Canyon, 161
Mellencamp, John, 195, 225
Messina, Louis, 64, 90
Metallica, 101
Metamodern Sounds in Country Music (Simpson album), 222
Miami Herald, 64
"Midnight Rider" (at Austin360 Amphitheater), 229
"Midnight Rider" (at Fort Worth Stockyards), 194
Miller, Gary, 200, 204, 207, 220
Miller, Roger, 49
Miller, Townsend, 10, 19, 40
Minick, Billy, 172–73, 176, 178, 181, 184–85, 189, 191

Minick, Pam, 173, 174, 177, 181, 182, 187, 188, 191, 192
Minnie Mouse, 104
Mithoff, Richard, 42, 43
Moman, Chips, 148
Moncrief, Mike, 173, 174, 175, 191
Monroe, Bill, 176
Montgomery, Maggie, 127, 128
Moore, Justin, 212
Moore, Scott, 205, 207
Moorer, Allison, 229
Morrison, Darren, 165
Morrissette, Alanis, 101
Morrissey, 197
Morrow, Cory, 125
Moulton benefit, 44, 46
Moyes, Doug, 156
Mueller, James, 147
Mueller, Marge, *146*, 147
Mull, Frank, 219, 225
Munson, Houston, 40, 42, 43–44, 46, 58–60, 61–62
Murphey, Michael, 44
Murrin, Steve, 176
Musgraves, Kacey, 216, 227, 229

Nacogdoches (Nelson album), 172
Nashville Skyline (Dylan), 32
Nashville Tennessean, 58
Neil, Vince, 104
Nelson, Amy, 201–2, 203, 208, 220, 221, 223, 226, 228
Nelson, Annie, 187
Nelson, Billy, 121
Nelson, Connie: on backstage atmosphere, 80, 203; on music's role, 237–38; on Picnic planning effort, 70, 83; on reunion of friends, 80–81, 82; separation from Willie, 105, 108; on Willie-Trader relationship, 73, 74
Nelson, Lana, 1, 127
Nelson, Lukas, 7, 186–87, 201–2, 211
Nelson, Micah, 7, 187, 201–2, 206, 211, 232, 233
Nelson, Paula: on O'Connor, 158; on Picnic atmosphere, 136, 197, 208, 210; as Picnic performer, 7, 136, 201–2, 221; on Poodie, 203; on reunion aspect, 142
Nelson, Raelyn, 218–19, 220–21, 223, 225, 235, 236, *color photo section*
Nelson, Susie, 21, 75
Nelson, Willie: albums, 36, 37, 67, 88, 89, 122, 124, 172, 230; character of, 74, 96–97, 118–19; in films, 66–67, 96, 105, 119, 172, 179; hand problem, 179–80; importance of friends, 80–81, 101, 227; IRS problems, 121; music mentoring role, 171, 227, 235–37; music scene transitions, 32, 84, 89–90, 124; son's death, 121
Nelson, Willie (career highlights): during the 1970s, 9, 18, 37, 69–70; during the 1980s, 66, 69–70, 72, 88, 89, 105; during the 1990s, 122; during the 2000s, 152, 172, 196, 214
Nelson, Willie (commenting on Picnics): backstage atmosphere, 28; Carl's Corner, 115; chaos factor, 60; Dripping Springs, 24, 28; Fort Worth Stockyards, 188; Gonzales, 43, 60; hassle factor, 60; Kansas City, 64; long term possibilities, 84, 227, 235; outdoor venues, 64, 212; Zilker Park, 120
Nelson, Willie (in Picnic planning): Carl's Corner, 107–8, 114; date options, 178; Gonzales, 40–41, 43; location selection, 191; Pedernales, 70
Nelson, Willie (performances): Armadillo venue, 10, 228; Atlanta, 87; Austin360 Amphitheater, 224, 225, *226*, 229, 230, 231; Backyard, 6, *201*; Carl's Corner, 112, 113; Dripping Springs, *17*, 18, 29, *31*, *color photo section*; Fort Worth Stockyards, 187–88, 212, 213; Gonzales, 38, 54, *57*; Houston, 195; Luckenbach, 141–42, 148–49, *color photo section*; Moulton benefit, 46; Pedernales, *238*, *color photo section*; Q2 Stadium, 232, 233, *color photo section*; South Park Meadows, 150, 236; Two River Canyon, 162–65, *167*, 169
Nelson Prospecting Corporation, 12

The (New) Backyard. *See* Backyard *entries*
New Jersey Picnic, 87, 241
Newton, Scott: at Gonzales, 51, 56; at Pedernales, 76, 84; on Picnic atmosphere, 237; at South Park Meadows, 93, 95, 98, 101; on Trader-Willie relationship, 74
The Newton Boys (film), 148
New York Picnic, 87
New York Times, 67, 71
Nightcrawlers, 29
"Night Life" (at Lubbock honkytonk), 92–93
Nitty Gritty Dirt Band, 193
No. 2 Live Dinner (Keen album), 35
"Nobody There But Me" (Hornsby song), 114
"no-Picnic years," 86, 150–51
Norris, Paul, 59
"Not Fade Away" (at Two River Canyon), 164
Nudie jackets, 98
nudity, 21, 22, 36, 56, 76, 112
Nunn, Gary P., 124, 126

Oak Hill Fire Department, 30
Oakley, James, 155–56, 158, 159, 160, 166, 169, 170–71
O'Brien, Derek, *236*
O'Connor, Tim: Austin Opry House, 64; background, 156–58; Backyard/New Backyard, 196–97, 204–5, 207, 209; Bee Cave mini-Picnic, 121; Carl's Corner, 105–6, 108, 109, 110, 112, 114–15, 117–19; Dripping Springs, 14; Farm Aid II, 104; on friendship benefits, 81; interview openness, 5; Jones relationship, 217–18; Luckenbach, 128, 130, 132, 134, 143, 145; no-Picnic years, 119; Pedernales, 70, 78, 80, 84; South Park Meadows, 103; on Trader's "heart attack," 85–86; Two River Canyon, 152, 153–54, 156, 160, 169–70; Zilker Park, 121
Oklahoman, 63
Old Five and Dimers like Me (Shaver album), 37

"On the Road Again" (at Q2 Stadium), 232
"On the Road Again" (at Zilker Park), 121
O'Rourke, Beto, 230, 232
Ottawa Journal, 76

Pace Concerts, 64, 217
Pace Management Co., 88, 100
Pancho and Lefty (Nelson and Haggard album), 89
"Pancho and Lefty" (song): at Austin360 Amphitheater, *224*, 225; at South Park Meadows, 99
Pankratz, Carlotta, 21
Pantera, 194
parking/traffic: Austin360, 219; Backyard, 204; Carl's Corner, 109; Dripping Springs, 19–20; Farm Aid II, 104; Fort Worth Stockyards, 186; Gonzales, 44, 52; Liberty Hill, 36; Luckenbach, 130, 139; Pedernales, 70, 71, 75–76; South Park Meadows, 102; Two River Canyon, 153, 159–60, 165, 170–71
Particle Kid, 232, 233
"The Party's Over" (at Dripping Springs), 29
Pasadena, Gilley's picnic, 86
Patoski, Joe Nick (commenting on): Armadillo's influence, 32; Austin360 Amphitheater, 225–26; Austin's music evolution, 214–15; Dripping Springs, 23; Fort Worth Picnics, 173, 193; golf, 72; Gonzales, 38, 46, 48, 51; Liberty Hill, 36; music transition, 123, 124; Picnic management, 91; Picnic spirit evolution, 215–16; South Park Meadows, 93, 100; Willie's music mentoring, 173, 236
Patterson, Rob, 78
Paul Masson Mountain Winery, 121
Paycheck, Johnny, 66, 77, 86
Payne, Jody, 79, 201
Payne, Waylon, 198, 201
Pearl Jam, 101
Pedernales Country Club, Willie's purchase, 64, 67
Pedernales Picnics: aftermath, 83–86;

artists listed, 241; atmosphere, 76–77, 81–82, color photo section; backstage activity, 79–80; opposition, 64–65, 69; performances, 77–78, color photo section; photos, 68, 69, 71, 81, 83, 85, 238; poster, color photo section; preparations for, 67–69, 70–71, 217; traffic problems, 74–75
Perkins, Billy (poster by), color photo section
Phases and Stages Production, 44
Pickens, Slim, 66, 78
picnic table idea, 102–3
Pine, Ava (Ava Mason), 131
Pipkin, Chisty, 120
Pipkin, Turk, 120, 217, 220, 227, 235
Pogue, Alan, 20, 22–24
Pointer Sisters, 36, 138, 236
Police, 101
Pollack, Sydney, 66, 67
Porta Potties. See sanitary arrangements
posters, 12, 93–94, 125, color photo section
power outages, 28–29, 114–15
Powers, Freddy, 200
Prewitt, Budrock: Backyard, 198, 199, 204, 207, 208, 209; Carl's Corner, 108, 109, 115, 118, 119; on chaos for Picnics, 197; Luckenbach, 134, 142, 149; Two River Canyon, 156, 163, 169, 170
Price, Margo, 227, 228, 229, 231
Price, Michael, 16
Price, Ray: at Billy Bob's, 176; career highlights, 66, 122, 172; death of, 227; Hall of Fame, 122; and Trader, 73
Price, Ray (at Picnics): Fort Worth Stockyards, 182, 184, 187, 211, 212; as frequent performer, 7; Luckenbach, 130, 138–39, 142, 144; Pedernales, 77, 81; San Antonio, 195
Pride, Charley, 213
Prince, Jeff, 47
Prine, John, 12, 24, 104
promotion/advertising, 12–13, 15–16, 45, 46, 49, 52, 93–94, color photo section
psychedelics, Carl's Corner, 111
"Purple Rain" (at Fort Worth Stockyards), 194

Q2 Stadium Picnics, Austin, 232–33, 249, color photo section
Quick Park, 186

racetrack settings, 34–35, 214, 220, 239–40
"Ragged Old Flag" (at Zilker Park), 120
Ragsdale, Randy, 181
Raitt, Bonnie, 104
Ranger Security Systems, 70–71
rapes, Gonzales, 56
Raphael, Mickey, 231
Rattlesnake Annie, 112–13
Rebel Meets Rebel (Coe album), 194
Red Headed Stranger (Nelson album), 36, 37
"Redneck Mother" (at Q2 Stadium), 233
Reed, John, 24
Reese, Pauline, 198, 199, 202–3, 205, 225
Reflectacles, 206–8, 211
Reid, Jan, 16, 18, 28, 30
R.E.M., 101
Reshen, Neil, 60
Rhodes, Kimmie, 6, 121, 122, 141–42
Rich, Charlie, 22, 27
Richards, James, 94
Ride Me Back Home (Nelson album), 230
Ride with Bob (Asleep at the Wheel album), 172
Ridglea Theater, 173
right-now-court, Pedernales, 70
"Ripple" (at Two River Canyon), 164
"The Road Goes on Forever" (at Luckenbach), 140–41
Roberts, Woody, 11, 12–14, 15–16, 18, 27, 28–29, 32, 103–4
Rodriguez, Johnny, 97
Rogers, Randy, 211–12
Rolling Stone, 1, 86
"Roll Me Up. I Die" (at Fort Worth Picnic), 213
"Roll Me Up . . . I Die" (at Austin360 Amphitheater), 225
Royal, Darrell, 9, 18
Ruddock, Upton, 42
Ruiz, Alex, 153–54, 166, 171
Runaways, 221

Run That by Me One More Time (Price album), 172
Russell, Leon: career highlights, 9, 152, 196; death of, 227; as Picnic inspiration, 1; Willie's admiration, 217
Russell, Leon (at Picnics): Austin, 223; Backyard, 206; Dripping Springs, 13, 16, *17*, 18, 19, 24, *27*, 29, *31*; Fort Worth Stockyards, *183*, 184, 187, 212; as frequent performer, 7; Gonzales, 37, 38, *39c*, 49, 53, 57; Luckenbach, 142; Pedernales, 65; South Park Meadows, 97, 98
Russell, Mary, 37, 49

Sahm, Doug, 13, 24, 54, *57*
Sam Houston Race Park, 195
San Angelo Standard-Times, 141, 148
San Antonio Express, 60
San Antonio Picnic, 194–95, 246
sanitary arrangements: Backyard, 204; Carl's Corner, 110; Dripping Springs, 15, 21; Fort Worth Stockyards, 180–81, 185; Gonzales, 38, 42, 44, 50–51, 60; Liberty Hill, 36; Luckenbach, 144, 146; Pedernales, 65, 70, 83; Two River Canyon, 165
Schatzberg, Jerry, 66
Scheske, Eddie, 43
Schulz, Sue, 95
Secret Service, LBJ's, 79–80
security services: Carl's Corner, 112; Dripping Springs, 1, 20–21, 22, 23–24; Fort Worth Stockyards, 185; Gonzales, 42, 44, 54; Luckenbach, 131–32, 137; Pedernales, 70; Two River Canyon, 155
Seeger, Pete, 225
Selman, Wally, 57–58
SFX Entertainment, 217, 218
Shaefer, Larry, 63
"Shakin' Things Up" (on S. Jones album), 154
Shaver, Billy Joe: career highlights, 9, 105, 214; death of, 4, 227, 232; Dripping Springs Reunion, 1
Shaver, Billy Joe (at Picnics): Austin360 Amphitheater, 229, 230; Dripping Springs, 18, 19, 26; Fort Worth Stockyards, 192, 193; as frequent performer, 7; Houston, 195; Luckenbach, 135, 147–48; South Park Meadows, *4*, 97; Two River Canyon, 167–68
Shaver, Eddy, 201
Sheldon, Thomas, 22
Sheridan, Peter, 46, 48
shopping center, Southpark, 101–2
Shotgun Willie (Nelson album), 37
Showco Sound, 28
Shreveport Times, 151
Shriver, Evelyn, 53
Sillerman, Robert, 217
"Silver Wings" (at Two River Canyon), 154, 161–62
Simpson, Mike, 70–71, 82
Simpson, Sturgill, 216, 222
Six Hours at Pedernales (Willie album), 124
Skanse, Richard, 125
Skynyrd, Lynyrd, 63
Smith, Bobby Earl, 24, 34, 35
Smith, Randy, 192
Smith, Rick (musician), 172–73, 175, 176, 188, 191–92
Smith, Rick (reporter), 82
Smith, Sammi, 12, 28, 201
Smith, W. T., 159
Smith Music Group. *See* Smith, Rick (musician)
Sosa, Norma, 235
South Austin Jug Band, 154, 161, 171
South Bend, Indiana, 195, 246
South Park Meadows Picnics (1980s): artists listed, 241–42; atmosphere, 88–89, 94–96, 98–100, 102; performances, 92, 96–98, 99, 102, 150; photos, *4*, *91*, *92*, *95*, *97*, *100*; poster, 93–94, *color photo section*; site location, 91, 101–2; stage setup, 103–4; work opportunities, 93
South Park Meadows (2000), 149–51, 245
Spicewood Airport, 78
Spirit (band), 124

282 / INDEX

Spuds MacKenzie, 111
Spurgers, Josh, 165
Stagecoach (film), 105
stage setups: Austin360 Amphitheater, 216; Carl's Corner, 108; Dripping Springs, 15, 16–17; Fort Worth Stockyards, 178, 183–84, 188; Gonzales, 50; South Park Meadows, 103–4. *See also* backstage atmosphere
Stamps, Roy, 47
Stapleton, Chris, 216
Stardust (Nelson album), 67
A Star is Born (film), 37
"The Star-Spangled Banner" (at Gonzales), 53
Steinbeck, Thom, 120
Sterling Kelley Ranch. *See* Gonzales Picnic
Stevenson, B. W., 53
Stimeling, Travis D., 89–90, 100–101, 237
Stone Mountain venue, 149–50
Strait, George, 90
Stray Cats, 87
Stroeher, Mark, 150
sunrise performance, Dripping Springs, 17, 18–19
Swanson, Gail, 206–7
Sweetheart of the Rodeo (Byrds album), 32
Sweet Willie (film), 55
Syracuse Herald-American, 87
Syracuse Picnic, 87, 241
Szal, Fran, 68, 71, 72, 74, 76
<LS>
Tarradell, Mario, 173–74, 175, 182–83, 187, 189, 191
Tatom, Charles, 96
Taylor, Laurie Kelley, 39, 58, 59
Taylor, Leslie, 70
Taylor, Spencer, 175–76
Taylor, Steve, 39, 58
Tedeschi, Susan, 236
temperatures. *See* heat problems
Tennessean, 78, 84
Texas Alcoholic Beverage Commission, 109
Texas Country Music Hall of Fame, 152
Texas Department of Health Resources, 60

Texas Hill Country Band, 135
Texas Jewboys, 148
Texas Mass Gathering Act, 36, 42, 69, 149–50
Texas Monthly, 194
Texas Rangers, 1
Texas State Fair, 220
Texas World Speedway, College Station Picnic, 34–35, 239–40
Texxas Jam, 64, 217
"This Land is Your Land" (at Backyard), 207
"This Land is Your Land" (at Farm Aid II), 104
Thompson, Greg, 32
Thornton, Billy Bob, 166, 172–73
Threadgill, Kenneth, 10, 31, *color photo section*
Threadgill's restaurant, 10, 11
ticket prices/sales: Austin360 Amphitheater, 216; Carl's Corner, 105–6, 106, 109, 115; College Station, 34; Dripping Springs, 15, 29–30; Farm Aid II, 103; Gilley's, 86; Liberty Hill, 36; Luckenbach, 144–45; Moulton benefit, 44; Pedernales, 70, 83, 88–89; South Bend, 195; South Park Meadows, 91, 100; Two River Canyon, 170; Zilker Park, 120, 121
Tillerson, Janis, 6, 109, 110, 111, 112, 115
Tillman, Floyd, 53, 96
Time (Price), 172
Tim's Porch, 195, 198
Tiny Tim, 86
Titty Bingo, 142
"To All the Girls I've Loved Before" (Nelson and Iglesias song), 89
Tolleson, Mike, 12, 14, 15, 16, 19, 20–21, 30
Tong, Perry, 53, 54–55
Trachtenburg, Jay, 77, 78
Trader, Larry: background, 72–74; death, 74; Dripping Springs, 9, 12, 21, 30; Farm Aid II, 104; Luckenbach, 127, 128, 130–31, 134, 141; Pedernales, 78–79, 84–85
traffic problems. *See* parking/traffic
trash: Dripping Springs, 15, 29; Gonzales,

39, 58, *59*; Liberty Hill, 36; Luckenbach, 144, 146; Pedernales, 65, 82
Travis, Marty: on Billy Bob's hosting, 189–90; Fort Worth Stockyards, 175, 178–79, 180, 182, 184, 185, 187, 188; on Rick Smith's death, 192
Trevino, Lee, 73
"Truckin' " (at Two River Canyon), 164
Trucks, Derek, *236*
Tubb, Ernest, 65, 189
Tulsa Picnic, 63, 217, 240
Tulsa World, 63
Turner, Tina, 176
Two River Canyon: aftermath, 169–71; artists listed, 245; atmosphere, 159, 160, 165–66; performances, 161–65, 166–68; photos, *155*, *163*, *167*, *168*; poster, *color photo section*; preparations, 154–56; site location, 152; traffic problem, 159–60; venue expectations, 152–53
"Two Sides to Every Story" (at Pedernales), 78
two-stage operations, 178, 183–84, 188, 216

"Uncle Willie" poster, 12, 93–94, *color photo section*
Underwood, Peggy, 127
"Up against the Wall Redneck Mother" (at Caesar's Palace), 86
Up against the Wall Redneck Mother (Hubbard album), 38
The Urantia Book, 111
Uranus Urethanes, 17
Urban Cowboy (film), 175
Urban Cowboy sound, 89–90

Valley News, 54
Van Zandt, Townes, 97
Varnon, Zeke, 107, 108
Vaughan, Jimmy, 115
Vaughan, Stevie Ray, 29, 104
vendors. *See* concessionaires
Victoria Advocate, 54
violence: Gonzales, 38–39, 51, 55–56; Pedernales, 76. *See also* guns
VIP areas, 102–3, 160

Virtual Picnic, 231–32, 248
Viva Terlingua! (Walker album), 18, 126
Vollentine, Henry, 42, 44, 46, 48–49, 54, 60
von Erich, Kerry, 111–12

Wade, Bob "DaddyO," 106
Wade, Roger, 159
Walker, Charlie, 217, 218
Walker, Jerry Jeff, 4, 18, 53, 97, 109, 124, 125
Ward, Ed, 78
Washington Post, 64
Washington State Picnic, 194, 246
Waterloo Records, 22
water supplies: Backyard, 199–200; Carl's Corner, 110; Dripping Springs, 21; Fort Worth Stockyards, 189; Gonzales, 60; Liberty Hill, 36; Pedernales, 76; South Park Meadows, 96
Wayne, Dallas: Austin360 Amphitheater, 218, 223, 225, 229; Backyard, 203, 205, 207; on evolution of Picnic, 216; on final years possibility, 227; on Picnic longevity, 235, 237; on Poodie, 211
weather conditions: Austin360 Amphitheater, 229–30; Carl's Corner, 112; Gonzales, 37–38, 57; Liberty Hill, 36; Luckenbach, 133–34; South Park Meadows, 102; Two River Canyon, 159, 161. *See also* heat problems
Wenk, Michael, 150
"We're an American Band" (at Fort Worth Stockyards), 194
Westby, George, 186
West Textures (Keen album), 140
"Where's the Dress?" (at South Park Meadows), 97
Where the Hell's That Gold (film), 119
"Whipping Post" (at Fort Worth Stockyards), 194
"Whiskey River": at Backyard, 207; at Fort Worth Stockyards, 187, 188; at South Park Meadows, 96
White, Jerry, 93, 94, 96, 99
White, Monk, 106, 107, 115
Wickman, Melinda, 23–24, 32, 55–56

Wier, Rusty, 53
Williams, Hank Jr, 87, 178, 186
Willie blog, Banks's, 181
"Willie Nelson Day," 35
Willie Nelson's 4th of July Celebration (Yablonsky film), 34
"Willie's Reserve" marijuana, 214
Wilson, Eddie (Dripping Springs Picnic): advertising, 15; aftermath, 31; arrival of fans, 19, 20; backstage conflict, 27; heat problems, 22; pistol accident, 23; power outage, 28–29; stage construction, 17; vision for, 9–11, 13–14
Wishoff, Bob: Carl's Corner, 110, 111, 114, 118–19; Luckenbach, 135–37, 143, 145–46; on O'Connor, 158

Yablonsky, Yabo, 34
Yoakam, Dwight, 148, 233
Yoder, Jack: Austin360 Amphitheater, 216; Backyard, 199, 206, 208; Fort Worth Stockyards, 184; Luckenbach, 129–31, 132, 134, 143; on Picnic legacy, 237; on Poodie, 203; Two River Canyon, 154, 169
Young, Faron, 77, 97
Young, Neil, 102, 152, 154–55, 168–69, 170, 225

Zilker Park Picnic, 118, 120–21, 243
Zimmerman, Zip, 132, 134, 137, 146
zip tie problem, Porta Potties, 180–81
Zurkirchen, Dale, 88
ZZ Top, 102, 176, 198